JOHN BROWN OF HADDINGTON

JOHN BROWN
OF HADDINGTON

ROBERT MACKENZIE

'For we preach not ourselves, but Christ Jesus the Lord; and ourselves your servants for Jesus' sake.
(2 Corinthians 4.5)

THE BANNER OF TRUTH TRUST
78b Chiltern Street, London, w1

Originally dedicated:
"To My Wife and
Daughter"

Set in 10/12pt Times Roman
Printed and bound in Great Britain by
Billing and Sons Ltd
Guildford and London

Contents

[5]

Preface

The eighteenth century witnessed struggles in Church and State that were of immense import. The shattering commotions of the seventeenth century, with its civil wars and sanguinary persecutions, were past. Men were weary of such methods of unifying a nation. Liberty had at last come to its own. But power strangely fascinates, and lures back the control it once possessed. George III was bent on securing the old supremacy of the crown which the Revolution had largely shorn away; and many were prepared to abet him. Happily his schemes were frustrated, and a constitutional monarchy confirmed.

In the Church there were like movements to assert its authority and clothe its leaders with unlimited powers. Their tendency was to strangle the spiritual life of the people. But the attempts were vigorously opposed, and liberty claimed for full expression of conviction and aspiration. The Wesleys in England refused to submit to the repressive policy of the established Church, and looked out on 'the world as their parish.' The Erskines in Scotland declined to be silenced by the stern decrees of the Kirk, backed though they were by military force. The former went forth on their own way, and organized new methods of life and polity; the latter seceded, but followed the same lines of worship and church government. They were ever longing for the day when the Church of their fathers would reform itself, and get rid of ministerial election by patronage, of a toleration of evils that were sapping its strength, and of an ill-concealed antipathy to evangelical doctrine. But both movements materially helped to keep the fires of the Gospel aglow in the land.

The Church the Erskines founded rapidly grew in numbers and influence; and the causes for which it stood have mainly been won. No better representative of its spirit and genius in the second generation could be found than John Brown of Haddington.

His early struggles read like a romance. Happily his unique gifts were quickly recognized in the new communion. While no University ranked him among its students, or recognized his services to religious literature, except a rising one in the new Republic across the seas toward the end of his days, he trod the path of a scholar, and in the later years placed the fruits of his learning before the world. While Pastor and Professor, he single-handed produced a Dictionary of the Bible that held its own for a hundred years; and a Commentary on the Scriptures, which he happily entitled *A Self-interpreting Bible*, on which Charles Simeon nourished his soul with great delight, and which is still a living book in America.

His life and labours have scarcely had their due presentation to the public. His brief autobiographical sketch, which his sons issued, had parts eliminated. Short biographical accounts appeared in the foreground of some of his works which were reissued during last century. His youngest son, William, in 1856, produced a fuller memoir than the rest. A Centenary Memorial by a grandson, in 1887, added to our knowledge: while one must not omit the cameo sketch by Dr. John Brown, the author of the immortal *Rab and his Friends*, in his famous *Letter to John Cairns, D.D.*

In producing this work, I have consulted all the original material available, and perused the minutes of the Presbytery and Synod of Brown's period, for over twenty years of which he acted as clerk in both courts. I have been specially indebted to Miss Rachel Brown, Bridge of Allan, a descendant of the fourth son in the fourth generation, for the original copy of the *Short Memoir of my Life*, which for the first time is given in full, for the manuscripts of works and pamphlets published and unpublished, and for other kindly help. I would also record with gratitude my obligation to Professor A. Crum Brown, M.D., Edinburgh University, for various manuscripts, and suggestions; to John Brown, Esq., Edinburgh, for photos of the St. Andrews Greek Testament, which is in his possession, and other material; to Miss Agnes Smith, and Miss Spring Brown,

Edinburgh, descendants, for helpful assistance; to the Rev. J. Thomson, M.A., Abernethy, for the privilege of consulting the Abernethy Church Records, and for other information; to the Rev. William T. Cairns, M.A., Edinburgh, for reading the manuscript of this work, and for the correction of details; to the Right Rev. Dr. Moule, Bishop of Durham, and Principal Tait, D.D., of Ridley Hall, Cambridge, for information regarding Simeon and Brown; to Principal Ritchie, D.D., Nottingham, and Professor Johnson of Cheshunt College, Cambridge, for matter bearing on the Countess of Huntingdon and Trevecca College; and to the Rev. Dr. Lee, St. Louis, U.S.A., in respect to Brown's works in America.

I am under special obligation for many hints and helps which I have received from my friend, the Rev. J. R. Fleming, B.D., London, and my brother Sir William W. Mackenzie, K.C., K.B.E.,; and to the Rev. Walter Brown, M.A., Edinburgh, for kindly reading the proofs.

ROBERT MACKENZIE

CLAREMONT MANSE,
ALLOA.
1918.

CHAPTER 1

Parentage and Childhood

John Brown was born in the year 1722, in the hamlet of Carpow, near Abernethy, by the river Tay in Perthshire. It was a unique period in Scottish history. Within a narrow range of years, most of the men saw the light who became the leaders in the intellectual awakening of Scotland. In 1718, Hugh Blair was born, whose eloquent sermons were the delight of Samuel Johnson and George III, and who was the first to occupy the chair of Rhetoric in Edinburgh University. In 1721, came William Robertson, who rose to be Principal of the same University, and who was to rival Gibbon and Hume as the historian of his day; and in that year also, Tobias Smollett, whose imaginative powers were to give fiction a new prominence in literature. In the same year as John Brown, John Home first saw the light, whose tragedy of *Douglas* was to cause such a stir among the ecclesiastics of Scotland, and in 1723, Adam Smith first drew breath, who by his *Wealth of Nations* was to reveal the value of economic factors in the building up of empires. In 1711, David Hume was on the scene, who was to unite in himself the philosopher and the historian, and to give such éclat to the intellectual renown of his country.

But in those days, when in the home of Carpow all that was heard was the puling cries of the child, the country was heaving with a religious crisis. The political disturbance of 1715, when 'The Old Pretender' made a futile attempt to regain the throne of his fathers, had died away. But in the ecclesiastical world, a controversy was raging that was to break up the outer unity of the Scottish Church. The 'Marrow' doctrine was permeating the Church, not yet thoroughly welded together after the tossed and troubled period of the killing times, only thirty years away. The 'Marrow of Moderne Divinity,' as set forth in a book that Thomas Boston found casually in the house of one of his flock in Simprin, and which had been brought to Scotland in the knapsack of a soldier returning from the civil wars, was welcomed ardently by some in the Church, and fiercely rejected by others. In the year 1722, twelve good men were rebuked in the General Assembly of the Church of Scotland for preaching its doctrine. One of the champions of the condemned book was the minister of Abernethy, Alexander Moncrieff, who owned the neighbouring estate of Culfargie, whose father had suffered exile for his faith, and who himself had been taught in the schools of Leyden. Abernethy was shaken with the controversy, the subject of which was discussed in every cottage and hamlet in the district. Into this atmosphere John Brown was ushered; and thus he grew up with the quickening lights of evangelical truth flashing around him.

But Abernethy and district has a further claim on the interest and gratitude of the generations, inasmuch as out of the dim mists of the past it emerges as an active religious centre. As early as the light of history falls upon it, it is a vigorous outpost of the Christian faith. With the advent of Pictish rule in Scotland, it gained in importance, and became, in the words of Walter Bower in the *Scotichronicon*, 'the principal royal and pontifical seat of the whole kingdom of the Picts.' Its Round Tower, of which it still proudly boasts, testifies to the high place it occupied in the political world, erected as it was in the ninth century as a means of defence, as some hold, against Danish attacks, a hundred years before its only other Scottish companion, that of Brechin, was built. With the passing of the Celtic Church, its fortunes as a royal and ecclesiastical residence declined, and other places in Scotland became the seats of power. But an interesting story this picturesque and ancient townlet has to tell, that weaves itself at times into the destinies of the nation, so much so that its latest historian avers that its parish history broadens out into an 'Historical Study' that must include the nation, with its own distinctive tale.

It was in such a centre of historic associations and at such a time of ecclesiastical stir that John Brown began his auspicious day. His father bore the name of John Brown, and his mother that of Catherine Millie. But the veil falls upon their ancestry, and upon themselves. Yet the stock from which he sprang must have been of remarkable vigour and rare quality to have helped to produce a character like his and the 'dynasty' that followed. Tenacity, grit, strength, were its main features, and—

> Lo, Strength is of the plain root-Virtues born;
> Strength shall ye gain by service, prove in scorn,
> Train by endurance, by devotion shape.
> Strength is not won by miracle or rape.
> It is the offspring of the modest years,
> The gift of sire to son.

In Carpow, a hamlet to the east of Abernethy, now entirely swept away, they had their home. The ruins of the little village on both sides of the purling stream that meanders on through the sylvan glades to the Tay, a mile or less away, still remain, with a couple of ash trees to tell of 'the days ayont, the days awa,' when to and fro sped busy feet. Some old trees stand near by that register immemorial years; and scarcely two hundred yards off are the bare, stript, crow-stepped walls of the old mansion of Carpow, then owned by the Oliphants, loyal supporters of the Stuart house. In the old mansion, Prince Charles Edward spent a night on his southern march, while his triumphing army lay at Perth. Through the hamlet passes the road between Newburgh and Abernethy; and today only fifty yards to the south of it, through a deep cutting, runs the railway that links the two places together.

Though vanished, Carpow can claim an older history than Abernethy. The remains of a Roman villa are still visible three hundred yards to the east of the old house. Indeed this region must have been an important centre in the remote past, guarded as it was by a hill-fort – whose formation speaks of its antiquity – on the top of the Castle Law, that commands with a watchful eye the whole district.

In the days of Brown's father, small patches of ground were allotted to the workers on the farms, on which they grew flax that was spun by the wives and daughters of their families. In the winter season, his father was one of the weavers of the place; in the summer he followed the salmon fishing, which is today and has always been, a profitable calling in the neighbourhood. Of education he received none; but he taught himself to read. He filled his home with the current literature of the period, which was peculiarly religious. Immediately the gift of reading was awakened in his son, he feasted upon what his father possessed, and strong meat it was for a youth of tender years.

Toward the end of his days, John Brown wrote a brief sketch of his life, a 'Short Memoir' as he called it; and in it we obtain a glimpse of those early years with their grim background, and hard but not joyless struggle.

'The more I consider the dealings between God and my soul, I am the more amazed at His marvellous lovingkindness to me, and my ingratitude and rebellion against Him.

'It was a mercy that I was born in a family which took care of my Christian instruction, and in which I had the example of God's worship, both evening and morning – which was the case of few families in that corner at that time. This was the more remarkable that my father, as I have heard, being born under prelacy, got no instruction in reading or next to none, but what he got from masters after he began to be a herd.'

The atmosphere of the home was serene. Religion shone in the background. If it burned low in other dwellings, its light gleamed brightly under one roof in Carpow. It deeply moved the young life, in particular at the one great religious festival of the year, the sacrament of the Lord's Supper, which was held in Abernethy in the month of July. In most of the parishes at that time there was only an annual celebration of this ordinance. Days were allotted to it. Thousands attended from far and near. Abernethy was a favourite centre. There they gathered on the green slope at the foot of the hill to the south of the village, sitting in plaids on the green grass, the preacher standing in an elevated narrow shelter, like a sentry box. Within the church, the Communion proper proceeded, where those only were admitted who were privileged to sit down at the table. In turn the groups of communicants took their places at the reserved seats, reverently covered with white linen, while preacher after preacher addressed them, and distributed the sacred symbols. It was a profoundly impressive occasion.

The awe and reverence of the people touched the hearts of the young folks as they beheld the continual succession of their elders moving in and out of the church. It may have repelled some; but it awakened the intense curiosity of young John Brown. On one occasion he ventured to mingle with the crowd that poured into the church, to learn for himself what took place. He slipped into the gallery. The sight of the worshippers below, partaking of the hallowed symbols, and the fervent utterances of the preacher, left an impression that was treasured for life. But the young eager face peering down from the upper chamber was ere long descried. Its presence was a sacrilege; and he was summoned to leave. The recollection, however, of the scene and the impressions produced so abode with him that, in later years, he instituted a reform in the Communion Services of the Church, by the admission of young persons as witnesses of the celebration, and by a more frequent observance of the supper.

In his autobiographical fragment he writes:

'About the eighth year of my age, I happened in the crowd to get into the church on the Sacrament Sabbath, when it was

[15]

common for all but intended communicants to be excluded. The table or tables which I heard served before I was put out, were chiefly served upon Christ, and in a sweet and delightful manner. This captivated my young affections, and has made me since think that little ones should never be excluded from the church on such occasions. Though what they hear may not convert them, it may be of use to begin the allurement of their heart.'

The school-days of John Brown were easily numbered. Scotland has always been proud of her educational system. Lofty ideals for the instruction of youth were outlined at the Reformation, for its value to the national life was deemed of the highest importance. But the 'Sturm und Drang'[1] of the seventeenth century, when Prelacy and Presbytery contended for the mastery, and were in turn overthrown, interfered sadly with the realization of these ideals. In 1633, again in 1643, and yet again in 1696, the Scottish Parliament enacted and re-enacted that a schoolmaster should be appointed for every parish, a 'commodious house' should be provided for a school, and that assessments be made, half from the tenants, and half from the heritors, for his salary. This beneficent law was almost completely disregarded. The sanction behind the law was ineffective. The tenants left it severely alone in deference to the landlords, and the landlords left it as severely alone in deference to themselves. Presbyteries were authorized to nominate 'twelve honest men' to carry out the law; but nobody was authorized to see if they did their duty. In consequence any kind of a shelter was allowed to serve as a schoolroom – it might be the church steeple, a cowshed, a stable, a granary, a family vault, a dilapidated hovel. Usually the schools were small, dirty rooms, the windows open to let in the light, or boarded up to keep out the cold, and the wind, and the rain. In winter they hung thick with the smoke of peat, kindled to warm the children. Often seats and desks were wanting, and

[1] i.e. tempests and tensions.

[16]

the scholars squatted on the floor, covered with the rushes or straw which it was the children's duty to supply. In 1725, the Town Council of St. Andrews was informed that 'the boys cannot sit for learning to wreatt; so that they are necessitat to wreatt upon the floor lying upon their bellies.'

The schoolmaster was kept in as dire straits as his school. The Act authorized his salary to be not less than 100 merks (£5), and not more than 200 merks (£10). The former was the common salary in a country parish; and the teaching consisted of Latin, mathematics, arithmetic, writing, and singing. Provisions, of course, were cheap at this period – a boll of meal 6s., a dozen eggs 1d., 1 lb. mutton 1½d., while shoes cost 10d. a pair, and the woollen shirts and the rough plaiding were spun at home. But the salary was poor and difficult to gather in from fifty or a hundred tenants or heritors, as the case might be, in sums of a penny or a fraction of a penny. Excuses for not paying were hurled at the dominie, as he collected his pittance – bad harvests or threats to withdraw the children. Payment in kind was offered; and the saying was but too literally and painfully true, that 'literature was cultivated on a little oatmeal.' Thomas Ruddiman (1674-1757), the renowned librarian of the Advocates' Library in Edinburgh for fifty years, and of still wider juvenile fame as the author of *The Rudiments of the Latin Tongue*, while schoolmaster at Laurencekirk, was paid chiefly in corn, which he sold to his uncle in the dear years that followed the Revolution

Happily the scanty months that John Brown spent at school at Abernethy were not affected by the building in which the lamp of instruction was dimly burning. It was to him an opening of the gateways of knowledge. They were entered with eagerness and the promised fruits seized with passion. He was not content with reading, but with 'learning by heart' what he read. When one considers what was read by this boy of eight or ten – the Catechisms of Vincent and Flavel, and the *Larger Catechism of the Westminster Assembly* – the mental grip must have early declared itself. Vincent's *Catechism*, the

[17]

general pabulum of the time, was a hard, dry book, but a book so highly esteemed by Alexander Cruden of *Concordance* fame that he founded an Exhibition of £5 in connection with Marischal College, Aberdeen, one of the conditions of holding it being a perfect acquaintance with Vincent's *Catechism*. Flavel's *Catechism* was another favourite of the period, its author, John Flavel (c. 1627-1691), being the son of a Non-conformist divine, who is described in contemporary records as a 'painful and eminent minister.' The *Larger Catechism of the Westminster Assembly* even, not the *Shorter*, which is held to be too stiff for the twentieth century, was also reckoned a work to be mastered by the youth of this earlier period, for its doctrine was both solid and sound.

Brown says of his school-days:

'My thirst after knowledge was great. My pride not a little instigated my diligence, particularly in learning by heart what Catechisms I could get. I have found not a little advantage by this, especially by my learning of Vincent's and Flavel's Catechisms, and the Assembly's *Larger Catechism*. My parents' circumstances did not allow them to afford me any more but a very few quarters at school, for reading, writing, and arithmetic, one month of which, without their allowance, I bestowed upon the Latin.'

That completed John Brown's school and university career. It is evident, as Carlyle said of Dante, that in those few months he 'with his earnest, intelligent nature, learned better than most all that was learnable.'

A youth so studious did not escape the keen notice of the watchful mother. Seeing her boy's absorbing eagerness to learn, she had a vision of a future for him, which she was destined never to see, of his one day standing among Scotland's preachers. Using the quaint language of the time, she was wont to say, 'Oh when will I see the craws fleein' ower my bairnie's kirk!'

Two brothers and a sister completed Brown's family circle. James, the elder of the brothers, found his way to Cupar, Fife, and died a burgess of the ancient burgh in 1799: a great-grandson of his is now (1917) minister of the parish of Bervie, Kincardineshire. William, the younger, turned toward the west and obtained employment on the Inverary estate of the Duke of Argyle, dying comparatively young, leaving a family that devoted itself to forestry. Janet married one John Heggie, and established her home in Newburgh-on-Tay in Fife.

CHAPTER 2

The School of Life

'My father dying about the eleventh year of my age, and my mother soon after, I was left a poor orphan, who had almost nothing to depend on but the providence of God.'

Such is the next pathetic sentence in the *Short Memoir of my Life*. Thus early did the struggle begin in life's hard school. Of what exactly the parents died is not known. But death demanded a heavy toll of human life in those days. Sanitation was unknown; the mansions of the great were without the most rudimentary and essential conveniences of cleanliness. Epidemics swept with fatal virulence over the land. Ague, arising from the marshy soil, yearly disabled thousands. Smallpox ravaged the community and fever abounded because of the prevailing filth. Medical skill was in an exceedingly crude stage; and the remedies prescribed would be amusing, were they not so pathetic: toads used inwardly for dropsy, outwardly for carbuncles; slaters, or woodlice, for colic, convulsions, palsy, and cancer; earthworms, slit up, 'well-washed and dried,' for jaundice and gout; vipers for dysentery, smallpox, and ague; and, of course, the inevitable panacea for every disease, blood-letting. Disease raged triumphantly. Yet it says much for the vigorous constitution of the people that, with the healing art in such a parlous state, the death-rate was so moderate. It was a case of the survival of the fittest. Before the onslaught of one of these prevalent diseases, first the father, in 1733, and two years later the mother of John Brown fell victim; and then the humble home of Carpow was broken up.

With what he calls a 'small religious family,' John found

a kindly shelter for a time, Fever, however, attacked his sturdy frame no less than four times in succession, and at the end left him in a state of great weakness. The sorrows and sufferings through which he passed, naturally aroused the religious sensibilities of this serious youth. The deep concerns of religion appealed to him, although he was only in his twelfth year; and life was established on the surest and broadest foundation on which a man can build – the personal surrender to the Lord of life. The religious books of the period were eagerly read and absorbed. Their titles may seem rather startling to an age which shrinks from the subjective, but they meant exactly what the writers intended. *An Alarm to the Unconverted*, by Joseph Alleine (1634-68), next to Baxter perhaps the most widely read of the Puritan writers, and one of the two thousand ejected preachers of 1662; *Trial of a Saving Interest in Christ*, by William Guthrie (1620-65), the keen angler, and the devoted pastor of Fenwick; *Guide to goe to God*, by William Gouge, D.D. (1578-1653), a member of the Westminster Assembly of Divines, and a leader of the London ministers who protested against sending Charles I to the scaffold – these works were not meant to catch with guile, but to do, or attempt to do, what they claimed. Such was the literature on which this youth barely in his teens feasted his young soul, along with the Scriptures, and the *Letters of Samuel Rutherford* (1600-61), which are still a joy and a profit to read. This was the result:

'Meanwhile in 1734, and especially in 1735, the Lord by His word read and preached, did not a little strive with and allure my soul. The reading of Alleine's *Alarm to the Unconverted*, contributed not a little to awaken my conscience, and move my affections. Some of his hints, made worse by my mind however, occasioned my legal covenanting with God. I made much the same use of Guthrie's *Trial of a Saving Interest in Christ*. Indeed such was the bias of my heart under these convulsions, that I was willing to do anything but to flee to Christ and His free grace alone for my salvation. In these times I had no small delight in reading religious books, the Bible, Rutherford's *Letters*, and the like; and by means of these, particularly by means of Gouge's *Directions how to walk with God*, was led into considerable circumspection in my practice. The sweet impressions made by sermons and books sometimes lasted days on end, and were sometimes carried to a remarkably high degree. Under these I was much given to prayer, but concealed all my religious appearances to the uttermost of my power.

'Four fevers on end brought me so low within a few months after my mother's death, as made almost every onlooker lose all hopes of my recovery; only I remember a sister, the most simple but the most serious of all us children of the family, told me that when she was praying for me, that word, "I will satisfy him with long life, and show him My salvation," was impressed on her mind, which she said made her mind perfectly easy with respect to my recovery. Apprehensions of eternity, though I scarce looked for immediate death in these troubles, also affected me.

'But the death of my parents, and my leaving a small religious family, to go into a larger, in the station of a herd-boy, for two or three years, was attended with not a little practical apostasy from all my former attainments. Even secret prayer was not always regularly performed. But I foolishly pleased myself by making up the number one day which had been deficient in another.

'It was my mercy, too, that in all my services I was cast into families, except perhaps one, [where] there were some appearances of the grace of God, besides useful neighbours.'

One of the families was that of John Ogilvie, who tenanted the sheep-farm of Muckle Bein. He was an elder of the Church at Abernethy, of which Alexander Moncrieff was at that time minister. Advanced in years, but yearning for knowledge, and unhappily never taught to read, he welcomed the service of the studious youth, not so much for herding his sheep as for his ability to read to him, and his delight in his spiritual communings. The two built a little shelter on the Colzie hill, where they might talk together in the utmost privacy far away from the gaze of men, long afterwards known as 'the Tabernacle.' It is like the delightful picture Pepys describes, 'the most pleasant and innocent sight that ever I saw in my life,' of the shepherd on Epsom Downs, and his little boy reading the Bible to him, 'far away from any houses, or sight of people.'[1] Pepys has recorded his experience in a passage which Stevenson regarded as the most romantic in all the *Diary*.

The farm lay to the south among the heights that half encompass Abernethy on that side. The youth, wandering over these hills, must have had his mind stirred and quickened by the magnificent views of the surrounding scenery that disclosed themselves, especially when the atmosphere shimmered with 'the clear shining after rain.' The Earn came winding down its well-tilled valley, joining the Tay as it broke out between the hills of Kinnoul and Moncrieffe. The river now pursued its broadening course on toward the North Sea, visible on the eastern horizon, with Dundee lying on the left bank. Between the Tay and the Sidlaw range, with Macbeth's Dunsinane standing guard, was spread, like a billiard-table, the Carse of Gowrie, while, beyond the Sidlaws, stretched the long broken line of the Grampians, enfolding between them the rich expansive valley of Strathmore. On clear days Schiehallion showed its lofty peaks, fully forty miles away. Toward the west, Ben Voirlich, Ben More, and the shoulders of Ben Ledi could be descried, and toward the south, not only the Lomond Tops of Fifeshire, but North Berwick Law, and the Lammermoors, sheltering at their feet the ancient town of Haddington, where the youthful shepherd was to spend his busiest days – all these could be seen with the naked eye. The far-flung, extensive view of nearly three-parts of Scotland, so

[1] *The Diary of Samuel Pepys*, July 14th, 1667.

[23]

varied in form, so rich in beauty, beating morning after morning upon the thoughtful and reverent shepherd lad, left memories that found suggestive and significant expression in the *Christian Journal*, that was to be a feast of soul to many a pilgrim long years after its author had passed to his rest.

A contemporary of John Brown's contributed in after-years a sketch of him up to the days when his ministry began. It was sent to his son John, who was minister at Whitburn, and was then issuing a Life of his father. For some reasons it was not made use of; probably it came into his hands too late for his purpose, like the more famous sketch by his great-grandson, Dr. John Brown, author of the immortal *Rab*, which he sent to Dr. John Cairns, the biographer of his father, but which was received too late for insertion in the first issue of the published Life. In this interesting letter, the companion of his youth said:

'Mr. Brown was born in poor circumstances. His infant life, through the death of near relatives, may be styled friendless, but as soon as he could do anything, Providence provided a friend for him in the neighbouring mountains to Abernethy in John Ogilvie, a shepherd, venerable for age, and eminent for piety. This worthy man, though intelligent and pious, was so destitute of education, as not to be able to read English. Knowing the narrow circumstances of your father's family, his serious disposition, his love of learning, his wonderful capacity, he was induced to engage him in his service, to help him with his sheep, particularly to tend his lambs, but chiefly to read to him. They were not long companions till they became dear friends, and both of them found their connection mutually beneficial. To accommodate themselves they built a lodge on Colzie hill, to which they repaired not only to screen themselves from the storm, but to read the Word of God, to pray, and to sing the praises of the Chief Shepherd. Thus "the wilderness and the solitary place was glad for them, and the desert rejoiced with joy and singing."

'The ruins of this lodge are well known, and from its sacred use obtained, and yet bears, the name of the Tabernacle. But, however, the pleasant period comes to an end; the farmer dispersed his flock, and the godly shepherds separated. The old man retired from business to Abernethy, of which parish he was an elder.'

The demands of the religious life seemed to the young lad to call for the rigorous observing of specified times of devotion. It was an age when 'method' was regarded as a prime essential in the Christian profession, and which found its most illustrious example in the Society that John Wesley and his brother founded at Oxford in 1732. It is curious to find that about the same time John Brown was endeavouring, with many failures, to put in practice on the hills of Abernethy the same ideas as to the religious life. The precepts of William Law and Joseph Alleine were treated with reverential deference; but the spirit of religion was apt to lose itself in the letter of religious duty. In a letter of August 6th, 1745, John Brown writes:

'After a formal slight using of Alleine's "Directions for Conversion," I dedicated myself to the Lord in solemn vow, as Alleine directs (summer 1735 or 1736); particularly, I vowed to pray six times in the day when I was herding, and three when I was not herding; so I continued to do this; and if I was deficient one day, I made amends the next. If I fell into any known sin, I prayed for forgiveness, and so was well. All movings of the affections I took for special enjoyings of God, and now thought myself sure of heaven, if I was not a hypocrite; to avoid which deceit, I kept the whole of my religion as hid as I could, especially prayer; and to that end prayed almost aye in the field, where, if I was not pretty sure nobody was near, I was exceeding low of voice; and, lest my head being bare might discover it, I cast my blanket over it, or else laid an open book before me, that so they might think I was reading; and so made myself, in my conceit, as sure of heaven as possible. In this way of doing I continued from that time till June 1740 or else 1741 at least, if not till now; still putting my fashion of religion in Christ's room, setting up my formal prayers, etc., for my Saviour, yea, for my God.'

The formal stage, ever fraught with disquiet, passed, and there broke the full splendour of the glowing sunshine. To revert to his autobiographical fragment:

'At length, after a multitude of ups and downs, glowings of affections, and sad coolings, I, after a sore fever in 1741, which somewhat awakened my concern about eternal salvation, was providentially determined, during the noontide, while the sheep which I herded rested themselves in the fold, to go and hear a sermon, at the distance of two miles, running both to it and from it. The second or third sermon which I heard in this manner, and I had no other opportunity of hearing, the greater part of the year, being preached on John 6. 64, "There are some of you that believe not," by one I both before and afterwards reckoned as a most general preacher, pierced my conscience as if almost every sentence had been directed to none but me, and made me conclude myself one of the greatest unbelievers in the world. This sermon threw my soul into no small agony and concern, and made me look on all my former experiences as nothing but common operations of the Spirit; and in this manner I viewed them for many years afterwards; and often in my sermons, after I was a preacher, described the lengths which common operations might go on this footing. But at last I began to doubt that I had been too rash in throwing aside all my former experiences as having nothing of the really gracious in them. And I saw that it was improper for a preacher to make his own experiences, either of one kind or another, anything like a discriminating standard of his conceptions or declarations on these delicate subjects.

'On the morrow after, I heard a sermon on Isaiah 53. 4, "Surely He hath borne our griefs, and carried our sorrows," which enlightened and melted my soul in a manner I had not formerly experienced; and I was made as a poor lost sinner, the chief of sinners, to essay appropriating the Lord Jesus as having done all for me, and as wholly made over to me in the Gospel, as the free gift of God and my all-sufficient Saviour, answerable to all my folly, ignorance, guilt, filthiness, wants, slavery, and misery. This sermon had the most powerfully pleasant influence on my soul of any that I ever heard.

'By a sermon on Isaiah 45. 24, "Surely in the Lord have I righteousness and strength," my soul was also remarkably affected and drawn to the Lord. By means of these and other ordinances, the sweetness which I felt about 1735 was not only remarkably returned to me, but I had far clearer views of the freedom of God's grace, and of the exercise of taking hold of and pleading the gracious promises of the Gospel.'

John Brown was then nineteen years of age. The deep impressions of this period of spiritual wrestling were not of a passing nature. Though reticent till near the end of his days about his inner life, he busied his pen frequently in after-years in writing 'Meditations,' soliloquies of the soul, intense, powerful presentations of the subjective truth of the Gospel. By this time he had emerged to see what was 'really gracious' in the thoughts and feelings stirred by the concentration of mind and heart on such high themes. There are two 'Meditations' that seem to have sprung out of this struggle towards the light. They are typical of one of the means he sedulously employed to fan the flame of religious truth in the land. The one is entitled, *Reflections of a Soul shut up to the Faith*. It is a call to look back 'to the rock whence thou wast hewn.'

'By a Christian education, God had shut me up from the more flagrant iniquities – cursing, swearing, lewdness, intemperance, and the neglect of the forms of religion. But, ah! with what earnestness I indulged myself in sins not less criminal, though less open and scandalous! – seeking righteousness, as it were, by the works of the law! When conscience upbraided me for neglect of former duties, particularly of acts of worship, how often have I redoubled, or even tripled the ordinary tale, in order to pay off my old debts. . . . In vain. . . . But

[27]

thanks be to God, He passed by me, and looked upon me, and said unto me, "LIVE." And, behold, my time was the time of love, the day of power, the day of espousals indeed! Determined to make an uncommon stretch of Almighty grace, He hedged me in. Before, behind, and on every side, I heard, I saw, I felt—not cherubim with flaming swords, but calls, but cords, of everlasting love.'

The other 'Meditation,' *Reflections of a Christian upon his Spiritual Elevations and Dejections*, is a vivid description of the sunlit heights and the deep dark depths that may be crossed in the pursuit of the highest.

'Sometimes He hath lifted me up, in allowing me sweet distinct views of divine truth, and of Jesus and His Father therein. . . . Anon, He casts me down into deep and darksome caves. I groped as a blind man at noonday. . . . Sometimes God, by His Word and Spirit, afforded me the most convincing assurance that He was my Saviour, my Husband, my Father, my Friend, my Physician, my God—my *all* and in *all*. Anon, He permitted me to fall into such darkness and doubts that I could be persuaded of scarce anything inspired. . . . Sometimes God hath lifted me up to a sweet serenity of soul. . . . Anon, He cast me "into deep waters where there was no standing." . . . Sometimes He hath so feasted me in His ordinances that the frequent return of Sabbaths, sacramental occasions, opportunities of family, social, or secret worship, were my delight. . . . Anon, ordinances became to me as "dry beasts," and their approach a trifle, a burden; and neither before, nor in, nor after did I enjoy the visits of Christ. . . . Sometimes God hath carried me up to Mount Pisgah, and shown me the celestial Canaan, and my irrevocable title thereto. . . . Anon, He held back the face of His throne, and spread His cloud over it. . . . Are thy frames, my soul, so changeable? Let me charge thee to have no confidence in thyself; but to live by faith on the Son of God, and His everlasting covenant, which are "the same yesterday, to-day, and for ever."'

CHAPTER 3

The Acquisition of Languages

A dominant passion of this friendless youth was to acquire a knowledge of languages. The means, however, were limited in the extreme: few, if any, were ever so devoid of the opportunity and the appliances of learning. A penniless orphan boy, who had only a quarter or two at school, and one month at Latin, toiling for his daily bread in the lone uplands of a country parish, far from centres that stimulate thought, had obstacles to face so stern and forbidding as to discourage all likely attainment. But he dared the impossible, and did it.

It is not to be supposed, of course, that a serious youth, who 'reined in' the spirit of frolic that was in him, would escape the gay tormentings of boys of his own age. It is youth's privilege to indulge in pranks that search and expose the supposed weaknesses of comrades. A solemn tendency provides fair sport for merry assailants. If it is manfully borne, there is that appreciation in the youthful nature to champion henceforth the victim, and courageously defend, and loyally serve him as a friend. On the farm of John Ogilvie was another youth, Henry Ferney, who delighted to tease and test the sober son of Carpow. One Sabbath evening he thought that he would call out the angry fires. He hurried his sheep to the fold, then strewed the entrance, on which an open gate hung, with whins, and stacked a bunch of rough prickly ones near the post where the gate was fastened. John Brown brought up his sheep, and, being last, was under obligation to shut the gate. He made his way bare-footed through the gorse, with sharp twinges of pain, and barred the gate. As he withdrew Ferney watched his opportunity, and sent him headlong into the prickly heap, with a roar of boyish laughter. Young Brown rose with face, hands, and legs bleeding. Henry expected that at last he would now hear an enraged tongue, or be summoned to fight. But he was more than astonished when the victim of his crude joke looked at him, and said in a kindly but injured tone, 'O Henry, what for do ye that on the Lord's nicht? I would have been loth to do that to you.' Henry was stung by the meekness of his comrade, and was distressed till he was frankly forgiven. From that hour, Henry Ferney became a staunch and steadfast friend.

The relations of the two afford a glimpse of the period and of the boy who was 'the father of the man.' Ferney afterwards acknowledged the interest young Brown took in his self-improvement, and aspiration toward a better life. Brown sought to fire him with his own spirit, and opened to him what treasures of knowledge he possessed. He awoke him to a high sense of duty, and to hear the call of higher things. At bedtime he would say, 'Henry, did you go about prayer this night?' 'Yes.' 'When was it?' Such time, he would say. 'Henry, you must have little to seek at a throne of grace. O Henry, if you but saw your many needs, and the many mercies God is ready to give you for asking, you would not be so soon through.'

John Brown, with his scanty tools for acquiring knowledge, especially of languages, made such use of them as to display remarkable originality. The little Latin he had been taught, instead of being lost when life's hard school began, where in truth there seemed so little use for it, was carefully treasured, and added to, until the mastery of the language was well within his grasp. He borrowed books wherever he could find them. In the midday, when for two hours the labours ceased, he bounded off to the minister at Arngask, three to four miles away, Rev. J. Johnstone, or to his own minister at Abernethy, Rev. Alexander Moncrieff, who for a time, at least, was his friendly counsellor and helper. Moncrieff would set him studies that he imagined days would be required to overtake, but in a short time, Brown was at his door, with the work prescribed finished, and ready for more.

His browsing in Latin fields led him to seek the richer pasturage of Greek, and acquaintance with the very words of the New Testament. He was too modest to ask guidance in this more exclusive region. Latin then was common property; not so Greek; and he conceived a plan to reach his goal by himself, rather ingenious and entirely original. He took his *Ovid*, an old Latin grammar, and the names of the New Testament, especially the genealogies of the first chapter of Matthew, and the third chapter of Luke. The last he divined to be transcripts of the Greek, and to suggest the key to unlock the door between the two languages. 'Reason told me,' he argued, 'that at least an unaccidented tongue could not much change names from what they were in the Greek.' With these he made a discovery of the Greek characters,[1] as true a *discovery* as Dr Young's of the characters of the Rosetta stone, or Rawlinson's of the cuneiform letters. He compared the names and the letters verse by verse with the English. He treated the Greek as an expert uses a cypher, and bit by bit with wonderful patience and ingenuity, he learned the sound of the letters. Though only making guesses at the meaning, yet, by comparing it with the English, he was able to read the Greek. Then, having acquired so much Greek, he pushed on to Hebrew.

He tells the story himself in a letter which he wrote to explain the mystery of his acquiring a knowledge of the Greek, without a grammar and without the assistance of any one, that seemed to those who knew Greek to be an achievement without the bounds of possibility, and as implying the necessity of being helped by none other than 'his Satanic Majesty'. The main part of the letter will be given in the next chapter; this portion bears on the subject in question.

'I learned the letters from *Orth. Tab. Gram.*, marginal words in *Ovid*, and names in the New Testament; for reason told me

[1] John Brown, 'Letter to John Cairns,' *Horae Subsecivae*, second series, p. 68.

that at least our unaccidented tongue could not much change
names from what they were in the Greek, as, *e.g.*: (1) words
authoritatively interpreted, as Eloi lama sabachthani, Talitha
cumi, Siloam, Corban, Golgotha, Gabbatha, Emmanuel,
Cephas, Aceldama; for if these be changed in any language —
as, for example, if Aceldama be made Acerdama, it would be
false; for it would say — 1st, that the Jews called that place
Acerdama; 2nd, that Acerdama, *Hebraicè*, signifies a field of
blood. And so in the matter of all words of this kind. (2) Words
authoritatively called alien, as Abaddon, Armageddon. (3)
Proper, obsolete, inequivalented names, as, *Hebraicè*, Cainan,
Arphaxad, etc., Luke 3, *Graecè*, Olympas, Priscilla, etc. (4)
Names changed in one place from what they were in another —
Noah, Genesis 10. 1, Noe, Luke 3. Now, both being alike to
our English, the reason of their change is the Greek, and, therefore, must be in the Greek as in ours. Now, all the Greek
letters may be found by comparing—

Eloi	lama	sabachthani	Arphaxad
Ελοι	λαμα	σαβαχθανι	Αρφαξαβ

Capernaum	Sem	Aceldama	Booz	Ragau	Salmon
Καπερναουμ	Σημ	Ακελδαμα	Βοοζ	Ραγαυ	Ψαλμων[1]

'Now, to prove the powers to be what you conceive or not,
look other words: as, for example, I would be sure of β that
it is equal to *b* — I look Αβρααμ, Αβιουδ, Αβια, Ωβηδ, in all
which, if I have hit right on the power β by calling it *b*, then
the second form in all these four words must be like it; but
this is true; therefore the former. This way I used.

'Another rule I also walked by is, cast your eyes on what
form you will and fancy it to be what power you will; then
compare it with other words having powers equivalent, and if
they confirm it not, fancy it to be some other power, and so do

[1] In the *Centenary Memorial of Rev. John Brown*, p. 63, by his grandson, Dr. J. Croumbie Brown, he remarks that the Greek character τ is
not included in this test, but this must have been the result of oversight.

till you find some words to confirm you in your fancy; and then you may take it for probable that you have really lighted on its power. And if it can be found to be no single letter, fancy it to be some double consonant, diphthong, or syllable; as, for example, I cast mine eye on β. I fancy it to be α. I look Aram, Asa, Josaphat, Graecè. I see nothing like it there; and yet the power α is there; *ergo*, it is not α. And, by the by, I remark that the power of *a* is found *Anglicè* four times besides capitals, and it only is so often found; but the Greek form α is found alone so oft; *ergo*, the form α has the power of *a* English. Again, I fancy β to have the power of our *d* by comparing Αμιναδαβ, Ωβηδ, Αβιουδ, Ελιουδ; I see the antepenult and ult letter in the other three is *d* English; therefore the antepenult form in Aminadab and the other three *Graecè* must have the power of *d*, by the rule anent obsolete names; but this form is δ, not β, and so β is not equal in power or sound to *d*. But observing such a form in Ωβηδ–now, the second power there is that of *b* English; therefore, I fancy it to be *b*, and by comparing it with Ζοροβαβελ, Ιακωβ, I found it to me proven to be *b*.

'Thus one might go through all the forms. Now, I knew proper names from the places they are put in with us *Anglicè*, the initiating capitals, their repetitions, etc. As for the other ways I used, it would weary you to hear them; so I forbear at this time.

'When I had, by these means, got myself into a probability that I had the letters, I came down and sounded them before Mr. Reid, and when he did not approve of my way, I called them his way, viz., *n, u*, etc.

'Now, the way I took to learn the sense was much the same, by comparing the Greek words with the words in our Testament, beginning at the shortest verses, as 1 Thess. 5. 16, etc.; and as I had observed many terminations with some of their oblique cases in Latin Greek rudiments, so as I went along I made it my study to notice verbal terminations, right and oblique, still allotting them to that person, time, mood, voice,

B   [33]

etc., their English agreed to. All this while, I never thought of its dual number, middle voice, etc., which the Latin has not. Also I noticed prepositions, adverbs, etc. As to construction, Ruddiman told me (*Rud.*, p. 98, I think) that the rules he has not distinguished by an asterisk are natural; therefore, I concluded, used in Greek. Some others I noticed, as Ακούω, 68, etc. All this time I got lessons now and then from Mr. Reid; then I got a grammar and rudiments, etc. As for Hebrew, I got a grammar one hundred and ten days before I saw another Hebrew book, and am far from so exact in any of them as they [*i.e.* his maligners] report.'

Having thus obtained a knowledge of the Greek alphabet, he was anxious to possess a copy of the Greek Testament for himself. He had now gathered sufficient money to purchase one. The nearest likely place where such a volume could be obtained was St. Andrews, with its University. Perth was only seven miles distant; but it was doubtful if the booksellers there would stock such a volume. In the university city there could be no such doubt. Taking his friend, Henry Ferney, into his confidence, and securing his promise to look after his flock during his absence, one evening, in the year 1738, at the age of sixteen, when the sheep were penned, he set out on the twenty-four miles of unknown road that lay between him and St. Andrews. He arrived early in the morning, footsore and weary. He found the bookseller's shop in South Street, near the University Library, then owned by Alexander McCulloch. Going in, he startled the shopman by asking for a Greek New Testament. He was a very raw-looking lad at the time, his clothes were rough, home-spun, and ragged, and his feet were bare. 'What would you do wi' that book? you'll no can read it,' said the bookseller. 'I'll try to read it,' was the humble answer of the would-be purchaser. Meanwhile some of the professors had come into the shop, and, hearing the talk and surveying the youth, questioned him closely as to what he was, where he came from, and who taught him. Then one of them, not unlikely Francis Pringle, then Professor of Greek, asked the bookseller to bring a Greek New Testament, and, throwing it down on the counter, said, 'Boy, if you can read that book, you shall have it for nothing.' He took it up eagerly, read a passage to the astonishment of those in the shop, and marched out with his gift, so worthily won, in triumph. By the afternoon, he was back at duty on the hills of Abernethy, studying his New Testament the while, in the midst of his flock.

This same Testament has been handed down in the family and is today in the possession of the fifth John Brown in lineal descent – the son of the beloved physician. It is a small, rather thick volume, bound in leather, bearing marks of constant use. It is still in good preservation, but wanting a part of the Gospel of Matthew. The name *John Brown* is written on the fly-leaf, obviously the writing of a youth, and resembling his handwriting in later years. At the end is the autograph of his son Thomas, afterwards Rev. Dr. Thomas Brown of Dalkeith, written when a young man at the University.

CHAPTER 4

Unjust Suspicions

It is manifest that by this time John Brown had fixed on the ministry of the Church as the goal of his ambitions. The way was beset with difficulties, but, to one of his mettle, difficulties only existed to be mastered. The passion for learning burned in his soul. Latin had been won, Greek was yielding, and Hebrew was being added to his conquests, the door of it being opened with the key that undid the bolt on Greek. He did not parade his learning; he did not boast of how he had triumphed over the obstacles that sealed the language of Plato and of Paul for the few. But when questioned about what he had so sedulously acquired, he returned a straight answer, as he naïvely says, he 'did not know the danger of saying the truth.' He had not studied Bacon's essay on Simulation and Dissimulation, or even its first sentence, 'Dissimulation is but a faint kind of policy or wisdom, for it asketh a strong wit and a strong heart to know when to tell truth and to do it.' There was no simulation or dissimulation in Brown's nature, and his shrinking modesty made him pay a heavy penalty.

His marvellous acquaintance with Greek, in his circumstances, simply staggered a few young men in Abernethy who were studying for the ministry. The priggishness of youth, struggling with Professors' help to acquire the language, whetted their jealousy of this unkempt, untaught herd-boy, daring to sip 'the nectar of the gods.' In conversation with William Moncrieff, son of the minister of Abernethy, William ventured to say, 'I'm sure the deil has taught you some words.' Brown laughed at the jest. But it turned out to be no jest; it was seriously meant. It is scarcely credible today; but the foul suspicion of using the black art was fastened upon him, and in that superstitious age was believed in, and persisted in; and five ugly years elapsed ere the stigma that was blighting all the youth's prospects was removed.

In continuation of his autobiographical fragment, Brown refers to this unhappy time:

'I had not lived much above a year after, amidst many delightful breathings of God's Spirit, intermingled with fears, temptations, and prevalencies of inward follies and corruptions together, when I was exercised with a new and sharp trial, especially on account of the piety and influence of some that promoted it.

'By means of my anxious pursuit of learning, as I could get any opportunity, I had, by the Lord's assistance, acquired some knowledge of the Latin, Greek, and Hebrew languages, and was beginning to fix my purpose to use it in the service of Christ, if He should open a regular door. My learning of these languages without a master, except for one month, occasioned some talk of me, and some small connection between some Seceding students and me, some of which proved my stedfast friends, while others took a very different course. Having no knowledge of polite manners, being never more than a bashful herd-boy, I did not know the danger of saying the truth. Accordingly I was simply drawn into imparting to an intimate friend a hint, which was thought not so honourable to one of the students, though I meant nothing but a simple declaration of truth, in answer to the question put to me by my friend.

'This was represented by the student as false. My words were misrepresented, as if they had borne that I was as, if not more, learned than he; and, to crown my afflictions, it was represented by him and his defenders that I certainly had got my learning from Satan.

'As scarcely any person had ever appeared noted for the knowledge of languages, but such as had learned at least some

[37]

of them by their own mere industry, it manifested either strong prejudice or great ignorance of what had passed in the learned world, to put this construction upon what my hard labour, by the blessing of God, had acquired to me. It was, however, thought necessary by the managers of it to hunt me down with this malevolent reproach. Nor did they spare to invent or hand about many mere fictions of their own, in order to make it gain credit.'

In this respect young Brown experienced, though not so severely, a similar fate to that which befell Roger Bacon, who, in the thirteenth century, for his intellectual daring and scientific discoveries – 'certain suspected novelties,' they were called – was accused of being aided by magic and 'communion of devils,' and suffered in consequence fourteen years' imprisonment. But a worse fate than imprisonment, even cruel torture and death, were meted out in the later centuries to those condemned for witchcraft. In 1740, Scotland was only emerging from the tyranny of this devilish spite against the efforts of some of her stronger spirits. In all countries the black art exerted its hateful spell. From the fourteenth to the seventeenth century it was specially active, and numbered its victims by tens of thousands. The Reformation made no change in its dismal rule, which indeed was never so virulent as in the seventeenth century. Catholic and Protestant theologians believed in the possibility and reality of compact with the devil, as firmly as they believed in the dogma of the personality of the devil himself. Both alike vigorously defended the prosecutions of those so falsely and wickedly accused. A physician of Germany, Johann Wier (1516-88), was one of the first to write in protest against the folly and cruelty of the witchcraft trials, asserting with withering sarcasm in the course of his argument that in the hierarchy of hell there were 'seventy-two princes, and seven million four hundred and five thousand nine hundred and twenty-six devils, errors excepted,' a number so precise that his opponents concluded that it could only have been communicated to him by Satan himself. But the firm protests of the few were angrily resented by the multitudes, led by the clergy, who found Biblical sanction for the extermination of the evil. The gradual dawning of a more humane feeling, with the advance of the centuries, and the spread of the principles of toleration, stirred by a revolt against its excessive cruelties, led to the belief in witchcraft being routed from its fastnesses, so long defended by ignorance, superstition, and malignity. But it died hard, even after Parliament had decreed that punishment for it must cease. In his Journal, John Wesley makes more than one allusion to it, uttering his strong protest against the growing tendency to toleration, and defending the old belief, by a number of what he calls 'well-attested facts.' Writing on May 25th, 1768, nearly thirty years after Brown suffered, he says:

'It is true that the English in general, and indeed most of the men of learning in Europe, have given up all accounts of witches and apparitions, as mere old wives' fables. I am sorry for it; and I willingly take this opportunity of entering my solemn protest against this violent compliment which so many that believe the Bible pay to those who do not believe it. I owe them no such service. I take knowledge these are at the bottom of the outcry which has been raised, and with such insolence spread throughout the nation, in direct opposition not only to the Bible, but to the suffrage of the wisest and best of men in all ages and nations. They well know (whether Christians know it or not) that the giving up witchcraft is, in effect, giving up the Bible.'

In Scotland, the trials for witchcraft were, as in other countries, a travesty of justice. The accused were hounded down with the merest pretence of a trial. The clergy in Scotland were blamed for the rigour with which the prosecutions were carried out. In Sharpe's *History of Witchcraft in Scotland*, there are many ghastly details of the tragedies of this fateful art. It was

[39]

only in 1736, two years or so before the allegation was made against young Brown, that the statutes imposing a death penalty were repealed. In 1697, in Paisley, seven persons suffered for bewitching a girl of eleven, Christian Shaw, of Bargorran. At Pittenweem in 1704, and Kinross in 1718, neither of them far from Abernethy, the scaffold claimed a victim. The last execution in Scotland was at Dornoch in 1722, where a poor old woman perished for having ridden her own daughter, according to the allegation, transformed into a pony, and shod by the devil, which made the girl lame for ever after in hands and feet, as well as her son after her. In 1730, one of the Professors of Law in Glasgow University, Professor William Forbes, proclaimed his firm belief in witchcraft in his *Institutes of the Law of Scotland*. He defined it as that 'black Art whereby strange and wonderful things are wrought by a power derived from the devil. Nothing seems plainer to me than that there may be and have been witches, and that perhaps such are now actually existing.'

What made the accusation the more serious for young Brown was, that when the statutes against witchcraft were repealed, many of the clergy in Scotland protested, and none more emphatically than those who had seceded from the Church of Scotland, and it was to the Church of the secession that Brown adhered. In 1743, in a confession of national and personal sins, they deplored 'the penal statutes against witches having been repealed by Parliament, contrary to the express law of God; for which a holy God may be provoked in a way of righteous judgment to leave those who are already ensnared to be hardened more and more; and to permit Satan to tempt and seduce others to that same dangerous and wicked snare.'

Brown felt keenly the cruel suspicion that was fastened upon him. The very retirement he sought on the upland solitudes for higher communion was twisted against him; and this perversion of his conduct was a double sting. He was charged, in the whirl of words, with compact with the devil, also with falsehood and hypocrisy. For he was now a member of the

Church of Abernethy. The Session,[1] who exercised oversight over the conduct of the members, naturally took cognisance of the *fama* raised against him, yet apparently not greatly daring to serve upon him a formal accusation. Some of its members still lingered in the dark supersitions of the past, others were casting them off, but not so resolutely as to stand out completely from under their shadow. Unhappily, Alexander Moncrieff, with all his perspicuity and force of character, in this matter leaned to the traditions of the centuries, and agreed with John Wesley in his protest that the giving up of witchcraft was, in effect, giving up the Bible. Unhappily for Brown, he evidently believed in the absurd accusation. Though at first he encouraged him in his studies, it would seem that when he saw that he was bent upon the ministry of the Church, he scouted the idea of this school-less youth making such pretensions. In spite of Brown's repeated attempts to get his character cleared by the Session, Moncrieff allowed the charge to hang round his neck. At last the disappointed youth resolved to shake the dust of Abernethy off his feet. But his heart clung to the faith of his fathers, whose spiritual treasures he had begun to realize for himself. The fellowship of Christian men and women, he wished, wherever he went, to cultivate; and the principal passport to their circle was a clean certificate of church membership; for then, as now, evil galloped its hundred leagues while truth was pulling on its boots.

The Rev. Alexander Moncrieff (1695-1761), Brown's minister, was a man scholarly, devout, and supremely zealous for the truth. He was a minister highly esteemed in many respects, deeply interested in the young of his flock, and greatly given to prayer; sometimes in the middle of his preaching he would pause, with face uplifted and lips moving, which led an old woman to say: 'See! Culfargie, he's awa' to heaven, and left us a' sitting here.' But withal he had a strong and stubborn temper that made him obdurate and unbending at times. He

[1] The name given in Scottish Presbyterianism to the collective body of elders in the local church.

was descended from those who had passed for their faith through fire and blood. His grandfather, the Rev. Alexander Moncrieff, of Scoonie, Fifeshire, stood beside James Guthrie of Stirling in the fierce persecution under Charles II. The one was taken, hanged at the scaffold; the other left, but condemned never to preach again. He was, however, of apostolic mould, and knew whom to obey. Ere his death in 1688, in many a highland glen, and in busier haunts, he proclaimed his Master. His son, the father of the minister of Abernethy, died when the youth was fifteen years of age. At Perth Academy and St. Andrews University young Moncrieff prosecuted his studies, and then, to perfect himself in theology, went to the University of Leyden in Holland, in those days, by the teaching of John à Mark and Wesselius, an acknowledged centre of learning in Europe. In 1720, he was called to his native parish, and ordained as minister of Abernethy. He was also proprietor of the estate of Culfargie in the near neighbourhood. He sided with the 'Marrow Men' in their attitude in the Assembly of the Church of Scotland in 1722; joined Ebenezer Erskine in his defence of the Church's rights in 1732 at Perth, and became one of the Secession 'Four.' When they were deposed and necessity was laid upon them to organize a Church, he became in 1742, the professor of divinity. In the burgess-oath controversy he upheld strenuously its disallowance, and separated from his brethren. He died in 1761, leaving two sons in the ministry, Matthew as his successor in Abernethy, and William in Alloa.

In order to obtain a certificate of his church membership, Brown wrote a long letter to Moncrieff, of extreme interest, in which he defended himself against the base calumny, explained how he acquired his knowledge of languages, and expressed his readiness to account for every step of his conduct before the ecclesiastical court. The letter is somewhat diffuse, jerky, and disjointed, and studded with uncouth phrases of common parlance. It has to be remembered that it was written by a youth, practically self-educated, who had devoted more time and strength to the study of ancient languages than to a mastery of his own. It bears the date, August 6th, 1745.

To the Rev. Alexander Moncrieff, Abernethy

'REV. SIR,—Although God has justly punisht me very sore for my exceeding great unbelief, pride, perjury, etc., by specially carrying as an enemy himself, yet at the same time he has let loose men and devils against me, as instruments in pleading his just quarrel. But among all other things the misunderstanding that is betwixt you and me is not the least part of the trial; therefore I humbly wish you would give me leave to inform you of the falsity of some stories which causes this misunderstanding; and also to tell you wherein you have wronged me in some things, as also wherein I have wronged you. The story runs thus:

'Somebody having (as I hear in a private unsubscribed letter) exceedingly defamed me—December 7th, I think. When I spoke to you, December 16th, the conversation was to this purpose—You: "Got ye a book from Roby Millar?" I: "Yes, *Quintus Curtius.*" You: "What was he doing when ye took it home?" I: "Bigging his father's wain." You: "Did you say to him that you could read it all?" I: "No, I said, when he said, 'Can you read it all?' 'Nay, for there are many sentences I cannot construct, and I mind of four or five words that I ken not the English of at all.'" You: "Did you speir [ask] these words at him?" I: "I tell'd [told] him them over that he might tell me their English." You: "Did he do it syne [at that time]?" I: "No. After this." You: "Do you pray evening and morning?" I: "Yes." You: "When began ye to do so?" I: "About seven or eight years since." You: "What put you first to it?" I: "My father, when I was a little chield, gar'd [made] me do it, but I often slighted it." You: "But did you never neglect these seven or eight years?" I: "Not that I mind of, but for the most part I did it at the fold when I let out and put in my sheep." These answers concerning this last you look on as both proud and false; and in order to discover its fallacy, John Ogilvie was brought, who, when asked anent it, said, "I cannot say I found him a person under the exercise of grace." But as it was impossible for him to know perfectly anent whether I did it or no, so his answer neither asserts nor contradicts; and, as for the pride of it, as I do not trust that ever I did an action all my days without pride at the highest rate before God, so really I do not see wherein my pride in the sight of men appears, seeing I know not of either its falsehood or its unnecessity at that time in order to vindicate myself; but, if you will, you shall hear the sum of the whole story. My father, having forced me to pray alone, when I was little, I, as oft as occasion served, neglected it, for which I had some disquiet of mind by Psalm 9. 17, and by Vincent *On Judgment*, and Alleine's *Alarm*. So, after a formal slight using of Alleine's directions I dedicated myself to the Lord in solemn vow, as Alleine directs (summer 1735 or 1736, viz. the last, or last except one, I was with John Ogilvie, for I went from him Nov. 1736); particularly I vowed to pray six times when I was herding, and thrice when I was not herding, in the day. So I continued to do this; and, if I was deficient the one day, I made amends the next. . . . If I fell into any known sin I prayed for forgiveness, and so was well; all movings of the affections I took for special enjoyings of God, and now thought myself sure of heaven, if I was not a hypocrite; to avoid which deceit I kept the whole of my religion as hid as I could, especially prayer, and to that end prayed almost ay in the field, where, if I was not pretty sure nobody was near, I was exceeding low of voice, and, lest my head being bare might discover it, I cast my blanket over it, or else laid an open book before me so that they might think I was reading; and so made myself, in my conceit, as sure of heaven as possible. In this way of doing I continued from that time till June 1740, or else 1741, at least, if not till now; still putting my fashion religion in Christ's room, setting up my formal prayers, etc., for my Saviour, yea for my God.

'Anent the other story it happened thus—December 18th,

1742 – when I was before the elders. You said: "You said you speired [asked] these four or five words at Roby Millar?" Said I: "I only tell'd him them that he might tell me their English." You: "But Henry Ferney says you said to them you speired them." I: "I don't think it, but if I said speired, it was a snaper [harmless misdemeanour]." You: "That was a fell way of snapering [a pretty considerable misdemeanour]." I: "It was much about one meaning, for I tell'd him them in a speiring way." You: "You use fell equivocating." I: "Henry Ferney said, 'I'll tell you just the way, as far as I mind, he said, he let Roby Millar see these words.'" You: "Roby, did he speir these words at you?" R. said, "No." I said, "I am not saying speired; Roby, did I not tell you over these words?" R.: "You told me no such words." I: "Well, Roby, I appeal to your brother and to your conscience to the contrary." R.: "If so, I did not hear you." I: "I do not ken whether you heard me or no; but am sure I told you them."

"You alleged that it was pride to say I knew all *Curtius* but five words, or to say Roby Millar did not tell me their English, and that it was as much as to say Roby knew them not. To answer which I shall narrate the whole story, and it runs thus: I said: "Roby, have there your book." Roby said, "Have you got a story out of *Quintus Curtius*?" I: "Yes." R.: "Can you read it all?" I: "No, for there are many sentences which I could not construct, and I mind of four or five words I know not their English at all." I mind not whether he speired what they were or no, but however I repeated them – Crudus, Arma, Maxæ, Diæ, and Calæ; at which time I affirm there was no natural impediment of his hearing. However, he told me not their English. Now I using whiles to read over a story of it to John and Henry Ferney, they missing this, said, "Where is your book?" I: "Home." They: "Could you read it all?" I: "No, for besides places which I cannot lay together, I mind four or five words which I know not the meaning of at all." They: "You should have speired them at him." I: "So I did, or so I did tell him them." They: "Did he tell you their English?"

I: "No." They: "It may be that he could not." I: "I know not whether he could or not, but he did not."

'At this meeting also you said to me: "Did you say, 'I can read all *Ovid* but five words'?" I: "No." You: "Alexander Blyth, said he it not to you?" Alexander said, "I cannot be positive, but I think he said so." I: "I said never such a word." He answered not a word. You said to me: "Said ye ever that for as good a master Mr. Caml [Campbell] is, some of his scholars are not very good?" I: "No." You: "Henry Ferney, heard ye ever such a tale about the hills?" Henry: "No." On the whole you concluded me to be proud with a witness, and said you thought it not fit such a proud chield should be a student.

'Some days after I desired conference to inform you more fully of these stories. You refused, May 1743, I think. Notwithstanding you knew of all this, you admitted to me to accede [obtain] an attestation from Andrew Ferney; but June in the beginning, I coming to speak with you before Stirling Communion, said you: "I'll have nothing to do with you, because you dissembled to me." I: "I dissembled not to you." You: "Did not the lad say so?" I: "Did I not say contrary?" You: "Well, I shall consider it the first week-day's session; and so you may wait on." You: "You said to Alex. Blyth you knew all Ovid but five words." I: "Alex. Blyth would not say so, and I'm sure I did it not." You: "John Macarsy heard you say so." I: "Let John Macarsy come, I'll widd [wager] he shall not say it before my face." He was not brought. You: "What was you doing when you was up in some hill?" I: "What hill?" You: "I ken not, some hill." I: "The way of that story is that I was in the Castel [Castle] Law four nights on end, when I was with John Ogilvie, doing nobody knew what; but I said it is a lie, for I never was in the Castel Law one night. I indeed watched my sheep some nights at the foot thereof, seeing it was my duty."

'So the first week-day's session was June 28th, which day I in some measure attended on the Session, but was never called in. That day I took occasion of some conferences, as 1st, with Mr. Millar. I said: "As I would end the matter as peaceably as possible, so I offer if you'll go to the session and say, *It may be I* told you those words, to seek no more." R.: "There is no matter betwixt you and me; all the matter is betwixt you and H. Ferney." I: "You said, I told you not these words." R.: "I said not you did not tell me them, for you might tell me them and me not hear you, etc." 2nd, with Mr. Macarsy. I: "The minister says you heard me say to Mr. Blyth, I knew all *Ovid* but five words, and you know you never heard me speak anything to Mr. Blyth bees [such as] that." Mc.: "I heard you never say it to Mr. Blyth." I: "Well, will you but tell Mr. Moncrieff you did not hear me say so?" Mc.: "I'll bear no such message to the minister." I said: "I hear there was an unsubscribed letter sent to the minister saying a deal of ill of me. Was it you who sent it, or know ye ought about it?" Mc.: "I know nothing about it; and for my part, as much as I have been blamed, I never said ought to your disadvantage." I: "I hear you would not let my letters be seen, but destroyed them." Mc.: "I did it out of love to you, for had they been seen they would have done you more ill than all that yet has appeared, for they were clatters [idle talk], and founded on clatters." I: "I doubt if the two last would have done me any ill, but, as for the first, I own there were some things wrong in it." Mc.: "They were full of wrath and malice, and also in a letter to Mr. Archibald, you endeavoured to make us all black." I: "There I said no more of you than that – 'Equidem audivi Joan Macartium in Strathmiglo me esse diabolice doctum dixisse.'"[1] Mc.: "I do not mind of ever speaking of your name in Strathmiglo. As for your learning, I'm in a strait about it, as well as far better learned men are." I: "You told me the contrary at Culfargie's [viz. that he spake of me to John Lumsden and Andrew Ferney]; but that is but a mistake of the memory, which is fallible." I answer if he had

---

[1] 'I have personally heard that John Macarsy in Strathmiglo has stated that I have got my learning by the help of the devil.'

been in any strait he was willingly in it, else he would have sought information.

'Now as there are several stories anent my learning as that it is unprecedented – from the devil – that I learned in hills and dens, without a grammar, and master, etc., I shall endeavour to satisfy you on this matter. Now I think it is not from the deil on these accounts: because, 1st, I am, as I solemnly appeal to the God of heaven as witness, in no compact with him, nor did he ever speak to me *viva voce*, nor yet learned he me ought (as far as I know) by enthusiastick impulse, in which if I lie, may God avenge it. (1) I sought it from God by beginning my lessons of times with prayer, as God is witness. (2) Its reasonableness further appears in that I had an occasional master, Mr. Reid, from whom I got many lessons, and at him I speired all the unknown words I minded. Now if a fixed master can learn, an occasional one may do it too, tho' more slowly, for *majus et minus non variant speciem*.[1] 2nd, It is well known that all arts use to arise from men's reason by learning. 3rd, Learned men, as Locke *on Education*, and Clarke in his *Introduction*, tell us one may learn by industry; "nay," says Locke, "one's mother might teach him the Latin tongue," etc. As to grammar, it is the consent I suppose of all men, it is not absolutely necessary, seeing it is only a superstructure founded on language. Now a foundation may well exist without a superstructure, at least Lilly, Watt, and Clarke, and Locke, are of this opinion. As the great question is anent the Greek, which I learned some of afore I got a Greek grammar, it runs thus:

(Then follows the portion already quoted as to how he acquired a knowledge of Greek with his *Ovid* and New Testament.)

'As to my letters the story runs thus: About November 10th, 1741, I had some conversation with Messrs. W. and Mat. Moncriefs, and John Macarsy. They caused me to read some

[1] 'Greater and less make no difference in the nature of a thing.'

[48]

lines of Terence and Greek Testament, then asked if I had a Greek grammar. I said "Not yet." W. said (I thought it had been in jest): "I'm sure the deil has told you some words." Mac.: "You begin at the top and build down to the bottom." Nothing more remarkable was here said. About November 29th, when I came to Mr. Blyth's school, without any provocation, I got two counts from them, viz. Messrs. M. M. and A. B. At this time I got some hard language. They also gave a count, as I was informed, to Mr. Reid, I suppose in mockery, which much enraged me; as also I heard it commonly that Mac. and Mr. M. M. had and were endeavouring to spread it that it was not possible for me to learn so without diabolick influence, with which I, being enraged, sent with the pretended answer to their count these railing words: "Audivi vos dixisse me diabolice doctum. Sed qui scitis? Queisque signis probatur? Expertine estis diabolum bonum esse doctorem? Egone diabolicus? Vosne diaboli? Imo videtur ratio est. Mimalloneis vestra impli cornua bombis. Τῳ Ματθαιῳ Μονκρειφῳ και τοις λοιποις με διαβολιζουσι.'[1]

'No more that I can know to be offensive is in it. With these I sent them a count. Some time after by means of Amos 3. 6, "Can there be evil," etc., I came in some way to see God's hand in the affliction, by means of which about June 15th, 1742, I sent them two letters, confessing the wrong I had done them, and begging forgiveness, intimating that I forgave them whatever they had done against me. These letters were, as I heard, sore misrepresented, but as God is my witness that thus the matter ran, I desire to rest careless, seeing He is judge, as I told them.

'But, to return. The consideration of my character being neglected, June 28th, I several times entreated you to do it,

---

[1] 'I have heard that you stated that I was taught by the devil. But how do you know? By what evidence is it proved? Have you learned by experience that the devil is a good teacher? Am I a devil? Are you devils? That indeed seems to be the rational account of the matter. Its mad music I've filled your trumpets with. To Matthew Moncrieff and others who call me a devil.'

according to your promise. At length, in harvest, 1743, Providence seemed (upon condition I brought a testificate [certificate] with me) to invite me to another place, but by the unreasonable refusal of a testificate, I was stopt. Then, as for bleatness [becoming modesty], I feared to complain *viva voce* to the session of this their unjust treatment, I sent two letters to them, which, excepting some circumstances, I just now [still] approve. They nothing prevailed, therefore I twice came personally to them and pleaded a cognisance [investigation] July 9th, 1744. You, in their name, I think, before them said: "John, if you will come to the next week-day session and insist, we shall consider or *think on* methods for considering not only the affair betwixt Mr. Millar and you, but your whole character." Said I: "But how shall I know when the session sits?" Said you: "You'll get word some way." But several week-day sessions after this were kept so close (why, I know not), that, in spite of my utmost enquiry, I could never know when they were till they were past.

'So, being again disappointed here, I came again to you (thinking it was just much as if I had gone to the session, seeing at the session you may give the answer) in December 1744. I desired you to cognise [investigate] my affair. Said you: "I am not to fash my head about it; but if you go out of the parish you shall get a testificate." Said I: "You did not give me one when I sought it." Said you: "You was not going out of the parish." Said I: "But I know I was (and I appeal to All-seeing God, that I was firmly resolved to dwell out of this parish, as soon as I got a testificate, both now and then)." Said you: "John, you want to be a scholar, and I do not want that." I said: "That is not the present thing I want; I want to have my character as it should be." Said you: "I did not break your character."

'Here I take occasion to answer: (1) That though I should seek to be a scholar, that is no reason why I should be unjustly punished. (2) You say you do not want me to be a scholar. Why? Say you, "His reason for it is but fancy." I answer it may be so; but thus it is: Considering of a particular calling, it was borne in on my mind, that everybody should serve God in that calling his faculty is best for, and, considering that my learning faculty was strongest, therefore I concluded it was my duty to serve God in some learning station. I rejected it because I thought I was not able to carry on learning; but that word, "The Lord will provide," Gen. 22. 8, about the same time, Isa. 43. 2, were borne in on my mind, so I yielded to essay it. Further, as far as I can discover, this impulse brings with it a sense of insufficiency and impels regularly, so that notwithstanding of irregular doors being opened, with invitations to enter in, yet hitherto the Lord has kept my feet from thus falling, which I look on as a token from God. I add that often I've laid the matter before the Lord, but could receive nothing like a prohibition. (Indeed, in 1743, March, I think, I was haunted with this: "The evil is of the Lord, why should I wait any longer." I observed that this impulse carried with it a deadening carelessness about religion, and so concluded it to be a diabolick impulse.) About the same time there was an impulse. "Thy way to God commit. Him trust, it bring to pass shall He," etc. This I took as savouring more of the Holy Spirit. This is it wherein I fancied my call to be a scholar lay. So if you would indeed convince me that it is all fancy I should be glad, and should no more seek to be a scholar. (3) Your other reason why you want me not to be a scholar, is my want of means. To this I answer, if the Lord ever shall open a door for my entrance to be a scholar, I hope to be in no way burdensome to the Presbytery or you either. But, to return. June 1st, I went away out of this parish (leaving commission to John Laurie to get me a testificate) and travelled in East Lothian some time, accounting it my residence (for I have none but a nominal residence here), but took no house till I was quite away. So coming back for my testificate, I caused Mr. Marshall write a common one, and came and bade you, by Janet Din, sign it. You refused. I by her bade you put what you would to it, and then sign it. You said: "I have nothing ado with it." Here appears a right cruel procedure, for: First, your promise of a testificate was that which moved me to seek one. Second, This, in my view, was equal to the greater excommunication materially, for it implies a total casting me out of your care, and so you would have nothing to do with my testificate. Thus you have punished me these two years on suspicion with a material excommunication, the evil of which I showed in my letters, March 1744, and January, I think, 1744, or December 1743. I add, thirdly, thereby I am exposed to the fury of men and devils; as (1), to soldiers taking me, as being under *mala fama*; (2), to adherents tempting to apostasy, of which tempting they make this, your unjust treatment, their occasion; (3), to devils and mine own lusts tempting me to vent anger at you, etc., to desert the cause, because of the bad usage I met with in it. Under which trouble, as I have acted most sinfully by trespassing more and more against the Lord, so I have been guilty of hatred at you, which I have especially discovered in not using due pains to restrain you in this course of injustice, and also in telling this your treating of me, unwarily, where I should not; for which as I wish for forgiveness of God, so I wish you'll forgive me it, humbly intimating that through the grace that is in Jesus, I desire to forgive you and all men, whatever they have done or said against me, as I would desire to be forgiven of God. So I earnestly beg and intreat you would from this time forth do me justice by bringing my character to trial, and if you find me then guilty of scandal, punish me with some formal censure, which thing I resolve to seek from the session as soon as possible.

'All this letter I write in presence of Almighty God, who punishes liars, Rev. 21. 8; 22. 16, and leave it to the management of Providence, desiring you to use it as the Lord shall direct you. So farewell. August 6th, 1745.

Your weak lover,

CARPOW.

JOHN BROWN.

'N.B.—Sometimes the sense (not the exact words, is only kept.

J. B.'

[52]

The letter, quaint, rugged, stilted as it is, so different from the flowing style he was yet to acquire, is a witness to the seriousness of the charge, though the charge seems to us today to savour of the ridiculous and the grotesque. His irreproachable character, his manifest purity of motive and of life, alone warded off the slander and its dire possible consequences. Time brought its test; and in the end truth and sincerity prevailed. But Moncrieff was adamant to the last. Another year of disquiet had to be endured. Then on June 16th, 1746, the clean certificate of full membership in the Church was granted by the unanimous vote of the elders and deacons of Abernethy, Moncrieff dissenting, and refusing to sign it.[1] Thus, after five years of persecution, his character was cleared. But the lash of the slander left its mark on the young spirit. The freeness and ease of talk with men in regard to his scholarship or literary aims, was gone. There was a certain reserve about him henceforth, as of a man who had to be on his guard, and a reticency to speak of the days of his youth. It is not without interest to recall what he himself said about witchcraft in his *Dictionary of the Bible*, which enjoyed such a wide repute in its day:

'WITCH is a woman and WIZARD is a man that has dealing with Satan, if not actually entered into formal compact with him. That such persons are among men is abundantly plain from Scripture, and that they ought to be put to death (Deut. 18. 10; Exod. 22. 18). It is plain, however, that great caution is necessary in the detection of the guilty, and in punishing them, lest the innocent suffer, as many instances in New England, and other places, show. Nor can I believe that people's standing in awe of persons, as suspected for this infernal power is anything else than an indirect worshipping of

[1] The minute of the court runs as follows: 'John Brown, having desired a testificate to be given him, the Elders and Deacons agreed *nemine contradicente* that the testificate should be given him, and the minister signified that he would not stand in the way of its being given him, seeing it was carried in the session, but that he could not sign it, but left it as a deed of the session to be signed by the session clerk.'

Satan. Witchcraft comprehends all kinds of influence produced by collusion with Satan, and excludes the user from the kingdom of God (Gal. 5. 20).'

The falseness of the charge against himself did not deliver him from the trammels of the long-standing tradition. In his *History of the Church of Scotland*, referring to Archbishop Sharp and his delinquencies, he says: 'There is not a little ground to believe that he had entered into a solemn compact with the devil, in order to preserve his life, and to carry on his designs.'

Hard is it for the human mind to divest itself wholly of the ghastly cerements that have clung to it from the days of youth, and been so universally worn. Perhaps in regard to himself, Brown concluded that, seeing it was the New Testament that drew him into the net of the inquisition, there was *prima facie* reason for the senselessness of the imputation upon him; for, as his great-grandson sagely observed, 'That shrewd personage, the devil, would not have employed him on the New Testament.'

CHAPTER 5

The Pedlar

The *Wanderjahr*[1] of many men at one time was regarded as
an essential part of their education. It carried them into strange
lands, and among people of strange tongues, which they were
expected to acquire. It opened the mind to new aspects of life,
and was considered a liberalizing agent in the mental development of the privileged youth, as no doubt it was. John
Brown had his *wanderjahr*; but it was of a different order
from that commonly enjoyed. To begin with, it was, in a
measure, forced upon him. It only included the counties of
Kinross, Fife, and East Lothian, with occasional adventures,
or sacramental pilgrimages, to neighbouring counties. Business
was conjoined with education. The one year stretched into five
years, with two exciting episodes between, one connected with
the State, and the other with the Church.

Abernethy, which had proved an unkind mother, he had
determined to quit, as soon as his character was cleared by his
Church. Meantime he assumed the role of pedlar, shouldered
a pack, and set off into the neighbouring county of Kinross,
crossing at times the Firth of Forth to the Lothians, and
offering his goods to selected customers.

A characteristic feature in Scottish life in that troubled
period of Church history was the formation of 'praying
societies.' In many places the lamp of religion burned low.
The services in the churches were cold and dead. But in nearly
every town and hamlet there were fervent hearts that hungered
for fellowship. Little societies sprang up, that met once a week

[1] Year of travel.

and kept the flame of the evangel bright and glowing. These societies were the saviours of evangelical truth in Scotland. John Brown sought them out in his wanderings and enrolled himself in their ranks. Their members, the sincere and devout of the time, scouted the calumny raised against him, and among them he found repose of soul. In later years, he expressed his gratitude by drawing up for their guidance a series of rules, which, by reason of their sagacity, breadth, and Christian spirit, proved of great service.

To the members of such societies mainly he carried his wares. Fashions changed slowly in the reigns of the first two Georges; but there was still a necessity for the household to renew its supplies. David Livingstone found, on his first visit to Cape Town, in 1852, after a number of years in the heart of South Africa, that his clothes were ten years out of date.[1] A hundred years earlier, ten years would have made no difference – he would have been still in the fashion. People in most cases made their own clothes, and the newest London modes were long in reaching them. Even the tailors who appeared occasionally at houses that preferred their services, and who were paid at the rate of 2d. or 3d. per day with food, believed thoroughly that the old ways were best. The shops, little earth-floored, dark, thatched houses, were poorly supplied through lack of capital and customers; and packmen carried round a varied if limited assortment of wares in their wallets, and waited upon cottage and mansion. In houses of the rich and poor, weaving went on, and travelling weavers made periodical visits and exchanged a tempting web for the home-spun product.

In this business John Brown spent five years of his life. But it did not prove a very profitable concern. His wares got sadly mixed up; a piece of ribbon would draw out needles and pins, thread, handkerchiefs, and lace, with the whole contents in inextricable confusion. To a few sympathetic and thoughtful housewives on his rounds, he was indebted for putting his

[1] W. G. Blaikie, *The Personal Life of David Livingstone*, first edition, p. 127.

wares in order, and making an attractive display. With him the passion for business was outrivalled by the passion for books. Wherever on the shelves of any household he discovered a few volumes, the pack was quickly forgotten, and he devoured the literature that was spread before him. The day would speed its course and night would often find him far from his lodging.

The great Church festival, observed at different times in different places, provided a change in the wanderings. Days were given up to the Communion seasons. To Dunfermline, Burntisland, Falkirk, Stirling, Glasgow, he walked and enjoyed 'ravishing' and refreshing times.

An interesting sketch of him at this period is presented by the acquaintance of his early days in the document already referred to:

'Some time after this Mr. Brown turned his attention to merchandise, and became a travelling merchant. His journeys were confined mostly to the inland parts of Fife and Kinross shires. In this line he did not much succeed; it was only families he called at who were reported to him as religious and given to reading, and, upon finding any intelligent person to converse with, or new book to consult, his merchandise was no more minded. Half days and more were spent thus, and when evening approached he had sometimes miles to travel to his lodgings, as he had what we call in this country only *feft* places he chose to lodge at. One of these, in this neighbourhood, was David Young's, in Balgedie. There, that sensible man told me, Mr. Brown would have stayed two or three days, and gathered in all the books he could get his hands on, about the town, which he could scarce be withdrawn from to take his meat. Mr. Young was acquaint with him from his infancy, and used great freedom with him, and often represented to him the propriety of attending to his merchandise, and not to spend his time in what at that time he thought did not so much concern him. But his remonstrances were all in vain, for, said Mr. Young, he was fit for nothing else but for being a scholar; and when he was but a child, his mother seemed to have some persuasion, or at least fondness, that he should. She would have said, "O, when will I see the craws fleein' ower my bairn's kirk?" But on his return to Mr. Ireland's, of Urquhart, or to Mr. Robert Low's in Roundil, from his trading excursions, for these were his headquarters and his home, his stock of goods stood in much need of a proper arrangement, which he was very well pleased to see accomplished by some of the family. His articles were often so displaced that upon laying hold of the end of a ribbon or garter two or three buckles were brought up, and these clasped some hanks of thread, and so on. About this time he was dressed in a whitish coat, which, with carrying his pack, was worn out on both shoulders, and mended with cloth darker than the coat.'

The writer proceeds to give a description of a journey to Stirling to attend a sacramental feast. The Rev. Ebenezer Erskine, pronounced by Dr. John Watson[1] to be 'the most representative type of sound spiritual character in the eighteenth century,' though he had separated himself from the State Church, had elicited the sympathy of many throughout the land, by the stand he had taken in defence of the Church's rights and the Church's faith. It found expression in the readiness with which these sympathizers travelled long distances to be present at the Communion celebrations of his congregation. John Brown and his company journeyed from Kinross and even beyond, twenty-five miles and more, down the vale of the Devon, to the City of the Rock. Hospitality was freely offered on such occasions. When they reached Stirling, Brown, with his rustic garb, was relegated to the humblest place in the house where he was entertained, which he accepted uncomplainingly; but his worth was soon recognized, and he was summoned to occupy the chief seat beside the master of the house.

[1] John Watson, *The Scot of the Eighteenth Century*, p. 284.

'At this period, he, in company with Mr. Ireland of Urquhart, and a number of people from this corner, went to Stirling to attend on the dispensation of the Lord's Supper by Mr. E. Erskine. Mr. Brown sometimes joined one company on the road, and sometimes another, but Mr. Ireland discerned his friend, if before him, by the back of his coat. At Stirling they were lodged in some respectable house near the town, in whose hospitality a considerable number of worshippers from various quarters also shared. Mr. Brown sat down in the kitchen in company with the servants and herds of the family. After supper the household and guests were called into a parlour for worship. The gentleman of the house requested Mr. Ireland to take the lead in divine service. He excused himself, as being at that time much fatigued with the long journey; but, reaching the Bible to Mr. Brown, said, "Johnnie Brown, you'll do this service for me," to which Mr. Brown yielded, and went through the service to the satisfaction of the company. On the after-days of the solemnity he was no more left in the kitchen, but preferred to a seat at the head of the table, close by the master of the house, and every respect shown him to which these talents, which his rustic garb could not conceal, evidently entitled him.'

Referring to this period, the 'Short Memoir' of his life gives a refreshing glimpse of a man under the cloud of a malicious calumny, who resolutely determined to steer the straight course in calm silence, till light should arise. With his own thoughts he communed as he carried his wallet to and fro; and the truth searched him the more keenly, especially in the gatherings at the sacred festival, because spiteful tongues had thrust this shame upon him. The retrospect of after-years revealed, however, that it was a spiritual snow summit which he had been climbing during this dismal period of obloquy and reproach.

'While for several years this calumny was carried on and spread far and wide, I enjoyed remarkable mixtures of mercy with the affliction. In my very entry on it, that word, "His loving-kindness the Lord will command in the daytime, His song shall be with me in the night, and my prayer to the God of my life," was peculiarly sweet to my soul. The members of the praying society to which I belonged all continued my steady friends. Not one that I knew of who knew me, as far as I discovered, appeared less, but rather more friendly to me than before, except such as were very nearly connected with the raisers or chief managers of the calumnious report. Nay, my acquaintance with the world being extended, many others upon my first acquaintance were remarkably sympathizing and friendly.

'Meanwhile the Lord, by powerful and pleasant impressions of His Word on my heart, particularly at sacramental occasions at Dunfermline, Burntisland, Falkirk, and Glasgow, marvellously refreshed my soul, and made these years perhaps the most pleasant that ever I had, or will have, on earth. Discourses on these texts – Heb. 10. 37; Ezek. 37. 12; Psa. 91. 2; and a meditation on Psa. 5. 7, were particularly ravishing. To some of these sweet transactions I allude in my *Journal of a Spring, Winter, and Sabbath Day*.

'Meanwhile I was led out to ponder my own heart and way, and made to see myself as bad before God as a devil, and much worse. This I took God to be calling me by the reproach. These things made me not a little content with my lot, and kept me from labouring to expose my reproachers, or even to defend myself, unless when I thought I had a plain call. And I then and ever since have found that the Lord most clearly delivered me and vindicated me, when I made least carnal struggling, but laboured to bear His indignation as quietly as I could. The sting I had found in my learning which I had so eagerly hunted after, tended to keep me humble under what I had attained, or afterwards attained. The reproach which I myself had met with, tended to render me less credulous of what I heard charged on others. On these and other accounts, I have since looked on that sharp affliction as one of God's most kind providences to my soul.'

CHAPTER 6

The Soldier

One day, in the autumn of the memorable year 1745, the pedlar was pursuing his occupation in the Howe of Fife, when a cloud of strangely apparelled figures appeared on the horizon. He slipped behind a cairn of stones, and watched them closely. Houses they entered, and farmyards they visited, and marched off with bags of booty. They were the Highland soldiers of Prince Charles Stuart, foraging for themselves or the army, on its march southward for the capture of a kingdom. It is said that 'during the long march from Perth they had been kept under perfect discipline; such provision as had been required was bought with legal money, and the Highland instinct for plunder was rigorously repressed.'[1] Exactions were laid on towns and country districts where Charles could command authority – at least on the outgoing expedition. On the return from Derby, when the Pretender felt that fortune was deserting him, and he rode sullenly at the rear of his army, discipline was relaxed. Liberty was given to men to supply themselves; and they fell on all convenient booty like 'caterans returning from a creagh.'[2]

The presence of the Highland host created a panic among the people. They feared the worst; and money, valuables, and even clothes were hidden away. Business was at a standstill; and the pedlars were the first to find that their wares were not wanted.

[1] Hume Brown, *History of Scotland*, vol. iii, p. 292.
[2] Scott, *The Tales of a Grandfather*, ch. lxxx. 'Cateran' = Highland cattle lifter; 'creagh' = plundering expedition.

John Brown was indifferent about the falling off of trade – it would give the more time for reading. But the sight of these marauders from the Highlands that had marched across the Grampians and down the Garry, and through the straths to Stirling, showed that his country was in danger. He at once offered for its defence. He took his pack and buried it in a peat-stack on the farm of Cameron, about two and a half miles to the south-west of St. Andrews. He then enlisted in the Fifeshire volunteer corps that was being raised in the county in defence of the Government. He was despatched to hold the fort at Blackness on the Forth, lying between South Queensferry and Boness, as Charles was marching rapidly on Edinburgh. He did not share in the 'Canter of Coltbridge,' as it has been cynically called, when an outpost of the King's dragoons, alarmed by a few pistol-shots from the Prince's approaching hosts, were seized with such panic that, doubling back on the main body, they threw them into such trepidation that the whole regiment fled as fast as horse could carry them through the fields on which the new town of Edinburgh now stands, and reined not bit nor bridle till they reached the village of Prestonpans, leaving Charles victorious, and Cope, the King's general, a public laughing-stock. But Brown was ready to go where the call sounded.

Such a spirit was characteristic of the men belonging to the young Seceding Church with which Brown had associated himself. They entered heartily into the defence of their country at this national crisis.[1] Perplexing questions were troubling their community at the time, but these were at once made to stand aside. The nation was needing the help of its loyal

H. G. Graham, *Social Life of Scotland in the Eighteenth Century*, p. 377, says: 'Scotland at the time was in rebellion and turmoil, parishes were disturbed by raids of wild Highlanders, men were enrolling as volunteers to resist the Pretender, and stolid ministers who could not wield a toasting-fork were anxious to tie on pouches for their ammunition, to shoulder muskets they could barely load, and to be drilled with their communicants; the Church was holding fast and humiliation days to stay the divine judgment in a civil war.'

citizens, and they were among the first to respond, organizing companies out of their own congregations. The Rev. Ebenezer Erskine, at Stirling, with the burden of sixty-five years upon him, formed a volunteer company, and himself acted as captain. When the town was in danger from the Highland host, he appeared in the guard-room in uniform. The officers on guard tried to persuade him that both his calling and his years unfitted him for active service; but he replied, 'I am determined to take the hazards of this night, for the present crisis requires the arms as well as the prayers of all good subjects.' While the rebels were in possession of Stirling, he acted in a twofold capacity, preaching to his congregation in the woods of Tullibody, five miles away, on Sundays, and leading the volunteers in weekdays against the enemy in assaults that again and again endangered his life. Ralph Erskine's son, Henry, settled at Falkirk as minister, led the volunteers of that town, and, as a recognition of his loyalty and bravery, was enrolled as an honorary burgess of Glasgow. Adam Gib, the doughty minister at Edinburgh, called upon his congregation for a corps to defend the city, and over 350 at once responded. While the rebels held the city, but not the castle, he preached for five weeks, at Dreghorn, near Colinton, three miles to the west of the town. There was a large detachment of the enemy in the neighbourhood; and often they sought the outskirts of his congregation. They had to listen to his denunciation of the rebellion, and his prayers for its speedy suppression and for the safety of the reigning sovereign. The spirit of loyalty fired the young Church; and where there were trucklings with the enemy, as, among other places, at Abernethy, where Alexander Moncrieff had to suffer the spoilation of his goods, and the seizure of his sons, the Session exercised its discipline. In many of the Session records of the time, there are instances of those who had served the usurping army, paying the 'cess' they demanded, and digging ditches for them, being 'rebuked' for their disloyalty to the King. Indeed every congregation was arranging to provide a corps of its own, when the rebellion ceased, and the necessity passed.[1]

John Brown's action was typical. Others as readily took up arms. At Blackness he helped to guard the Forth from a French descent, that was momentarily expected. Shortly after the Pretender set out on his ill-fated march to England, he was transferred to Edinburgh Castle. There he remained till the end of the civil war. The return of the Prince and his hapless host was checked at Falkirk by the battle with General Hawley, a man noted for two things, his ignorance of war, and his despotic tyranny. At Culloden, on April 16th, 1746, the decisive blow was struck which ended Charles's hopes and those of the Stuart dynasty. With the escape of the deluded Prince to France, to dribble out his days in his cups, the commotion of the conflict speedily died down. The Fifeshire regiment was disbanded, and Brown returned to his calling.

But Edinburgh had a special attraction for him. Then, as now, it had its famous bookshops. Allan Ramsay's circulating library, the first of its kind, was a fascination to the student.

[1] D. Fraser, *Life of Ebenezer Erskine*, pp. 437-46; D. Fraser, *Life of Ralph Erskine*, pp. 353-61; *Works*, vol. ii, pp. 251, 268, 277; Mackerrow, *History of the Secession Church*, p. 200; McEwen, *The Erskines*, p. 114; Rev. Adam Gib, Edinburgh, in *Scots Magazine*, vol. xxvii, p. 272, says: 'At the time of the rebellion in the year 1745 and 1746, the Seceders were spread as now through all the Lowlands of Scotland, from Dunkeld to Cheviot, from St. Andrews to Air, and in the counties of Angus, Mearns, Banff, Elgin, Nairn and Ross. But not only did not one of them join with the rebels, but all of them, men and women, took all opportunities to manifest their abhorrence of the rebellion, as they took all opportunities to join in public prayer and fasting for the suppression of it, and in public thanksgiving for the same after the great day of Culloden. All the Seceding Ministers were this day employed in their congregations with express supplications in behalf of our Sovereign, King George and his Government.' The records of these congregations practically confirm this. Where any of the members were found trading with the enemy, they were instantly dealt with, and it was shown that such trading was done more or less under compulsion. In a number of records we have examined there are no references, because there was no call for interference; but others show how scrupulously Sessions guarded their communion. In Falkirk a blacksmith was examined before the Session for having forged ramrods for the Highlanders on the Sabbath Day. His defence was that they stood over him with their bayonets, and compelled him to do the work. He was cautioned to be more careful in the future.

When released from military service, Brown set off, down by the Castlegate, where the author of the *Gentle Shepherd*, having now retired from wig-making, and bookselling, and even from the haunts of the Muses, had built his octagon house, commanding a magnificent view of the distant heights of Fife, beyond the Forth. Allan's shop was easily recognized with its heads of Ben Jonson and Drummond of Hawthornden above the door. Perhaps he dropped into the establishment of Alexander Symmers, the bookseller in Parliament Square, into which about this time, or later, Thomas Ruddiman, the famous grammarian, was wont to step, to play with the worthy bookseller the fascinating game of chess, regarding which play, Ruddiman's biographer states: 'They did not play for money; but, being both pertinacious players, they generally parted in a wrangle.'[1] More than likely the young soldier pressed on to the shop of John Gray, in the Grassmarket, the son-in-law of Ebenezer Erskine, who was later to be his own publisher. There he found what suited his taste, and read with avidity and ease works in Latin as well as in English. The Luckenbooths were then a feature of the broad avenue of the High Street, guarded by its lofty crow-stepped gables; and the Tolbooth, 'like a long black snail crawling up the middle of the street, and defiling its beautiful esplanade.' Edinburgh was not only still radiant after the gay doings of the Prince at Holyrood, but it rang with the memories of the turbulent cries of the mob that slung Captain Porteous on a pole in the Grassmarket nine years before – an officer over-officious in discharge of his duty, forgiven by the Crown, but slain by the incensed citizens.

But all the glory and the stir of the past and present faded with the studious soldier before the attractions of the shops of John Gray and other booksellers. His humble pay was spent upon them. When the rebellion was over and the regiment dispersed, John Brown left the city, not by the Queensferry coach, whose fare was 2s., but on foot, with 3d. in his pocket, sufficient to carry him across the Forth. He hastened along

[1] Chalmers, *Life of Ruddiman*, p. 170.

through Burntisland, and Kirkcaldy, Leven, and Largo to the Cameron farm, to find his precious wallet intact. In the somewhat quaint words of the friend of those days, 'Upon his return to Cameron, the stack of peats, which had been gradually removed for the use of the family, was greatly reduced, and on the very next day after his arrival they came to the pack, which was perfectly safe, and all things in good condition.'

CHAPTER 7

The Schoolmaster

Shortly after John Brown's return to his travelling occupation, he received the welcome intimation that the office-bearers of his church at Abernethy had granted him a full certificate of church membership. This closed his connection with Abernethy. He never crossed its borders again. Once (1752) he came within five miles of it to preach, at Auchtermuchty. A few loyal souls climbed the mountain road to hear him, which kindly act of theirs was a grave offence in the eyes of Moncrieff and the religious leaders of Abernethy. They were summoned[1] to the Session to account for their conduct, and were rebuked for venturing to go to hear John Brown, 'a pretended minister.' Prejudices die hard.

It was Brown's ambition to enter the ministry of the Church, but the means to obtain a university education were not available. The next step that was possible to take, he took, and became a schoolmaster. By his incessant self-culture, he was well equipped for the profession, which in those days lay open to any one, without compulsory courses of training. He started at Gairney Bridge, two miles south of Kinross, where a monument stands today to commemorate the event of thirteen years earlier, when the Secession fathers met and founded their Church. As a teacher he was eminently successful. He drew scholars from a wide radius. With a passion for learning in his own soul, he communicated the fire of it to his pupils.[2]

[1] On three separate occasions, May 31st, June 21st, and July 5th, 1752 (Session Records, Gen. Assoc. Church, Abernethy).
[2] 'The school was but an old disused hut, a few seats or blocks of wood serving as the benches' (Graham, *Scottish Men of Letters in the*

Saturdays were not then devoted to holidays, as today prevails throughout Scotland, but were usually employed by schoolmasters for special religious teaching. Those Saturdays in John Brown's mastership were better remembered afterwards than the other days of the week. Says the writer who has preserved the recollections of those early days of his career :

'He was accustomed on Saturdays seriously to address his scholars. His discourses on these occasions were very warm and pathetic. The late Mr. Adam Low of Barclay informed me that, for his part, he was often, by Mr. Brown's rousing lectures, terrified from sin, and so strongly convinced of evil that it cost him many nights' want of sleep, until he got clearer views than he had of the way of salvation through Jesus Christ.'

While at Gairney Bridge, it was not unusual for him on Sundays, as he relates in his closing days, to tramp over the hills of Cleish to Dunfermline, eleven miles distant, 'to hear that man of God, Mr. Ralph Erskine, whose ministry, he felt, was brought home by the Spirit of God to his heart.' In his post as teacher of this school, Brown had a famous successor, Michael Bruce, the author of the 'Ode to the Cuckoo,' a poet of rich promise, who died at the early age of twenty-one, too soon for the ripe fruits of his genius to be garnered in.[1]

While engaged in teaching, the way opened up for Brown to reach his long-looked-for goal. Abernethy was one of the burning centres of the religious controversy that had raged in Scotland for nearly twenty years. One Church in Scotland, holding the Presbyterian faith, had sprung out of the covenant-

---

Eighteenth Century, p. 365). Graham quotes no authority for this statement, and I have been unable to find any verification. A sketch of the school is given in James Mackenzie's *Life of Michael Bruce* (1914), p. 88, which shows that Graham's assertion is absolutely apart from the truth.

[1] Of the three poems, Wordsworth's 'Ode To the Cuckoo,' Shelley's 'To the Skylark,' and Bruce's 'To the Cuckoo,' John Bright, greatly admiring all these, preferred that of Bruce to the others (Trevelyan, *Life of John Bright*, p. 424).

ing struggle in 1690. In it were men who had steadily sought the favoured side of fortune, and men who refused to be 'bought', who cared for nothing but the purity of the Gospel, and the rights and liberties of the Church of Christ. For a period all went well. But differences emerged; and majorities began to crush minorities. The first divergence was a fundamental one over the relation of the sinner to grace. The book, *The Marrow of Modern Divinity*, was welcomed by those who upheld the evangelical view that faith in Jesus Christ is the very essence of the Gospel and that every sinner is warranted to lay hold on Christ freely offered therein. The opposing view was that a sinner must prepare himself by repentance and the forsaking of sin before he is entitled to trust in the Saviour. The Marrow teaching placed the sinner's warrant solely in the free promises of the Saviour, the opposing view qualified the promises by the conditions which were first to be met by the seeker. The latter theology led to a legal presentation of the Gospel and this was much favoured at the time; it triumphed in the General Assembly of the Church, so much so that, as has already been mentioned, twelve earnest and faithful men were publicly rebuked by the Assembly for asserting the 'Marrow' principles, one of whom was Ebenezer Erskine of Stirling, and another was Alexander Moncrieff of Abernethy. The rebuke was humbly submitted to; but it left a rankling in its wake, the more deeply felt that others who seemed to deny the divinity of Christ, and verged on a doctrine, as David Hume said, of 'heathen morality,' were left untouched.

This singular indifference on the part of the majority to the purity of the Church's doctrine was followed by an invasion of the rights of the congregations in the election of their ministers. These rights had been freely conceded in the settlement of 1690. They were snatched away by Parliament (the Union Parliament) in 1712. Scotland had little knowledge of the deed. When it did know, it so deeply resented it, that the Act remained for a while a dead letter, the Assembly of the Church annually protesting against it. However, when patrons, to whom the power of choice was given, declined to act, it lay with the Assembly to determine how ministers should be chosen. The Assembly granted the liberty to congregations till 1731, when it decided to entrust the choice to heritors and magistrates acting with the elders. Ebenezer Erskine,[1] a son of the covenant, with its struggles for the rights of the people and the honour of the Church bred in the bone, blazed out against such disloyalty to the Church's charter, in a Synod sermon at Perth, in 1732. For this, he and three steadfast adherents, Moncrieff of Abernethy, Wilson of Perth, and Fisher of Kinclaven, were censured by the Synod. They were suspended by the next Assembly from the ministry. But, as Erskine's father had told 'Bloody Mackenzie' that 'having a commission from Christ,' he could not be silent, these men continued to preach, and to administer sacraments in their own parishes, and wherever they were invited. On December 5th, 1733, they met in an inn, where roads converge at Gairney Bridge in Kinross-shire, on the great North Road, and, after three days spent in prayer, they, along with two others, Ralph Erskine[2] of Dunfermline, and Thomas Mair of Orwell, formed an 'Associate Presbytery.' The Assembly repented of its haste, and made repeated attempts to get these stalwarts to return.

[1] Ebenezer Erskine (1680-1754), of the house of the Erskines, in whose veins ran the best blood of Scotland, born at Dryburgh, Roxburgh-shire; studied at Edinburgh University; became minister at Portmoak, on the banks of Lochleven, in 1703, and continued till 1731, when he removed to Stirling; marked by the majesty of his person and his preaching. On Sabbath, May 18th, 1740, he was excluded from his charge in the West Church, but continued to minister to a large congregation in a new building that today bears his name. He died in the seventy-fourth year of his age, and the fifty-first of his ministry.

[2] Ralph Erskine (1685-1752), a younger brother of Ebenezer Erskine, born at Monilaws in Northumberland, gentler, more ideal, more mystical than his brother, fond of music and proficient on the violin; became minister of Dunfermline in 1711; sympathized with the stand his brother and others took before the Assembly, and eventually cast in his lot with them; his *Gospel Sonnets*, published in 1734, had a wide repute; his collected works in ten volumes passed through numerous editions; his church in Dunfermline today bears the name of Queen Anne Street Church, and his statue graces the entrance. He died in the sixty-eighth year of his age, and the forty-second of his ministry.

But they believed that this change of front was dictated more by policy than by principle, and they refused. They had now found a 'free platform,' and it was for Scotland's good that they reached it. The action they took represented 'a real step in Scotland's progress towards full religious liberty.'[1]

The marvel is that throughout the prolonged controversy, and with things said and done that future generations could not but condemn, no riots and no outrages such as have attended other contendings in the Scottish churches, marred the course of the spiritual struggle. Orderliness was a marked feature in the procedure of those who seceded. They faithfully followed the course kept by church courts, and as directed by church law. They held strongly that they, and not the Assembly, were loyal to the constitution of the Church of Scotland.

It was to this band of men, fired by a holy zeal for the rights of the Redeemer and His Church, that John Brown adhered. Into their ministry he desired to enter. Small encouragement, however, was given him by those who should have been the first to have helped. Moncrieff scorned the idea of this orphan lad, in the lap of poverty, attempting such a course. The students of the time and neighbourhood, outstripped in their own kingdom by this school-less, college-less youth, raised an evil clamour against him. Attempts were made, in view of this, to win him back to the Church he had left. Offers of assistance were held out. The chance was a tempting one, but the choice he had made had been too deliberate to permit of turning back. He was well aware of the meaning of the questions at issue, and, with his strong grasp of principle, he felt that the only men he could follow were such as the Erskines, who would rather suffer than that the Church should lower her standard of evangelical truth, or the people lose their Christian rights. In spite of the vile calumny cast upon him by those among whom he sought Christian fellowship, he had sunk his shaft too deeply into the principles for which they stood, to be turned aside by the malice of a few.

[1] J. R. Fleming, *The Burning Bush*, p. 104.

This is what he says of this period of his life:

'During those trials I had my own share of solicitation to desert the Secession, in which I was so ill-used by some of the chief managers. But, as I had not taken that side from regard to men, the Lord enabled me to take no offence at His cause because of their maltreatment of me.'

After teaching for a time at Gairney Bridge, he crossed the Forth to Spittal, near Penicuik, Midlothian, where, he says, 'I had a large school, and I hope was useful in training up, among others, several young men in the learned languages, who were afterwards eminent ministers of Jesus, as the late Archibald Hall of London and others.' But the calm that followed in affairs of State after the Pretender's eruption into Scotland found a fierce conflict bursting forth in the young Church, whose fires had been smouldering during the rebellion, and which was to rend it in twain. Again the eager youth had to make his choice.

Prior to the Prince's coming, a bone of contention had been hurled among the adherents of the Secession by the resuscitation, on the part of the Government, of an old oath imposed upon the burgesses of Scotland. The burgess-oath originated in 1591. For a century and a half it had been taken without a scruple. But in 1744, for the burgesses in three towns in Scotland, Edinburgh, Glasgow, and Perth, it was preceded with this religious clause: 'I protest before God, that I profess and allow with my heart the true religion, presently professed in this realm, and authorized by the laws thereof. I shall abide therein and defend the same to my life's end, renouncing the Roman religion called Papistry.' It was of no small value for one to be a burgess in those days. Only burgesses could carry on business within the burgh, enter the trade guilds, or exercise the franchise. A considerable proportion of the adherents of the Secession belonged to the cities mentioned. The question was, did those words of the new clause in the oath, 'the true religion presently professed in this realm,' imply approbation of the errors and defections complained of in the Church of Scotland, or did they simply mean approval of the true religion itself? Moncrieff and Adam Gib[1] strongly adhered to the former position, the Erskines to the latter. Supporters ranged themselves on both sides, and the contention was keen. The Church, now numbering thirty-two congregations, had already divided itself into three Presbyteries, with a Synod, meeting once or twice in the year, as need arose, as the supreme court. In the Synod a large majority condemned the oath, but others – and this was the rock on which they split – insisted on making disapproval of the oath a term of communion. At the spring meeting of the Synod, April 8th, 1747, the decision was taken. Of the 55 members present, 23 (13 ministers and 10 elders) voted for the extreme view; 20 (9 ministers and 11 elders) favoured mutual forbearance; the remainder, who did not take part in the final vote, wished delay, but sided with the Erskines. Moncrieff and his party withdrew, and formed a new Synod – the General Associate Synod – that at once proceeded to excommunicate the majority. The young Church had grown with amazing rapidity, an evidence to the value of its testimony, but this division, pathetically known as 'The Breach,' drove its wedge into every hamlet where adherents had gathered, and effected an absolute cleavage.

The root of the controversy was in the interference of State law with religion; it brought the civil magistrate in and put a stumbling-block in the way of the religious conscience.[2] But it was a melancholy affair; the more melancholy that the oath

---

[1] Adam Gib (1714-88), born at Castletown, his father's property, in Muckhart, Perthshire; studied at Edinburgh University; a man of strong heroic features; signed a covenant with God in his own blood; a theologian of no mean order; a generous-hearted friend, who tore up the will by which his father bequeathed his estate to him that the elder brother, who had been foolish, might obtain the inheritance; a courageous defender of his country in 1745; but all his life a restless controversialist, to whom the burgess-oath was anathema, and who was the main cause of the 'Breach' in his Church in 1747. He was the first minister of the Bristo Church, Edinburgh, but after the Breach had to leave it, and founded Nicholson Street Church.

[2] W. Blair, *Handbook of the United Presbyterian Church* (1888), p. 34.

was soon abolished. It took seventy-three years[1] to heal the 'Breach' in Scotland, though in America, where the young Church had already planted a vigorous branch, only twenty years elapsed before the two parts were knit together. But, as it has been truly said, 'It is the one dark spot upon the history of the Secession, and consequently the only fact in its history of which many of its detractors seem to be aware.'

John Brown in this crisis threw in his lot with the Erskines. He regarded Moncrieff and his party as too strict in their interpretation of the oath. He himself would not have taken it,[2] but he had no objection to church fellowship with those who might be required to take it, and could do so without violence to their conscience. But the ill fortune that befell the young cause was his opportunity. The 'Associate' Church required preachers. He offered himself, and was accepted. He continued his teaching for three years longer, until he had acquired a training in philosophy and divinity. Then the door to the ministry opened, and he passed within its portals.

[1] When the reunion took place in 1820, the thirty-two congregations at the 'Breach' had increased to 262. Under the title of the United Secession Church, it pursued a course of uninterrupted prosperity. It applied itself with great enthusiasm to the cause of missions, and planted stations in Jamaica, Trinidad, Africa West and South, and elsewhere. In 1847, it maintained more than 60 missionaries. In that year it united with the Relief Church, founded by Thomas Gillespie in 1752, whose congregations now numbered 114, while the Secession Church numbered 384 congregations. It then became the United Presbyterian Church, with 140,000 members. In 1875, it gave off 100 congregations in England, with 20,000 members, to form the English Presbyterian Church. In 1900, when it united with the Free Church of Scotland, it numbered 593 congregations, with 200,000 members, 150 missionaries on the mission field, which now included India and Manchuria, and an income of £392,000; and the United Church assumed the name of the United Free Church of Scotland. For its history, see David Woodside, *The Soul of a Scottish Church*, 1918.
[2] J. C. Brown, *Centenary Memorial*, p. 90.

CHAPTER 8

The Divinity Student

The disaster that had befallen the young Church played havoc with the Divinity Hall, which it had established for the preparation of its preachers, as surely as it had rent the congregations. The hope reigned supreme for a while among the Erskines and their followers, that a few months would lead to a better understanding, and the reuniting of their forces. They took no step to embarrass the situation by making new appointments. They waited patiently to see if a *via media* could not be reached, by which both parties could co-operate, where co-operation was so desirable. But their patience was unrewarded, and their hopes doomed to disappointment. Alexander Moncrieff of Abernethy was the Professor of the young Church at this exciting period; as leader of those who protested against the oath, he carried the Divinity Hall into the new Synod that had been formed.

The other party had no choice but to summon their adherents to a special meeting of Synod, which was held in Dunfermline, in September 1747. They urged Ebenezer Erskine to undertake the professoriate of the Church. He pleaded his years – he was now sixty-seven. A strenuous life had been his, and domestic sorrows of late had darkened his path. He would rather a younger man were entrusted with the office. Ultimately he consented on the understanding that, should his strength fail him, his remaining colleague in the Secession struggle, James Fisher, now of Glasgow, should relieve him of the burden.

Erskine's church was at Stirling, and it was in that town

[75]

that the Theological Hall of the new Church was first held. The first student who presented himself at Stirling was John Brown. A university career was demanded of all entrants to the ministry, but Brown had made such progress by his self-education in classes and general literature, that in his case a university curriculum was dispensed with. He was now twenty-six years of age; and he had mastered more than most after a university training, Latin, Greek and Hebrew, and was even knocking at the gates of Arabic and Persian. What theological works were available he had devoured. His qualifications in the matter of learning none could gainsay. But when for the day he left his school at Penicuik, and presented himself at his Presbytery at Falkirk to be received as a theological student, he was again to hear the echoing shouts of his persecutors, happily for the last time. The kindly and courageous defence of Ralph Erskine of Dunfermline, whose ministry he used often to attend while at Gairney Bridge, shielded him at the critical moment. When he was proposed as a candidate for the ministry one of the members raised the objection that the young man's learning he did not dispute, but he understood that he had got it from 'his Satanic Majesty'. Ralph replied with the soft answer that turneth away wrath, 'I think the lad has a sweet savour of Christ about him.' The gentleness of the rebuke silenced the harsh grumble.

Just before he went to Spittal, while at Gairney Bridge, Brown appeared before this Presbytery, as a commissioner with others from the congregation at Kinross, in support of a call to John Swanston, afterwards Professor in the Associate Church. Mr. Swanston hailed from the parish of Stitchel in Roxburghshire, and, in spite of the dissuasions and remonstrances of his family and friends, his conscience compelled him to withdraw from the Established Church and join the Secession. He took a full course of classical and philosophical instruction at Edinburgh University, and studied at the Theological Hall at Perth under William Wilson, for the Secession ministry. Various congregations claimed his services, Kinross among them. To urge the claims of Kinross, Brown accompanied a deputation to Falkirk. His appearance, eager, studious, with dark, flashing eyes made him a marked figure. A minister present pointed to him, and asked who that was. With a twinkle in the eye, he was answered, 'Do you not know the man that got his learning from the devil?' Quick came the reply, 'I warrant you he's a dungeon, then.'

The theological session was confined to about three months in the year, which enabled the students to keep on their situations, if engaged in teaching. These months brought the student into very close fellowship with the Professor. With Ebenezer Erskine, there was not much of the professional method or manner. His life had been cast in other moulds. But the privilege of profiting by the mature wisdom and the ripe experience of one who had not only been amongst the most commanding preachers of his country and generation, but who had been foremost in the struggle for the Church's liberties and rights in Scotland, was highly prized, and deeply impressed the young, ardent students that gathered around him. He did not deliver any regular lectures. In a less formal style he communicated his instruction from the rich fields of his own reading, experience, and observation. The *Institutio Theologiæ Elencticæ* of the Genevan professor, François Turretin (1623-87) was the principal text-book of the Universities at this period. From this Erskine read, commenting on the leading doctrines. Examination, however, was a marked feature of his work; and by it he skilfully elucidated doctrine, and tested the knowledge of the students. They had also to submit discourses, and his critical remarks upon them enabled him to give many valuable hints on preaching, an art in which he excelled. Literary style did not appeal to him, he being as indifferent to it as George Whitefield; but this defect, that weakens his discourses when read, disappeared, as with Whitefield, in the impression made on the multitudes that listened to them.

After two years, the professoriate passed from Ebenezer

Erskine – he died five years later at the ripe age of seventy-four – to his son-in-law, James Fisher. In 1741, Fisher had been removed from Kinclaven, in Perthshire, to a church in Glasgow. He had been singled out at Erskine's appointment as the next theological Master. John Brown, after the refreshing and stimulating experience of Stirling, moved to Glasgow, to sit at the feet of the accomplished Fisher, whose intellectual culture and refinement, studious habits, and aptitude for teaching eminently fitted him for the post. Minister of a large and growing charge, in the rapidly extending city of Glasgow, he so equipped himself for his task that the students received a new and wholesome stimulus under him; and from his classes, during the fifteen years he taught them, came forth some of the ablest and most accomplished ministers within the Church. Brown was conscious of his influence, and grateful for his illuminating guidance both in theology and philosophy.

A prominent feature of the class work was the delivery of discourses, and the reading of critical and exegetical exercises. Training in exact interpretation of the Word, and effective preaching of it, was the dominant aim. Pulpit-work was never lost sight of. A considerable proportion of the time, in consequence, was spent in hearing and criticizing students' sermons. The students shared in the criticism. When one of their number had delivered a discourse, or read an exercise, the members of the class were invited and expected to offer free comments, and they usually took full advantage of the opportunity. The Professor followed, summing up the merits and demerits of the production.

For the students to act as critics was a long-standing custom. But, whether the fires became too hot, and the opportunity abused, or the Professor felt that his judgment was weakened or diverted by the candid opinions of over-daring youth, it fell gradually into desuetude. John Brown, in the days of his own professorship, encouraged the practice, but under his successor, Dr. George Lawson of Selkirk, it began to decay, and ultimately expired.[1] When the exhilarating practice began, it is difficult to say. Wodrow, historian of the Church of Scotland, tells how his father, who was a Professor of Divinity in Glasgow from 1692 to 1707, conducted his class. He describes the assistance which a student could obtain from the Professor in the preparation of an exegetical exercise; and then he says:

'This and all other discourses were delivered without reading, to habituate scholars in that way, though their papers were allowed to lie before them in the delivery. Then the Professor usually asked the observes and censures of the students, who were very narrow and exact in their remarks upon this and all other discourses before them, both in matter and style, and manner of delivery. The deliverer was allowed to make his defences; and the Professor, in the last room, gave his observes, and ordinarily he had little left to do but give a general judgment.'

'The deliverer was allowed to make his defences.' This salutary part of the process seems to have fallen out by the middle of the century; and the student critics had it all their own way. The victim's opportunity would come when his neighbour stood in the pillory; and the fear of this perhaps restrained the intemperate ardour of the critics.

With the close of Professor Fisher's first session Brown emerged from the Divinity Hall. Licence, with its necessary 'trials,' now awaited him. He had little difficulty in meeting this test of his examiners; and on November 14th, 1750, at the age of twenty-eight, he became a licentiate of the Church, receiving licence from the Presbytery of Edinburgh. He was a man deeply affected by such occasions. For years this had been the goal of his ambition, and for a long period the way had been effectually blocked. Now that the eventful day had arrived he

[1] John MacFarlane, *The Life and Times of George Lawson* (London, 1862), p. 287.

was profoundly moved by the responsibilities involved. Curiously it coincided with the fate that befell the man who had been mainly instrumental in spreading broadcast and keeping alive the calumnious charge against him regarding his acquisition of knowledge: his base conduct descending to deeper depths of infamy, wrought vengeance on his own head.[1] Thus Brown refers to this time in his 'Short Memoir':

'Micah 7. 7-10 had been not a little impressed on my mind under my sore trial of about five years' continuance; and the Lord, by a connection of providences, gradually opened a way for my getting some regular instruction in philosophy and divinity, and I was licensed to preach the Gospel in 1750; and could not but be affected that about the same time, if not the very same night, my primary calumniator, whose part had been so earnestly maintained in opposition to me, was, after he had been several years a preacher, and a zealous preacher in appearance, necessarily excommunicated by his supporters, as guilty of repeated acts, or attempts, of uncleanness (even with married women). "Behold, O my soul, the goodness and severity of God, towards him severity, and towards me" – who was perhaps ten thousand times worse before His all-seeing eye—"goodness." Let me never be "highminded, but fear."'

[1] Robert Millar entered the Secession Church while a theological student in connection with the Established Church, followed the Moncrieff party, but was never called, and in consequence of his unworthy conduct was deprived of his licence.

CHAPTER 9

Called to Haddington

The fully-equipped student was now at liberty to perambulate among the vacant Churches, with a view to a settled charge. The life of a Probationer of more modern times has been portrayed by Dr. James Brown of Paisley,[1] in narrating the career of Thomas Davidson, a licentiate of brilliant parts whom death snatched ere a congregation called him. John Brown's itinerating of the Churches lasted less than a year. The journeys were on foot, by pony or stage-coach; and hospitality was received from generous friends in the congregations ministered to.

A Probationer's thoughts, as he makes his way from place to place, are usually exercised as to the sphere in which his lot may be cast. While this did concern our licentiate, he was more eager about being fit for the calling, in which he so ardently longed to serve. He has left an interesting tractate, entitled *Reflections of a Candidate for the Ministerial Office*, which reveal his mind and outlook. As was his wont, he turned the searchlight in upon himself, scanning narrowly every cranny and nook where unworthy motives might lurk. He pours forth a series of interrogatories that penetrate all round. He wishes to examine, with deep concern, the 'preparation for, the call to, and the end in,' offering himself to this important work. After testing and questioning the personal attitude, he asks:

'What furniture of gifts hath Christ bestowed upon me, what aptness to teach, what knowledge of the mysteries of the king-

James Brown, *The Life of a Scottish Probationer*.

dom, what skill to instruct others, bringing forth out of my treasures things new and old, what ability to make the deep things of God plain to weaker capacities, what quickness of conception, what due inclination to study, as one devoted to matters of infinite consequence, what peculiar fitness for the pulpit, qualifying me to commend myself to every man's conscience in the sight of God, preaching not in the enticing words of man's wisdom, but in demonstration of the Spirit, and with power?'

He fears lest the glamour of the preacher's address might captivate a congregation, or the preacher be a mere professional proclaimer of divine things.

'Say, then, my conscience, as thou shalt answer at the judgment-seat of Christ, am I taking this honour of myself, or am I called of God as was Aaron? Is Christ sending me, and laying a necessity upon me to preach the Gospel? While He determines me to follow Providence, and to take no irregular step toward thrusting myself into the office, is He breathing on my soul, and causing me to receive the Holy Ghost? Is He endowing me with tender compassion for the souls of men, and with a deep sense of my own unfitness, and earnest desire to be sanctified and be made meet for the Master's use? In the progress of my education, am I going bound in the spirit, with the love of Christ burning in my heart, and constraining me; rendering me willing cheerfully to suffer poverty, contempt, and hatred of all men, for His name's sake; willing, if possible, to risk my own salvation in winning others to Christ?'

He gathers into one thrilling paragraph a striking combination of all the Scripture passages bearing upon his calling, and subjects himself to examination by each. While deeming it right and wise to be gentle, faithful, and earnest, he is anxious to know if the courage and tact are there to deal faithfully yet tenderly with the shortcomings and failures of men.

It is manifest that, wherever his sphere was to be found, no low ideal was to be the standard of his work.

Two congregations, with great unanimity and heartiness, invited him to their pastorate—Haddington in East Lothian, and Stow on Gala Water. His choice lay with the former, although it was the smaller and less attractive sphere. But the Church at Stow held a warm place in his heart, and he rendered it frequent service in the course of his ministry.

The Haddington congregation had just passed through the fires. It traced its origin to the 'praying societies' that flourished in East Lothian. In 1737, the members made request of the new Associate Church for a regular ministry. Initial difficulties were overcome. A congregation was formed. An election was made, but the preacher preferred Perth. Another was called, but of him, the curious minute in the Presbytery records reads: 'Mr. Walter Loch, Probationer, being, in adorable providence, removed by death since last meeting of Presbytery, the calls to him from Stitchel and Haddington do fall, of course.' A third responded to their invitation, Robert Archibald, from Perth or its neighbourhood, and was ordained. The new cause rapidly grew. But the burgess-oath descended with its angry sword, and clave the congregation in twain. The minister and a portion of his people protested against the oath, but, being in a minority, they separated, and formed themselves into a new congregation of the General Associate Church. For four years they continued their service in the manse garden, though in winter some kindly shelter must have protected them, till a suitable structure was provided. The remaining members petitioned for fresh 'supply.' After one more declinature, they set their hearts upon John Brown, and he was ordained among them on July 4th, 1751.

While the succession of candidates was being heard by the congregation, an old lady of advanced Christian experience was asked which of the preachers she specially approved; she replied, 'Oh! the lad wi' the tattit head; there's a sweet savour of Christ about him.'

Her description silhouettes the figure of this ardent student, now commencing his ministry. He is twenty-nine years of age. His matted hair, in dark ringlets, clung to a brow broad and high, beneath which gleamed a pair of dark, eager, sparkling eyes. A full, ruddy countenance was supported by a mouth and chin that spoke of resolution and mastery, while the bodily frame, well-knit and vigorous, measured in height about 5 feet 8 inches. Behind was an indomitable spirit, a mind keen, active, of wide outlook, but specially directed, and that passionately, into one broad channel of sacred truth, a memory of extraordinary tenacity, and a conscience painfully sensitive, ever moving under the 'great Taskmaster's eye.'

Haddington ranks with Abernethy as a noted place in the ecclesiastical history of Scotland. It was never a large town, but stood on the highway to England, although today the railway passes it by. The English armies often penetrated to its precincts when the contests between the two countries were raging; and in 1549, while held by the English, it suffered a long siege. It is interesting to note that it was at the abbey outside Haddington (July 7, 1548) that Parliament accepted the hand of the French Dauphin for Mary, being careful at the same time to secure Scottish independence though a French prince she was to wed.[1] Two years before that event, George Wishart preached in the Abbey Church, long known as 'The Lamp of Lothian,' just prior to his capture at Ormiston and martyrdom at St. Andrews. Among the devoted band whose hearts were stirred by his message was John Knox, tutor in the family of Longniddry, then a young man of thirty-one, by the new reckoning, who, if Thomas Carlyle be correct, was born in Haddington.[2] Knox would fain have followed the dauntless Wishart to his doom, carrying the two-handed sword which had been entrusted to him as Wishart's bodyguard; but on the eventful night of his arrest Wishart took the sword from him,

[1] Andrew Lang, *History of Scotland*, vol. ii, p. 12.
[2] Carlyle generously purchased the reputed site of the house in which the great Reformer first drew breath, railed it off, erected a suitable monument, and presented it to the community.

and dissuaded him with the words, 'Nay, return to your bairns, and God bless you! Ane is sufficient for a sacrifice.'

Of the town itself about the middle of the eighteenth century, we have this account from the vivid pen of John Wesley, written three months before Brown was settled there as minister. It may have been that the two men were pacing the streets about the same time. Writing in his *Journal* on April 24th, 1751, about which time not unlikely John Brown was preaching for two or three Sundays as a candidate, John Wesley refers to this as his first visit to Scotland, and gives his impressions of the Scottish towns and people as he passed through Haddington.

'The Scotch towns are like none which I ever saw, either in England, Wales, or Ireland: there is such an air of antiquity in them all, and such a peculiar oddness in their manner of building. But we were most surprised at the entertainment we met with in every place, so far different from common report. We had all things good, cheap, in great abundance, and re-markably well dressed.'[1]

While the church in which John Brown ministered was in Haddington, it drew its membership from a wide area round about. It was a rich, fertile country that caused the hearts of Cromwell's soldiers to leap for joy when they beheld it a hundred years before. 'It contained the greatest plenty of corn they ever saw.' Most of Brown's flock were engaged in agricultural pursuits, or supplied with merchandise, in the various communal centres, the usual needs of the population.

As the pastor faced his work, and felt himself now in close contact with it, he again turned the light in all its intensity upon his inmost being, and he poured forth his reveries in a paper found after his death, *Reflections of one entered on the Pastoral Office*. He subjects himself to a series of sharp, searching

---

[1] Next day he says, 'We rode to Edinburgh' (only seventeen miles distant), 'one of the dirtiest cities I had ever seen, not excepting Cologne in Germany. We returned to Musselburgh.'

questions, in order to guard against any faithlessness in his high and sacred trust. He dreads his ends being selfish, or himself unenthusiastic. To be a 'graceless preacher' would be an unspeakable calamity; to be an ignorant messenger would be a disastrous experience. 'Am I set here at the gate of heaven, as a candle to waste myself in showing others the way, in lighting up the Bridegroom's friends, and must my lamp in the end go out in obscure darkness?' Urgent is the call for the fullest use of one's gifts, in view of the tremendous tasks imposed. The honour and privilege of the office and one's relation to the Great Master ought to impel to faithfulness. 'What self-denial, what pure regard to the honour of God, what prudence, what diligence, what humility, what zeal, what spirituality of heart and life, what entire dependence on Jesus by faith, what order, what plainness, what just tempering of mildness and severity, are necessary in dealing with the souls of men!' The consciousness of personal shortcomings almost overwhelms him. Pride ever threatens to rule the will, the factious spirit to assert itself, sloth to lay its heavy hand on duty. Let conscience bestir itself, and the Divine Spirit's help be claimed, that neither time nor talents be wasted, that 'I may not tear God's Church, mangle His truths, betray His honour, nor murder the souls of men.'

Few avoided the perils more successfully and rose more nobly to the higher heights of their calling. The supreme devotion to his life-task, manifest from the outset, became fruitful in results as the years proceeded.

CHAPTER 10

The Pastorate at Haddington

The pastorate opened with an extraordinary tale of pulpit and pastoral labour. When it was all discharged, the wonder arises where the time was left for the enormous literary and professorial work which Brown accomplished in the six-and-thirty years of his ministry. In the congregational records the statement is given in precise terms what his labours were to be. Whether it was his own wish that such duty was assigned to him – for it will already be gathered that he was voracious for work – or the wish of his people, who must have had great expectations if such was their request, there it is, set forth in his own handwriting:

'1. There is a lecture, a sermon, and an evening exercise on Sabbath in the months of November, December, January, and February; and public worship begins at eleven o'clock forenoon. During the other eight months there is a lecture, two sermons, and an evening exercise; and public worship begins at ten o'clock. Only in the east country is there ordinarily no exercise on Sabbath evening.[1]

'2. The congregation is visited once, and examined twice every year.

'3. The members of Session meet for prayer about the first Monday in every month, except September; – and the minister, with three of the elders or deacons, ordinarily pray on such

---

[1] What would he have thought of Robert Hall's oracular sentence to his grandson: 'A man of genius, sir, may produce one sermon in the week; a person of average talent may compose two, but nobody but a fool, sir, can write three'? (John Cairns, *Memoir of John Brown*, p. 88).

occasions, with singing of Psalms, and spiritual conference between prayer.

'4. The tokens[1] are distributed by the minister in presence of the elders, constituted with prayer.

'5. Young communicants are admitted with a solemn renewal of their baptismal engagements, in presence of the Session, and with suitable exhortations.'

To be furnished with material for Sundays so crowded meant considerable drain on both the physical and mental powers. But Brown was a master of the Scriptures. His extraordinary knowledge of them, unparalleled in its way, joined to a most retentive memory, served him well. Specimens of his outlines still preserved show the grasp he took of a subject and a marvellous wealth of Scripture illustration. His style aimed at simplicity and directness; his manner was not demonstrative; but earnestness was visible in every feature. To the end the tale of regular pulpit work seems to have remained what it was at the beginning.

On the week-days the visitation was carried out. His congregation drew from a wide area – from the parishes of Spott, Whittinghame, Dunbar, and Pencaitland, places seven to ten miles apart. On an appointed day, duly intimated from the pulpit the previous Sunday, he and one of his elders would set forth to visit the families in a particular district. They passed into a house, where were assembled the parents, the children, and the servants, if there were any. The heads of the household were first catechized, and afterwards the children, on matters relating to the doctrines and duties of religion. An exhortation to all followed, and prayer concluded the visit. In the next family, and the next, till all had been waited upon, the same procedure was followed. Night found the visitors weary with their exhausting yet stimulating labours.

Another day was fixed for a 'diet of examination.' A centre was decided upon, and duly announced the preceding Sunday.

[1] The token was a piece of metal like a coin given to those who intended partaking of the Lord's Supper.

To this, all, old and young, were expected to come at the appointed hour. The occasion was open to all; it might be held in the church, as it would be for those in Haddington, or in Dunbar, or North Berwick, or Tranent. Usually they met in the evening. Into their midst passed the minister at the fixed hour. After brief devotions, the examination commenced. The *Shorter Catechism* was the standard text-book. He would call on one of the members to repeat the answer to the question, for example, 'What is effectual calling?' With this as a basis he would proceed to ask of others further questions in order to elucidate and enforce the truth it contained. The answers were mainly monosyllabic; but they afforded the opportunity of imparting knowledge, of removing difficulties, of strengthening the foundations and rearing the fabric of Christian character. Twice in the year in the various centres were these examinations held.

Such methods of maintaining and developing the spiritual knowledge of the people were characteristic of the age. The school years were then of short duration; labour claimed youth at an early stage; books to read were few. The days of Sabbath Schools, Bible Classes, Young Men's and Young Women's Christian Associations, had not dawned. Literary societies were unheard of. John Wesley recognized the clamant need for some system of regular instruction in Scripture in England, and devised his 'Classes.' In Scotland, where the habit of learning prevailed, examination and visitation were the means adopted to foster and encourage the intellectual and spiritual development of the people. Changing circumstances as time went on led to change of methods; the diet of examination fell into disuse, the method of visitation altered; but throughout the ministry of John Brown this was the system that prevailed. Besides this plan of getting into touch with his flock, the care of the sick and the infirm was ever upon his heart. In the wide area he had to traverse he was assiduous in his attentions, not merely confining himself to his own people, but going wherever sickness or sorrow cast their dark shadows.

[89]

These pastoral labours, abundant though they were, did not oppress his spirit. There was a lambent humour that played around his life, making it gay with its brightness, and strong in the sharpness of its thrust. Such a burden of toil as the members of his congregation seemed to think necessary for a new pastor, made some of them doubt his fitness for the post. One absolutely refused to adhibit his name to the 'call,' when it was agreed to invite him to Haddington. He waited for a few months after the pastorate had commenced, and, seeing the grit of the man that had been chosen, he was anxious to explain to him why he did not sign his call. 'I have nothing against ye, sir,' he said, 'but I think ye're ower young and inexperienced for the work.' 'That is just what I think myself, David,' was the reply, 'but it would never dae for the like o' you and me to go in the face of the whole congregation.'

In the course of his visitation, he was passing through Tranent riding on his pony, which was halting. A scoffing blacksmith, seeing him jogging up to a house near the smithy on his limping steed, shouted to him, 'Mr. Broun, ye're in the Scripture line today – the legs o' th' lame are not equal.' 'So is a parable in the mouth of a fool,' was the ready retort.

He knew also when to strike as well as how. His tact was as alive as his wit. On one occasion he was crossing the Forth by the usual Ferry boat that then plied between Leith and Kinghorn. The waters were rough, and the temper of the passengers was tried. An old Highlander gave somewhat vigorous expression to his feelings in language so impolite that it grated harshly on the ears of his fellow-passengers. Some were disposed to rebuke his ferocity. But Brown waited till the shore was reached; and, slipping up to him as he passed along the quay all alone, he civilly but seriously reproved him for language so brutish. The irate Highlander took it in good part, and thanked him for his thoughtful courtesy in not humiliating him before the crowded boat. 'Had you said this to me while in the boat, sir, I believe I would have run you through.'

The manse of which John Brown took possession when he

commenced his ministry, and in which he continued till its close, still stands in Haddington. It occupies a site facing a short street that emerges into Market Street, which runs parallel to that off which is the house in which Jeanie Welsh, destined to become the wife of Thomas Carlyle, was born, and is not far from the early home of Samuel Smiles. It is a two-storey building with low-ceiled rooms, as was the fashion of the time. Behind it stood the church with its four lancet windows, its entrances from the sides, a gallery round three parts of the building and the pulpit between the high windows. Into the little fireless room over the doorway of the manse, Brown crowded his books of many languages, and there spent every available hour of his time, not only in preparation for the pulpit, but in mastering all kinds of knowledge, and issuing works for the press. His stipend began at £40 per annum, and never rose above £50. Small though it was, it met his necessities, and therewith he was content. Indeed it went further: he had always something to spare to help the poor and needy in their struggle. In these economies, he was indebted to the prudence and the care of the two help-meets who shared his lot—Janet Thomson, who died in 1771, and Violet Croumbie, who long survived him.

Janet Thomson was the only daughter of a Musselburgh merchant, John Thomson. He was a remarkable man, in whose veins ran the blood of staunch defenders of the faith. He was born in the parish of Strathmiglo, Fifeshire, in 1700. His people had suffered for their fidelity to principle in the days of the Stuarts. In 1727 he went to Musselburgh, and there built up a large and prosperous business. In 1745, when Prince Charles Stuart summoned the clans to regain his father's throne, like John Brown he shouldered his musket in defence of his country, and suffered considerably from the Jacobites of Musselburgh for his attachment to the house of Hanover.

Just before the battle of Prestonpans, a Highlander entered his shop and demanded his money. He simply and flatly refused. The Highlander wheeled round, slammed the door, and turned the key. Drawing his claymore, he gruffly said, 'Don't you know your life is in my hands?' 'I'm not so sure o' that,' was the answer from behind the counter. 'My life is in God's hands.' Ere the burly Northman got further, an officer of his regiment opened the door behind him. He had heard the loud shouting as he passed, and, scenting mischief, entered the shop and arrested the interloper. The Highlander had been too eager to secure his quarry, and had turned the lock before the door was shut. Thus was the trapper trapped. John Thomson was one of the fine types of the period, of high principle and clear vision, ready for sacrifice if such was demanded, and unswerving in his attachment to the truth. He died on December 1st, 1774.

His daughter, Janet, shared his independence and courage. Married to John Brown in September, 1753, she brought to the home in Haddington the fidelity and the piety that shone so brightly in the merchant's house in Musselburgh. Eight children were born of the marriage, only two of whom survived. Both followed in the footsteps of their father, John becoming minister of Whitburn, and Ebenezer minister of Inverkeithing.

CHAPTER 11

The Pastorate at Haddington (continued)

The widespread area from which the members of the congregation at Haddington were drawn would have made it almost impossible for a pastor, however diligent, to keep in touch with them all. The Presbyterian Church, by calling in the laity for special service, has broadened and strengthened its own foundations, and at the same time has developed and ennobled the character of the laymen whom it calls to office. The responsibility of office in the Christian Church has been for the making of the men appointed; and they in turn have contributed largely to the Church's activity and strength.

John Brown had the assistance of a Session of twelve elders, with six deacons whose duties were more concerned with the temporal affairs of the congregation. They met at fixed times, and prayer and conference formed a regular part of their proceedings. The Sessional duties covered a wide area of the individual life of the members; sometimes the contents of the old church records almost raise a smile. Wanderers from the fold, as we have already seen in connection with Abernethy, were even gravely rebuked for their forgetfulness. Brown himself was the innocent cause of two members being called in question by the neighbouring congregation (in Haddington) of Antiburghers. He had been visiting members of his flock at Samuelston, a hamlet three miles from Haddington, and had remained overnight at the house of a farmer, who invited one of his men to meet him, and Rev. W. Hutton, of Dalkeith, at breakfast. After the meal, the morning praise was rendered; and, while it was proceeding, the grieve of the farm entered and sat down. The two servants belonged to the other regiment.

Such intercourse in religious fellowship was apparently perilous, and was considered subversive of discipline. The two men were both summoned to the church court; the grieve was admonished, because he had gone in inadvertently, and the other was censured because he knowingly remained while the family joined in worship. It was a remnant of the old spirit of intolerance that reached its height in the days of Charles II. These were light judgments compared with what was then meted out. Only seventy years before, Marion Harvey, a servant-girl in Bo'ness, had been executed in Edinburgh for going to hear Donald Cargill, and helping his escape at South Queensferry. Isabel Alison from Perth suffered along with her, because she, too, had sought out and sat at the feet of the great preacher, and refused to submit to the tests Episcopacy would thrust upon her. The Wigton martyrs, Margaret Wilson and Margaret Lachlison, the one little more than twenty years of age, and the other over threescore, and both blameless and gentle, suffered for the simple offence of attending field and house conventicles. The narrowness of the age was passing, a dawn was breaking, and toleration was coming to its own. Liberty in time triumphed along the whole line of the Presbyterian Church. But to this day exclusiveness still reigns in certain branches of the Church in Scotland and elsewhere, and if not censure, a severe frown would follow a wanderer from their particular fold.

Towards the end of 1753, there came to Brown an honour that usually does not reach a man till near the end of his ministry. Though only a little more than two years since his ordination, he was called to occupy the Moderator's chair of the Synod – the supreme court of the Church – that met in the November of that year in Edinburgh. Two others were nominated along with him, James Erskine, nephew of Ebenezer Erskine of Stirling, and James Bennett, the first minister of St. Andrews; but the choice fell on the minister of of Haddington. That Synod meeting was one of historic importance, not so much because of the application for services from many parts of the country, nor because of the difficulties that the Supreme Court had with some Probationers, especially with one Forrest, under call to Stow, who refused to be settled where the Synod said they should, but because of the Testimony the young Church felt bound to record at this point in their history, as to the steps that had been taken to organize their Church, and the principles and practice for which they stood. They had come through the fires, first in their conflict with the Established Church, and then with their own brethren over the burgess-oath. Necessity was laid upon them to lay down with clearness and accuracy the principles for which they had contended and the course they had pursued in upholding them, so as to justify their action to those who might adhere to them, and to succeeding generations. In a long and full record covering no less than thirty-eight pages of the large folio volume of Minutes, they narrated 'the Rise, Progress and Grounds of the Secession.' Out of the animated discussions that ensued, various other questions arose that were not deemed so urgent, but yet required consideration, and to a committee of three, of which Brown was a member, it was remitted to prepare 'a draft of additional teaching.' Another subject that received the sympathetic consideration of the house was a pressing request from parties in North America, beseeching the Synod to have regard to 'their deplorable circumstances for want of faithful ministers'; and it was delegated to James Fisher and John Brown to write a 'consolatory letter,' and to ask for a fuller account of their number and circumstances.

It is generally the privilege and distinction of the Moderator during his year of office to visit congregations celebrating some event in their congregational history; it was the fortune of this Moderator to be more apostolic, and to be present at the beginnings of new congregations and assist in their organization. In this same year, Brown was also called to be Moderator of the Presbytery of Edinburgh, a post he occupied for the next three years.

These honours accorded to Brown were a tribute to his

character and standing, and no less to his business aptitude. The confidence his brethren reposed in him is seen by his being sent to confer with new congregations, and to guide them in their early developments. He journeyed across the borders for this purpose to Alnwick, and to Newcastle-on-Tyne, in which latter city he was requested 'to travel as he should see cause in that perplexing affair' of the minister of Newcastle and his congregation, who had come over from the Church of Scotland, and to bring matters to a satisfactory issue. At the frequent meetings of Presbytery, requests kept pouring in for 'supply' of sermon, and readily and freely the ministers in charges rendered assistance, taking the young congregations by the hand, till a pastor was settled among them, and they in turn were able to render help to others. In the manifold work of his Church Brown took an active share, becoming, later, clerk of the Presbytery of Edinburgh, and of the Synod of the Church. From the presbyterial and synodical records of the time, it can be gathered that he was as loyal, faithful and trusted as a presbyter as he was devoted and zealous as a pastor. Many questions appertaining to the doctrine and government of the Church naturally pressed on the young communion, framing a constitution; and not an important committee was appointed to consider these, but he formed one of its members.

In 1756, Brown introduced what was regarded as a daring innovation at the time. It was a simple matter in itself, but it occasioned much controversy. It was the observance of the ordinance of the Lord's Supper twice in the year. Such a plethora of services had grown up around the celebration of the Supper that it was declared impossible and unwise to have a repetition of these more frequently than once in the year. For example, there were two services on the Wednesday or Thursday preceding the Sunday fixed for the solemnity, another on the Friday, two on the Saturday, and on the Sunday itself services were continuous from morning till night, sometimes till midnight, and two more on the Monday. For over a hundred years this method of celebrating the ordinance in certain districts had more or less prevailed. Where religion was at a low ebb, there were no such celebrations, sometimes no observance for years. Among the more earnest and faithful, the plan of elaborate services met with favour, and Brown himself in earlier days had often frequented such gatherings. But he began to question the wisdom and the value, as well as the authority for such a succession of meetings, and doubted whether the true nature of the Sacrament was not in danger of being occluded by them.

From earliest times there has been a tendency to cumber the simple ordinance with what diverts attention from its main purpose. The early Corinthian Church surrounded it with the love feasts of the heathen days and degraded it, receiving the sharp reproof of the Apostle Paul. The Roman Catholic Church in process of years reached the transubstantiation conception, and developed the ornate and elaborate ceremonial of the 'mass' out of the plain original rite. They also withdrew the cup from the laity as being too sacred for common hands. Indeed the question as to the meaning and the method of the observance of this rite became prominent in the controversies of the Reformation movement. More and more clearly was it seen that the only way to overthrow sacerdotal domination was to purify the so-called 'Sacrament of the Altar' from the superstition by which it had been converted into a miraculous act depending on human intervention. 'It was a question,' says Creighton, 'which the Lollards handed on to the Hussites, and the Hussites to Luther. Wycliffe challenged the belief in a miraculous change in the nature of the elements; the Hussites attacked the denial of the cup to the laity; and Luther warred against the doctrine of the sacrifice of the mass.'[1]

Brown perceived that the Church of his time and country was pressing along a route that would obscure and pervert the purpose of the ordinance in another way by the multiplicity of services in connection with it, leading to what he termed a

[1] Mandell Creighton, *A History of the Papacy*, vol. i, p. 129.

kind of refined Popery. After careful study, he resolved to do his utmost to arrest the tendency. Where sympathies are strongly enlisted on behalf of an object, it requires considerable courage to advocate a course different from that pursued, which may seem contending against it, but is really conserving it. Brown faced this resolutely. His action in consequence had not a little to do with freeing the ceremony from the encumbrances that were overloading it, and securing for it that simple dignity and grace with which it is observed today.

The enormous gatherings that were wont to assemble at certain centres, where the celebration was held, were natural in the circumstances. Where so many services were deemed requisite on week-days and Sundays, it necessitated the assistance of a number of ministers. These ministers, in most cases, had to leave their flocks pastorless for the Sabbath, owing to the difficulty of obtaining 'supply.' Why, therefore, should not the flocks follow their shepherds to the rich feeding-grounds?

Unhappily, a by-product of these great gatherings sometimes revealed itself in the outer fringes of the vast assemblies. All classes were brought promiscuously together, and there was conduct that was not worthy of the object for which they had met, and occasionally led to grave scandal. This grieved the hearts of many, and Burns swept it with the lightning fire of his keen satire, as in the 'Holy Fair.'

In the beginning of the controversy, Brown wrote a letter to a fellow-student, William M'Ewen, of Dundee, the second minister of School Wynd Church, one of whose successors was the gifted George Gilfillan. M'Ewen began his ministry with rich promise, and published a work, *A Treatise on the Scripture Types, Figures and Allegories*, which enjoyed a wide reputation, Dr. John Erskine classing him with Hervey, the author of the *Meditations*, and which Carlyle 'even liked for its glib smoothness.' But the bright promise was sharply cut off by his death from fever at Leith, immediately after his marriage, at the age of twenty-eight. His loss was deeply mourned by a wide circle. Michael Bruce wrote an elegy on him, in the course of which he says:

> The righteous perish! is M'Ewen dead?
> In him Religion, Virtue's friend, is fled.
> Modest in strife, bold in religion's cause,
> He sought true honour in his God's applause.
> What manly beauties in his works appear!
> Close without straining, and concise though clear.

Brown's letter is the answer to a request for assistance from M'Ewen, at the celebration of the ordinance in Dundee.

To the Rev. William M'Ewen, Dundee

'I received yours, but can't perform what you desire, as I am to be at Linton Sacrament on the third Sabbath of this month. It is no wonder to see us disagreeing about the time of our Sacraments, when I fear it will be no easy task to prove that our way of administering the Supper is agreeable to the Word of God, or the Protestant principles of our covenants, or Directory for worship, or Acts of reforming Assemblies, all which we pretend to espouse in our Testimony. I see that communicating once a year was not known in the Church of Christ till the Papists, to please a careless generation, who could not give themselves the trouble to attend frequently, introduced it. I find not one of the Protestant Churches but has condemned it, and as few of the Greek Churches that deserve the name.

'I confess it is hard for me to think the present race of Ministers and Papists wiser than all the Apostles, Primitive Christians, and whole body of Reformers. That its unfrequency tends to make it solemn I do not see, for if it is so why not administer baptism but once a year also, as it, in its own nature, is as solemn as the Supper? Why not pray seldom, preach seldom, read God's Word seldom, that they may become more solemn too? How is it that the persons that communicate perhaps twelve times in a year have as solemn impressions of this ordinance, and get as much good by it, as those who cause once in two years to serve them?

'If the Passover being received once a year is a reason for our custom, then how is it we keep it not at Pasch – and that the remembering Israel's deliverance out of Egypt is not a main ingredient in the work of communicating? And how is it that the Apostles and other great men in the Church never took up the force of this reason? Is the withdrawment of the Spirit, in comparison of what it was in the Apostolic or reforming times, a reason for the seldomer administration of it? Then why should we not be unfrequent in prayer, reading, etc., when the Spirit is away? What if the unfrequency of this ordinance, through which the Spirit doth in an especial manner communicate His influences, be the spring of the want of His influences? If the pipes of a conduit be kept stopt can much water run out? Can even human appendages of a fast, or two or three sermons on Saturday and Monday, make up for the unfrequency of it? Can what is of human institution, though of itself very good, make up for the want of what is of divine institution? Might we not as well take it into our heads to set apart two or three days for reading God's Word, when we had a mind to pray in secret; and then only pray in secret once every half year, because no oftener could we get the destined time for reading – would the reading much on that occasion make up for the long neglect of prayer?

'If the prejudices of custom are laid aside, is it any plainer from the Scripture that the Supper should be administered once a year only than it is that a man should pray only once a month?

'Is the notion I am seeming to favour being independent-like? Then why is the Apostolic practice Independent-like? Why the first book of Discipline, the Assembly 1638, and 1645, so Independent-like in their words? Why the Westminster Directory so Independent-like? Why the Testimony espouse the books of Discipline and Directory, and our ordination vows espouse it, if this notion be so Independent-like?

'These doubts are the issue of my unbiased essay to examine the conduct of the Secession. I have hinted it then to you because we have had questions formerly together, and because I know you want, if you can, to be at the bottom of things.

Rev. dear brother,

Yours affectionately,

JOHN BROWN.'

The concluding utterance, 'I know you want to be at the bottom of things,' is exceedingly characteristic of Brown himself, whatever it was of his correspondent. To the bottom of this matter he went, and it baffled him to discover why there should be such infrequent observance of this important ordinance. The reasonableness of his contention seems to us so manifest today that we forget the prejudices of the age, and how strong these are, even with ourselves, when hallowed by the custom of years. Brown reasoned out his action, and wrote a defence, which he entitled an *Apology for the more Frequent Administration of the Lord's Supper*. He did not publish it, as his action in his own congregation, and his advocacy of it in other ways, commended itself to those with whom he was intimate. But nearly twenty years after his death, when the question became urgent in other communions, it was issued to the public. There he declares:

'I am not averse to the custom of a fast preparation, and a thanksgiving day, if the exercises on these days are considered as means for encouraging strangers to attend, as they have it so seldom at home; and when they are considered as means for deepening the solemnity of the approach to God in this ordinance, which in our present case is quite, or next to quite, worn off in the long intervals between ordinances of this nature. But is it not plain, that in case the Church were returned to the primitive custom, there would be no need to encourage strangers to attend, because they would have weekly opportunities for partaking at home? And there could be less need to use means of this nature to fix or deepen those impressions; the conscientious approach to God in this solemn ordinance,

[101]

the Sabbath before, and the Sabbath after, would more effectually prepare the soul for receiving and riveting divine impressions than all the work of these three days.

'When these days' exercises are considered as well-meant human helps, during the present unfrequency of administration, nobody regards them more than I do; but if anybody considers them, as too many ignorant people do, as essential parts of this ordinance, and plead the absolute necessity of them, as a reason against the more frequent administration of the Supper, can I, in consistency with our *Confession of Faith*, chap. xxi, sect. 1, refrain from detesting that view of them, and the usage proceeding therefrom as refined Popery? Are they not of human invention? Was not the invention of them merely occasional? Are they not still unknown in many Protestant Churches? Were they not unknown in the Church of Scotland for about seventy years after the Reformation? Do we not find one of our best Assemblies, namely, that of 1645, prohibiting to have any more than one sermon upon Saturday and another upon Monday? Did not Mr. Livingston,[1] as long as he lived, refuse to allow any more sermons on the Saturday and Monday at his sacramental occasions? Now, is it not plainly Popish to count human inventions and occasional additions, essential parts of this great ordinance?'

Then follows an elaborated analogy of private devotions observed on the same principles as alluded to in the above letter, and he concludes as follows:

'In fine, whether is it grace or corruption that most affects to add human devices to God's worship, in order to make it more splendid than Christ has left it? May not persons be as really guilty of Popery by doting on the splendid pomp of divine ordinances that consists in the variety of days, sermons, and ministers, as by doting on the variety of fantastic cere-

---

[1] John Livingstone (1603-72). On Monday after communion in June 1630, at Kirk of Shotts, Lanarkshire, he preached a sermon that touched the hearts of 500 hearers.

monies used in the Popish Mass? Ought we not to beware of adding to God's ordinances, as well as of taking from them? Is God content to barter with us in this point, by giving up with the frequent administration of the Supper, if we will annex a few days' sermons, ministers, and people to it, when seldom administered? Where does He either make or declare His acceptance of this proposal?'

The passing of the old custom was somewhat slow; but in time the more frequent administration found general acceptance. Three, four, and six times in the year are not uncommon throughout the Presbyterian Church, liberty being allowed each Kirk Session of a congregation to determine the times for itself. In the remote parts of Scotland, especially in the Highlands, the old method still lingers, and has gathered to itself, as though it were something unique in the Church's history, the title of a 'Highland Communion.'

Brown's other plea, namely, for the admission of young people as witnesses of the celebration of the ordinance, also gradually prevailed; and universal today is the delightful spectacle of the children watching with awe and reverence the observance of the impressive feast.

CHAPTER 12

The Preacher and the Student

Augustine, in his work on Homiletics, *Dei Doctrina Christiana*, sets forth his idea of preaching in the memorable words: '*Sapientia* (divine wisdom) without *eloquentia* (the best human expression) will do good; *eloquentia* without *sapientia* will do no good, and will often do harm; but the union of *sapientia* with *eloquentia* is ideal.' These kinds of preaching were being illustrated very strongly in Scotland in the eighteenth century. Of *eloquentia* there was an abundance; but a fashion prevailed of deprecating the *sapientia*. It was the day when the star of Moderatism was in the ascendant – a Moderatism that delighted in a merely moral atmosphere, and the vitality of religion seemed to be ebbing away.

It is to men of the stamp of John Brown we owe it that Scotland was saved from the full effect of the strong current that was bearing religion to an arid desert. His work in the pastorate, and still more in the professoriate, where he left the impress of his own ardent, Christ-fired spirit on young men being trained for the ministry, and not less in the books that issued from his pen, did much to keep in full flow the stream of his evangelical truth that was in time to fertilize the land.

Dr. Alexander Carlyle, minister of Inveresk, Musselburgh, has left us, in his entertaining *Autobiography*,[1] a vivid picture of that period, especially as it was lived in his own circle, which, with all its array of loud-sounding names, was not a particularly wide one. It is a picture stained by many dark blots that do not add lustre to the reputation of the clergy of

[1] *The Autobiography of Dr. Alexander Carlyle of Inveresk*, 1722-1805.

that age. Dr. Carlyle prided himself on his standing among the ranks of the Moderates, on their 'culture', their autocratic rule in the Church, and their glorious conviviality. His pen portraits of the leaders of the evangelical school are not very flattering. John Brown was a fitting representative of this group of men, loyal to the cause of learning, and passionate in his defence of vital religion; and certainly and happily, from this school, 'have sprung the preachers who have shaped and coloured the religion of Scotland.'[1] Not only in the ranks of the Secession, but in the Established Church were such to be found. They held tenaciously on, while religion was being driven into barren wastes, and Scotland threatened with a dearth of Christian truth. In the end, victory lay with them. But in the long, stiff struggle, the outer garb of the Church was severely torn. Moderatism compelled the Erskines and others to secede from the prevailing party; and later it thrust out Thomas Gillespie, the gentle but high-principled minister of Carnock, who, with a son of Thomas Boston, founded the Relief Church. These men were under the necessity of unfurling a standard under which they could worship, albeit inscribed with the same Confession and the same polity as that of the Church they had to leave. They resolutely kept the *sapientia* to the front in the preaching of Scotland, and helped the country to recover its faith and the Church to regain its freedom.

As to the character of the preaching of John Brown, we have an interesting light from the testimony of one who heard him in the course of his ministry. In his early manhood Robert Simpson, theological tutor of Hoxton Academy, London, was in Haddington in 1770. He went to Brown's church.

'I well remember,' he says, 'a searching sermon he preached from the word, "What went ye out for to see? A reed shaken with the wind." Although at that time I had no experimental acquaintance with the truth as it is in Jesus, yet his grave

J. Watson, *The Scot of the Eighteenth Century*, p. 191.

appearance in the pulpit, his solemn, weighty, and majestic manner of speaking, used to affect me very much. Certainly his preaching was close, and his address to the conscience pungent. Like his Lord and Master, he spoke with authority and hallowed pathos, having tasted the sweetness and felt the power of what he believed.'

It is still more interesting to hear the comment of David Hume upon his preaching. The occasion on which he heard John Brown preach was a public function at which an aspiring young clergyman spoke along with the minister of Haddington. The former delivered his message first, in an eloquent, florid style, typical of the age. Brown followed with his sermon, marked by his usual simplicity and earnestness. 'The first preacher,' remarked Hume to his friends, 'spoke as if he did not believe what he said; the latter as if he were conscious that the Son of God stood at his elbow.'[1] His son, Dr. William Brown, declares that 'as a preacher he was distinguished by great plainness, faithfulness, seriousness, and earnestness. His learning he never brought into the pulpit, unless by bringing down the great truths of religion to the level of common capacities.'[2] Archbishop Ussher's golden saying was a great favourite of his, 'It will take all our learning to make things plain.' The doctrines and duties of religion in his message were charged with tremendous power. In his appeals to those without the fold, he touched chords that vibrated with his own passion. He was never moved so deeply as when pleading with men that despised the light. Tears only wet his cheeks when entreating them to return to the Redeemer's fold. He was blamed by one of his former students, himself then in the ministry, for expressing disapproval of Richard Baxter: 'Mr. Brown, you are often speaking against Richard Baxter, but I see no man so like Richard Baxter as yourself.'

[1] Hay and Belfrage, *A Memoir of the Rev. Alexander Waugh* (1830), p.51.
[2] William Brown, *Memoir and Select Remains of the Rev. John Brown* (1856), p. 72.

In his delivery, he acquired a 'sing-song' then not uncommon among preachers. Such a method of utterance is usually offensive; but in his case it seems to have been rather effective, being described as 'singularly melting' to serious moods,' and as 'touching and overpowering.' 'I can have no recollection of his delivery myself,' says his son, William – he was only four when his father died – 'but I have heard it imitated by my brother Ebenezer, and I felt it so touching, and overpowering, that I question if the highest flights of oratory would have had anything like the same impression on my mind.' He was a strong advocate of brevity in religious exercises. 'Be short,' he was wont to tell his students, 'in the pulpit and the family; in the closet you may be as long as you please.' Intense souls are never long in public prayer; it is the thin-verdured who exhaust prayer and patience both. There was one occasion only when he disregarded this rule – at the observance of the Lord's Supper. Then he poured out his soul with the fervour of a man who stood in the inner depths.

It was an age when the sterner aspects of the faith were by no means kept in the background. But the conscientious pastor of Haddington welcomed the sharp, keen-sighted answer that came from a saintly member, whose foundations he was probing, as she lay dying. 'Janet, what would you say if, after all He has done for you, God should let you drop into hell?' 'E'en's (even as) He likes,' was the instant reply, 'if He does, He'll lose mair than I'll do." His honour as the righteous and faithful God was involved.

It is characteristic of him to regard his own work with extraordinary depreciation. We shall draw again from his *Autobiography,* and hear what he says about his preaching.

'The morning before I was licensed, that awful Scripture, Isaiah 6. 9, 10, was much impressed on my spirit; and it hath since been I know not how often, heavy to my heart to think how much it was fulfilled in my ministry. I know not how often I have had an anxious desire to be removed by death from being a plague to my poor congregation. But I have often taken myself, and considered this as my folly, and begged of Him that if it was not for His glory to remove me by death, He would make me successful in His work; for as to transportations I had not a good opinion of most of them, and I looked on it as so far my mercy that my congregation was so small.

'After all, I dare not but confess Christ to be the best Master ever I served. Often in preaching and otherwise, I have found His words the joy and rejoicing of my heart. He hath often laid matter before me in my studies, and enabled me with pleasure to deliver it. God in our nature, and doing all for us, and being all to us, free grace reigning through His imputed righteousness, God's free grant of Christ and His salvation, and of Himself in Christ, and the believing appropriation founded on that grant, and the comfort and holiness of heart and life flowing from that, have been my most delightful themes. And though I sometimes touched on the publick evils of the day, yet my soul never so entered into these points.

'No sermons I ever preached were, I think, sweeter to my own soul than those on Psalm 142. 7, first clause; Isaiah 44. 5, first clause; Isaiah 46. 4; and 60. 20, last clause; 1 Timothy 1. 15, 16; Rev. 3. 21, and John 11. 28. The little knowledge which I had of my uncommonly wicked heart, and of the Lord's dealings with my own soul, helped me much in my sermons. And I observed that I was apt to deliver that which I had extracted thence, in a more feeling and earnest manner than other matters.'

The pulpit was enriched by the labours of the study. The preaching was as if only one book was read. 'Notwithstanding all my eager hunting after most part of that lawful learning which is known among the sons of men, I was led to preach as if I had never read a book but the Bible.' 'The eager hunting' covered wide fields. It was his custom, says his son, to rise in the summer between four and five in the morning, and in winter at six, and to study till eight in the evening. He was a firm believer in the old German proverb, "morning has gold in its mouth." With the necessary duties of the ministerial life that called him apart, and in the discharge of which he was most assiduous, he managed to spend twelve hours of the day in the little room above the doorway of his house crammed with books. The procuring of these volumes out of his small stipend showed that the passion of the bookman glowed in his soul. He regretted that he had no one to guide him in the choice of books, nor money to purchase the best, but he acknowledged that, after all, he was led to acquire the most useful.

He possessed the gift of a quick mastery of languages, rivalling George Borrow in this respect. To the knowledge of Latin, Greek, and Hebrew, with which he commenced his ministry, he added that of Arabic, Persic, Syriac and Ethiopic, and of European languages, French, Spanish, Italian, Dutch, and German. He was an eager student of natural and moral philosophy, but his favourite reading lay in the realms of history and divinity. All the masters of theology he laid under tribute. As to Bible commentaries, he epitomized them in his *Christian Journal*, where he speaks of the 'elegant Calvin, laborious Poole, sagacious Patrick and Lowth, practical Henry, copious Gill, literal Calmet, sensible Clarke, plain Burkitt, soft-flowing Doddridge, judicious Guise, learned Vitringa, penetrating Owen, pious Horne, curt Bengel, dry Schultens, and critical Whitby.' As he read, pen and paper were beside him, and he summarized as he went from paragraph to paragraph. The multitude of his commonplace-books, which he happily entitled 'Books for holding Bright Thoughts,' bears testimony to his industry and to the wide range of his reading. *The Ancient Universal History*, published in twenty large octavo volumes, and Blackstone's *Commentaries on the Laws of England*, he abridged and compiled an abstract of for himself. Like Francis Bacon, he took all knowledge for his province. Only toward the end of his days, when he realized the vastness of the ocean on which he had launched, he declared, 'From experience I have found that it is vain to attempt

[109]

to be a universal scholar.' While rejoicing in the mastery of nearly a dozen other tongues, he was fully abreast of the literature of his own land and time. He was familiar with the works of the men whom he called the 'lofty Milton, witful Cowley, elegant Pope, sprightly Thomson, awful Young, ingenious Blacklock, soaring Browne, spiritual Gray, divine Watts.' As for the literature that 'tickles the imagination' he was not so enamoured of it, and held that it should be read 'at most, very sparingly.'

His notebooks are written in a clear and legible hand, packed with résumés of the different works he had read. Wodrow's *History of the Church of Scotland*, Robertson's *History of America, Miracles* by Bonnet, a work on *Universal Restitution*, with many others, are all epitomized, while there are also engrossed numerous statistical statements of the population of different countries, and various other matters.

But, first and foremost, was his intimate acquaintance with the Scriptures. They held the supreme place in his reading and thinking, and nothing was allowed to dislodge them. He knew them from cover to cover. Let a text be quoted, instantly he would repeat it, assign its place and connection with the context, and explain its meaning. He delighted to number at leisure moments not only the books and chapters and verses, but the very words and letters of the Bible. He had an extraordinary grasp of it in the mass and in detail. His miraculous memory, his oceanic reading, his intellectual power, and his deep religious spirit, united with his tireless industry, made him a fit instrument to produce a *Dictionary* of its contents, and a *Self-interpreting Commentary* on its chapters.

CHAPTER 13

The Beginnings of Authorship

Before John Brown undertook the works that were to give him enduring fame, he devoted his powers to other fields of study. The ground in which he sought to reap is largely neglected at the present day, but it attracted considerable attention at the time—*The Westminster Confession of Faith*, and the *Catechisms*. His aim was to get to the foundations, and induce men to build upon them from their earliest days. Seven years after his settlement in Haddington he first broke ground as an author. The work he issued was a volume of 400 pages, with the rather cumbrous title, *An Help for the Ignorant, being an Essay towards an Easy, Plain, Practical, and Extensive Explication of the Westminster Confession of Faith and Catechisms.*

'Essay' is a term that has lost its original shade of meaning. His work is not an 'essay,' in the sense of a short, written composition, but an attempt to explain by question and answer the subordinate Standards of the Church. Such a work demands clear thinking and clear writing. These are manifest on every page of this respectable production. Somehow, while Romanists and Episcopalians have used this method of instruction in recent years to enable the young and the 'ignorant' to grasp their distinct tenets of belief, Presbyterians have allowed it to lapse. Something after the manner of Brown's *Explication*, though not so elaborate, might well be revived for the benefit of Presbyterian youth throughout the world.

It is of importance to observe that the first production from his pen was directed towards the quickening and informing of of the mind of youth, and the last of his twenty-nine works had for its object the same purpose. His eyes from the first were directed up-stream, and he felt, in days when the young and growing mind received scant attention, that the destiny of the human race was after all in the hands of the coming generation. Let it be safely anchored, and the ship of Church and State will surely outride all threatening storms.

The *Explication* met with a ready acceptance. But soon, in that keen-scented age of controversy, the dread charges rang out that impiety, blasphemy, heresy, and other deadly evils lurked in its pages. The Rev. John Dalzell of Earlston led the attack with great asperity. Dalzell began his ministerial life in the same year as Brown, but in the other branch of the Secession Church. He possessed remarkable gifts as a preacher, and laboured for fifty-three years in the one sphere. Dalzell assailed Brown in a pamphlet, *The Imputation of Christ's Righteousness*, which is all that remains from his pen today. The point in dispute was the practical extent of the righteousness of Christ. Brown declared that though Christ's righteousness is infinitely valuable in itself, yet believers receive it only in proportion to their need, and to the demands which the law laid upon them; they were therefore perfectly righteous in law, as the law required them to be, but not infinitely righteous. 'Not infinitely righteous!' exclaimed Dalzell and his fellow combatants. The righteousness of Christ, they held, is imputed to believers in its whole infinite value, as it is the righteousness of a God-man, and therefore it constitutes us in law-reckoning as infinitely righteous as the person of the Christ, the God-man. The controversy raged with considerable fury, and pamphlets, as became the time, were shot with speed between the parties. One of eighty-four pages is before me, defending Brown with lucidity and force, and not wanting in severe language. The temper of the assailed author is revealed in his one reply to his bustling antagonist. In a small pamphlet entitled *Brief Dissertation concerning the Righteousness of Christ*, he marshals his arguments skilfully for his contention; and his wide reading stands him in good stead, as he submits the authorities, whose orthodoxy none disputed, that upheld his views. In his Foreword he writes with dignity and self-restraint, and shows the spirit in which he deemed controversy of such high themes should be conducted, and how distasteful this method of reaching the heart of these mysteries was to him:

'I have much more charity for the ministers of that party than to suspect the bulk of them are capable of imbibing, even through inadvertency, an old Antinomian and Familistic error; or have so small acquaintance with the writings of Protestant divines, as to imagine that I am the first who ever asserted that Christ's infinite righteousness is imputed to believers precisely in proportion to their need, and the demands of the broken law upon them, or so as to make them perfectly and completely righteous in law, but not in such proportions as to render them infinitely holy, righteous, comely, or valuable in law; and had these few, who, it seems, are otherwise disposed, signified their scruples to me in a Christian manner, either by word or by writ, I doubt not but I should have offered them such replies and solutions as might have prevented that conduct, which (though charity obliges me to hope, was entirely an inadvertent and well-designed mistake) some will readily reckon a wounding of truth, a dishonouring of Christ, an instructing of their people to revile, and in the issue, an injuring of their own reputation among impartial men. But now that the fact is committed, though I reckon it my duty to contribute my weak endeavours towards the support of injured truth, and to restore to the Scriptures and the most eminent Protestant divines their due honour of being my instructors in this point, yet, instead of intending to resent, with similar conduct, the injury these reverend brethren have done me, I reckon myself, on account thereof, so much the more effectually obliged by the Christian law (Matt. 5. 44; Luke 6. 27, 28; Romans 12. 14, 20, 21; 1 Peter 2. 23 and 3. 9), to contribute my utmost endeavours towards the advancement of their welfare, spiritual or temporal – and am resolved through grace to discharge these obligations, as Providence shall give opportunity for the same. Let them do or wish me what they will, may their portion be redemption through the blood of Jesus, even "the forgiveness of sins, according to the riches of His grace"; and, call me what they please, may the Lord call them "the holy ones, the redeemed of the Lord, sought out, and not forsaken."'

Six years after the appearance of his *Explication* of the Church's Standards, he published two Catechisms, one introductory to and the other explanatory of the *Shorter Catechism*. They had a very extensive circulation, and passed through numerous editions. They were familiarly known in many a household as 'Little Brown's,' and 'Big Brown's,'[1] and were translated into various languages both in Asia and Africa. Dr. Robert Moffat, in South Africa, rendered them into the Sechuana tongue. Other manuals have been issued since; but Brown's *Short Catechism for Young Children* is still being published and meets with a ready sale. It is as impossible to estimate the value of these *Catechisms* as it is to enumerate the hundreds of thousands of them that have proceeded from the press, and found their way all over the world.

'Once an author, always an author,' says Cowper in his diverting and delightful letters; 'this you know, my friend, and it admits of no dispute.' It was so with the busy pastor of Haddington. In the year 1765 he published what perhaps was the most popular of all his writings, judging by its countless

[1] Readers of *Marjorie Fleming* will recall the amusing paragraph where the faithful old servant of the household, Jeanie Robertson, instructing the children in the faith, put the question of the *Short Catechism* to Marjorie's brother, William, who could show his 'Calvinistic acquirements when nineteen months old.' Jeanie's glory was 'putting him through the carritch' (catechism) in broad Scotch, beginning at the beginning with 'Wha made ye, ma bonnie man?' For the correctness of this and the three next replies, Jeanie had no anxiety, but the tone changed to menace, and the closed *nieve* (fist) was shaken in the child's face as she demanded, 'Of what are you made?' 'DIRT,' was the answer uniformly given. 'Wull ye never learn to say *dust*, ye thrawn deevil?' with a cuff from the opened hand, was the as inevitable rejoinder. (*Horae Subsecivae*, Third Series, p. 210.)

issues in the course of the next fifty years and more. He called it *The Christian Journal; or, Common Incidents, Spiritual Instructors*. Its first publishers were 'John Gray and Gavin Alston,' at their printing press in 'Jackson's Close, Edinburgh.' As edition after edition was called for, the author was altering, adding to, amending, and sometimes not improving his pithy, pungent expressions. It is a work that looks upon nature as 'God's great green book.' It might have been prompted by the spirit that animated his renowned namesake, Sir Thomas Browne. 'There are two books,' he wrote, 'from whence I collect my divinity. Besides that written one of God, another of His servant nature, that universal and public manuscript that lies expansed unto the eyes of all.'

The *Journal* has five main divisions – the journal of a day in Spring, in Summer, in Harvest, and in Winter, and of the Day of Rest. He calls up a traveller on one of the days of these seasons, and with a swift, brief word he describes his thoughts, actions, sights, throughout that day, and follows in each case with a pointed spiritual application. One could easily reproduce the life of the period in town and country from his pages. You see the man awaking in the morning, rising, dressing, viewing himself in the looking-glass, passing out into the day's varied experiences, seeing nature arrayed in her ever-changing garb, and returning at night to his rest and to dreamland. All sorts and conditions of men, all the sights and scenes to be met with in any of the seasons, and on the Sunday, pass before the reader; and all are brought under one point of light, that penetrates with searching ray every incident and aspect of nature and of life – the 'Light of the World.' In the 'Summer' Journal he carries his traveller to a mountain-top, where before him march the nations, ancient and modern. With a graphic phrase each is described, and the application follows. Anon he passes into a library, rich in the literature of the world; rapidly is it reviewed, an apt adjective summing up each author and his style.

On the first page are happy quotations that justify the work.

One is from Hesiod: 'Let us begin with God; all things are full of God.' Another is from Cadha: 'The ear that is always attentive to God never hears a voice that speaks not of Him; the soul whose eye is intent on Him never sees an atom wherein she doth not discern her best beloved.' A third is from Job 12. 7, 8: 'Ask now the beasts, and they shall teach thee; and the fowls of the air, and they shall tell thee; or speak to the earth, and it shall teach thee; and the fishes of the sea shall declare unto thee.'

In his Preface he vindicates his method by asking—

'Does not the divine Spirit, in His invaluable oracles, constitute the puny ant, the lazy cur, the wallowing sow, the troubled sea, with its mire and dirt, our spiritual instructors? Does not Jesus, the wisdom of God, draw His instructive, His inestimable parables from sparrows, fishes, nets, bottles, grains of mustard seed, dough, and other common objects? Why may not we, though at infinite distance, follow His blessed example, and, with the skilful chemist, extract a precious spirit from things outwardly base and contemptible?'

To give an illustration, we might dip into the *Journal* anywhere:

'"How pleasantly the dew falls!" Lord Jesus, canst Thou not be as the dew to my soul! canst Thou not make me one of Thy young converts who are like "the dew from the womb of the morning"! Cursed unbelief, how hast thou resisted the power of this divine promise, and robbed Jesus of the honour of accomplishing it! "Here the worms creep out of the earth, to acknowledge their debt to Him that waters it, and to sip this early dew." When, my soul, wilt thou creep forth from thine earthiness and carnality, to thank the divine Father of the dew for all His kindness towards thee? When wilt thou desire and feed on Jesus, who is as the dew of Israel, and refresh thyself with the influences of His grace?

' "Without the warmth of the sun, and moisture of the clouds, the care of the husbandman could produce nothing." Without the concurrence of Jesus' blood and Spirit, no human labour could convert a soul, produce a good work, or produce a grain of felicity. Nay, He must do all and we nothing, but stand still and see His salvation. "How sweetly, in this vernal rain, the clouds consign their treasures to the field!" God's paths drop down fatness. Ye sons of men, muse, praise, and look forth lively gratitude. In lovely spring, and her soft scenes, I see my smiling God; I feel a present Deity, and taste His joy, to see a happy world. Sweet vernal fields! Thrice sweeter sacred Word! How Jehovah pours His stores of love, His melted heart, into thy darling page, that messenger of grace! Where rapture flows on rapture; every line with rising wonders filled; how from its rainy pools, my soul, enraptured, drank the spirit of eternal joy, of that unutterable happiness which Love alone bestows upon her favoured few! How soars my mind beyond the blooming earth! On swelling thought, my heart flies to the bosom of her distant, her ETERNAL FAIR: My Lord and My God.

' "Yonder the sparrow chirps." Pretty bird, but Jehovah's care, my Father's charge. Am I not much more so? though, when forsaken of Him I mourn, yet le me cleave to His house; nestle in the walls of divine perfections and promises, and in the covering of Jesus' righteousness.

' "Here runs a beautiful stream." Thrice more beautiful river of Jesus' blood and blessed Spirit, which makes glad the Church, the city of God. O the plenty, the purity, freeness and easy access to Thee! Here we may drink and wash; all may drink and wash; filthiness can never pollute Thy stream. Wash here, my soul; wash seven times and be clean.

' "How stately the steps, how great the strength, how bold the looks of this horse!" Rather, how gloriously the divine power and greatness shineth in him! how infinitely more august the aspect and goings of my God and my King who made him! How surpassing, that God should make this strong and stately creature so submissive to man! how much more so, that the Almighty Himself should submit to bear my sin, my curse, my woe! and to bear and carry me to everlasting rest! Never more doubt, my soul, of all things working together for thy good; and be thou as the Lord's goodly horse, strong in Christ, and courageous in His way; but beware of neighing after thy lusts or rushing into temptation, as the horse rusheth into the battle.

'Souls will soon become empty, which are always letting out, but not careful to let in from Christ. We should lay in Christ, lay up with Christ, and then lay out for Christ. We ought to beware of being always wooing Christ without ever marrying Him. . . . Opinion-sowing and church-railing professors have commonly more self than grace. . . . Young Christians commonly need a curb, and old ones a spur. . . . Sins die and fall off true Christians, as leaves fall off trees in harvest. . . . True Christians are like flint stones, which keep their fire under water itself. . . . Our care ought to be to wait on God, to walk with God, work all our works in and for God; and to bring our will in everything to the will of God; and the worse we see others, to be the better ourselves.

'"Now comes a light from my father's house, but my sight fails." O the dazzling beams, the tides of glory from above, which burst into my inner man! how Jesus, my everlasting Sun, enlightens my soul! how He leads me to His bleeding mercy, that quiet sea of infinite sweetness, for faith to drink of and bathe in, till I become without spot or wrinkle or any such thing! How He guides me into the green pastures of His comforting Word – Thrice happy prospect of the blind! no more can I read the letters of the precious, precious book of God, but I feel it written on my heart; no more can I see outward things, but I see Jesus formed in my soul; I see my name written, and myself lying in His heart; I see the things within the veil, whither the Forerunner is for me entered. I rend the curtain of time, and look into eternity. I give up with all creatures, life, heart, flesh, eyes, and all, that I may have all in God. O to appear before, and be near enough Him! O to be unearthed, unselfed, that I may be like Him! that my soul may be in perpetual ascension to Him! my love going forth in ever-lasting raptures after Him!'

In a letter to a correspondent, dated Haddington, August 20th, 1765, Brown says: 'The Christian Journal, I suppose, is now published. You may send for what copies you need, and O pray for its doing some good. No doubt it will be the savour of death and a stumbling-block to some carnal and profane readers; but if Jesus render it useful to the serious, it is my business to bear patiently the scoff of the profane.' The years it held its own, and the generations it influenced, bear witness to the great good it did.

Publishers found it to their advantage to issue edition after edition of it. James Nisbet, the founder of the firm of Nisbet & Co., states that when he resolved to leave his native Kelso and start business in London, the first work he issued was John Brown's Christian Journal. That was in 1810, nearly fifty years after its first publication, and twenty-three years after its author's death. He acknowledged that it was a happy and profitable venture.

The insight into the hidden meaning of animate and in-animate nature was a gift Brown passed on to his descendants. It was a particularly marked possession of his famous great-grandson, the author of Rab. The words of the Imitation might be fitly applied to both: 'If thy heart were sincere and upright, then every creation would be to thee a looking-glass of life.'

CHAPTER 14

The Dictionary of the Bible

The doors of authorship were now open, and works surging in the author's brain were struggling for egress into the marketplace of literature. His wide reading and enlarging vision made for a clear and confident grasp of the many subjects he longed to handle. Few helps did the people possess to a comprehensive understanding of the Scriptures; and the minister of Haddington, having gathered so much of the treasures of knowledge, boldly conceived the idea of preparing a *Dictionary of the Bible* for the reading public. There was no thought of calling in helpers in this great enterprise, as is so manifestly necessary in these days of specialized knowledge. Singlehanded was the work to be done. To design and dare such a task, with congregational and church duties that carried the pastor over a wide area and demanded a heavy tale of pulpit and synodical work, was an heroic thing to do. No one had attempted such an undertaking in Scotland before; and in England *The Christian Dictionarie* of Thomas Wilson (1563-1622), a rector of Canterbury, had long passed into oblivion.

As he proceeded to gather material for his great work, Brown threw off dissertations on some special subjects that interested him. In 1766, he issued *An Historical Account of the Rise and Progress of the Secession*, a small work, as befitted a history that might be supposed to cover only twenty-six years. He starts, however, with the Reformation, and proceeds in a fair and impartial spirit to detail the salient features of the Church's struggle till 1730. The events that follow are firmly handled. The deposition of the eight men who were jealous of the rights and liberties of the Church is vividly contrasted with the treatment that was meted out by the same Assembly to John Glass, 'an impenitent and furious Independent,' who was restored to the ministry, and who, the historian affirms, had plainly broken his ordination vows, and continued to declare against Presbyterian government. The work, vigorously written, gives an insight into the condition of Church life in Scotland at the time; it shows the kind of Gospel that was preached and the loose conditions of Church membership that prevailed, calling for a protest, if the country was to be saved from slipping into sheer paganism.

In the following year came from his active pen, *Letters on the Constitution, Government, and Discipline of the Christian Church*, nineteen letters addressed to 'My dear Amelius,'[1] who is regarded as a person with lax notions as to the constitution of the Church, and the admission of members within its pale. They are written with unflagging spirit, are weighty in argument, and rich in their Scriptural background. They show that Brown was reaching down to root causes, and laying the groundwork of a history that later years were to see.

The succeeding year, 1768, led him into a study that had a great fascination for many in that age – the typology of Scripture. His own mind was captivated by it, and he felt that he had light of his own for a subject that has so many facets. Out from the little sunlit, crowded study of Haddington went forth that year, *Sacred Typology; a Brief View of the Figures, and Explanations of the Metaphors, contained in Scripture*. An age that does not concern itself much with types, except of the scientific order, will be interested to know how they appealed to an earlier generation.

'The advantage,' says Brown, 'of a clear, comprehensive and regular view of the Figures, the Types, and the Predictions of

[1] It was a prevalent custom of the time to use classical names as representative of persons who held certain opinions, e.g. Berkeley's *Hylas and Philonous*, Hervey's *Theron and Aspasio*, Johnson in *The Rambler* frequently adopted it; while Pope spoke of Addison as 'Atticus.'

Scripture is obvious. In the first, we observe the surprising eloquence of Heaven, and discern, in almost every form of nature, a guide to and an illustration of inspired truth. By the second, we perceive the whole substance of the Gospel of Christ, truly exhibited in ancient shadows, persons, and things: in laws apparently carnal and trifling. In the third, we observe how astonishingly inspired predictions, properly arranged, and compared with the history of nations and churches, do illustrate each other; and modern events, as with the evidence of miracles, confirm our faith in the oracles of God.'

Of the trilogy here mentioned, the first appeared in 1768, the second and third not till 1781. These works, as one might expect, are often very arbitrary in their elucidation of the type or figure. The imagination is apt to run riot in such a field, and the analogy to become somewhat strained. Yet the views of truth presented at times are striking, and the whole is characterized by an extraordinary richness of Scriptural knowledge. The *Harmony of Prophecy* in particular is a manual exhibiting extensive reading, and judicious application of the prophetic word to the facts of history.

But all this was more or less the by-product of a larger work, which was to carry the author's reputation far beyond his native land. All his strength was now concentrated on the *Dictionary*, materials for which he had been gathering during the past ten years. In 1769 it first saw the light, and for a hundred years it was to hold on its way, by the issue of various editions, revised and brought up to date by various editors, the last appearing in 1868. British scholarship had practically neglected this field of Scripture study; and Brown's predecessors were, with the exception of Wilson, continental scholars, only one of whose works had been translated into English, that of Augustine Calmet, and the translation was an abridgement.

The story of Bible Dictionaries has never been told, but it is one of considerable interest. Like most great enterprises, they had a humble origin, a quiet beginning. They sprang from the simplicities of the concordance, a word leading to the summation of its varied meanings, a doctrine to the statement of its truths, a place to the account of its history, a person to the story of his life. The first to attempt a concordance was Cardinal Hugo de Saint-Cher of the order of St. Dominic, who died in 1261 or 1262. He called in helpers from five different monasteries to assist him. The difficulty he had to contend with was the lack of the division of the books of Scripture into chapters and verses. He overcame it by using the letters of the alphabet to indicate the lines of the pages of the MS. There was not the minuteness in detailing words as in a concordance of today; indeed that was impossible, but leading words were set forth with care and accuracy, and it was a decided help in the comparing of Scripture with Scripture.

His successors were a couple of enthusiasts, who worked together, Conrad d'Alberstade and Arlot. They added considerably to the material contained in Hugo's *Concordance*. Their work was issued in 1290.

A long period now intervened ere the next step was taken. It was not until the time of the Council of Bàsle in 1430, when Jean de Ségovie carried forward the plan, producing what he called, *Une Table alphabétique des particules indeclinables*.

Another century had to pass before developments were possible. The enthusiastic and enterprising Parisian publisher, Robert Stephens, by his bold division of the Scriptures into chapters and verses (chapters were partly acknowledged before), gave a great impetus to the work. His Bible, to publish which he had to retire to Geneva, that citadel of liberty for the men of progress and reform, was sent forth in 1551. The numbering of the Scripture writings by this ardent son of the Reformation abides to this day. It has often been condemned as unsatisfactory; and so it is, chapters chopping up paragraphs meant to stand as one, and verses dividing thoughts that are knit by the closest ties. Yet none have dared to produce anything better. Where the verse system has been modified or abandoned, the result has not proved satisfactory, at any rate from the point of convenience. Indeed stand it must, as practically the whole earth in its numberless tongues possesses the Scriptures, and with them Stephens' versicular division.

The path of bibliographers was now materially improved. George Bullocus, in 1572, sent forth a new concordance from Antwerp, in Latin, in which not merely the word, but the content of the word according to Scripture usage is supplied. His work bore the title, *Œconomia methodica Concordantiarum Scripturæ Sacræ.*

About this period also Matthias Flaccus Illyricus produced his work, which shows the development from the chrysalis stage of a concordance to the fuller growth of a dictionary. He called it *Clavis Scripturæ Sacræ*. It was in Latin, and runs to about 1,000 pages. Flaccus was for a time a colleague of Luther and Melanchthon in the University of Wittenberg; after the former's death he became a leader of the strict Lutheran party and fiercely assailed Melanchthon from Magdeburg and Jena, whither he had gone. But his exclusive narrowness and bitter polemics, in spite of his great ability, made him latterly acceptable to none, and he was driven from town to town, dying at Frankfort in 1575, at the age of fifty-five. He was the originator of the work called the *Magdeburg Centuries*, in which a number of scholars took part, and an attempt was made to write the history of the Church from the evangelical point of view, a work with a controversial tone, but of immense learning, that inaugurated the free study of Church history.

In 1612, the rector of St. George's the Martyr, Canterbury, Thomas Wilson, published his *Christian Dictionarie* which reached its eighth edition in 1678. In his short 'advertisement' he points out the difference between his production and that of William Knight, which is a 'concordance; mine is a dictionarie; his axiomatical, mine is partly verbatical, partly pragmatical.' This William Knight was rector of Little Gransden, Cambridgeshire, and in 1610, published in folio form, his

Concordance Axiomatical, containing a Survey of Theological Propositions, and their Reasons and Uses in Holy Scripture.

From Geneva in 1650, came the work of Petrus Ravanellus, in Latin, in two folio volumes. It was entitled *Bibliotheca Sacra, seu Thesaurus Scripturæ, canonicæ amplissimus*, a work more elaborate than its predecessors, and more comprehensive in its treatment of Biblical themes.

In 1693 appeared *Le Grand Dictionnaire de la Bible* of Honoré Richard Simon, a priest and doctor of theology at Lyons. It was a work of two large folio volumes of about 750 pages each. His aim he describes on his title-page, to set forth 'the lives and doings of important personages, spoken of in the Old and New Testaments, and in the history of the Jews, names of animals, pure and impure, precious stones, feasts and solemn festivals of the Jews, etc.'

A quarter of a century further on, in 1722, the year in which John Brown was born, came the monumental production of Augustine Calmet. It appeared in French in two volumes, supplemented by another two six years later. It carried on its title-page a full account of its plan and purpose: *Dictionnaire historique, critique, chronologique, géographique, et literal de la Bible, enrichi d'un grand nombre de figures en taille-douce, qui représentent les Antiquitez Judaïques.* The Introduction is a contribution of considerable interest, referring to the labours of some of his predecessors in this department of study, and to a review of the writings of Scripture, as dealt with by commentators up till that time. Calmet was a most voluminous writer, issuing a Bible commentary in twenty-three volumes, a *History of the Jews*, and an attempt at a *Universal History*, which reached seventeen volumes. He also produced a *History of Lorraine*, in four volumes. He was born at Mesnil-la-Horgue, near Coumercy, in 1672. He entered the order of St. Benedict, filled several important ecclesiastical offices, and, after a laborious career, died as Abbot of Simones in 1757. His *Dictionary* was translated into English in 1732, by Samuel D'Oyly, Vicar of St. Nicholas, Rochester, and John

Colson, Vicar of Chalk in Kent. It was an abridgment of the main work, and published in three large folio volumes and somewhat fully illustrated.

It was in the footsteps of these men that John Brown courageously followed, when in 1769, he brought out his dictionary of the Scriptures in two volumes, with this title –

A
DICTIONARY
of the
HOLY BIBLE

containing

An Historical Account of the Persons; a Geographical and Historical Account of the Places; a Literal, Critical, and Systematical Description of other Objects, whether Natural, Artificial, Civil, Religious, or Military

and

An Explication of the appellative Terms, mentioned in the Writings of the

Old and New Testament

The Whole Comprising

Whatever important is known concerning the Antiquities of the Hebrew Nation and Church of God; forming a Sacred Commentary; a Body of Scripture History, Chronology, and Divinity; and serving in a great Measure as a Concordance to the Bible.

The work contained a few illustrations, such as the camp of the Israelites, with the Standards of the Twelve Tribes, the Pyramids of Egypt, the Sphinx, the Ancient City of Jerusalem, maps showing the travels of the Apostle Paul, the countries mentioned in the New Testament, the Dispersion of the Nations, and one, the most curious and interesting of all, 'A

Map of the World, agreeable to the Latest Discoveries,' in which the western shores of the United States are represented as 'British Empire,' India as the 'Mogul's Empire,' Australia as 'New Holland,' and the northern half of Africa as 'Sarrah, or the Desert.'

There was no man in Scotland so well equipped for issuing a work of this nature as the minister of Haddington. His interests were encyclopædic. His knowledge of oriental languages, in which Calmet was markedly defective, of classics, of history, of divinity, and natural sciences was beyond anything possessed by any of his contemporaries in the Scottish Church. He had the works, it is to be gathered from his Preface, of Illyricus, Wilson, Simon, Ravenall, and Calmet before him, but he formed his own plan, and pursued his own method. His articles show independent treatment, and include subjects that hitherto had been left untouched. His extraordinary command of Scripture and his wide reading gave him an easy mastery in the many subjects that a Bible dictionary must embrace. What was unhistorical was omitted; 'few fancies of the Christian Fathers, or of the Jewish or Mahometan writers are here inserted, as I knew not how they could be of use.' He courageously faced difficulties, whether the solutions commended themselves to others or not. 'I have not wilfully kept back,' he naïvely says in concluding his brief, modest Introduction, 'the solution of any difficulty; but it is often given, especially in historical articles, without the least critical noise or parade.' The fires of criticism that rage so fiercely today had not then begun to burn round the books of Scripture. The *Conjecturings* of Jean Astruc (1684-1766), the French Professor of Medicine, which struck the first spark in the ceaseless inquiry as to the Elohistic and Jehovistic strata in the Pentateuch, had only recently been published (1753). No knowledge of them had apparently penetrated to the study-table of the manse at Haddington. If they had, their fire would most likely have been quickly quenched by a sharp drenching from the Scriptures themselves.

To produce such a *Dictionary* was a high adventure for one to undertake, compassed round with other duties, but it was admirably executed. If popularity be the standard of success, its triumph was complete. Edition after edition was called for. 'The author,' said Rev. Dr. Fletcher of London, issuing an edition early in the nineteenth century, 'could never have anticipated the remarkable, and extensive, and established countenance it has obtained from the students of theology.' Not only students of theology gave it countenance, but it found its way into the homes of the people. It 'embraced both the situation of teacher and taught.'

Three editions were called for during the author's life-time; and he 'bestowed no small pains in rendering each edition considerably more perfect than the former.' As to the number that followed it is impossible to say,[1] but few years elapsed down till 1868, when a publisher did not announce a new edition of *Brown's Bible Dictionary*, revised, corrected, and added to by some editor. No less than five spurious editions were published by persons anxious to propagate their own peculiar tenets, containing, as his sons (John, Ebenezer, and Thomas) say in issuing the fifth edition in 1807, 'sentiments diametrically opposed to those of the author, and replete with inconsistency and error.' The law of copyright held good then for fourteen years. But detection led to warning and suppression. It was, however, a striking testimony to the great value in which the reading public held the *Dictionary* of the minister of Haddington that it was exploited in these ways.

It need scarcely be said that a work of this kind, produced in 1769, is bound to be largely superseded today. But it was well abreast of the scholarship of that age, and practically for the first time put its results in an interesting form in the hands of the people. The whole work is written with unfailing spirit, something quaint, racy, and memorable glittering in almost every page. The articles cover all Biblical subjects and often

[1] In the British Museum there are ten editions of Brown's *Dictionary of the Bible*.

supply information which is not normally included in more recent works of this kind. The author's keen interest in natural history shows itself in his graphic description of Bible animals. His linguistic gifts find full scope; and his ample knowledge of divinity and history is manifest throughout. Altogether it is a work that would have made the reputation of any author. While it revealed Brown's extraordinary powers, it proved of immense service to Biblical study. It was treasured as being a source of information on Bible themes, and acknowledged by not a few as being in addition a means of spiritual quickening.

To complete the interesting bibliographical record which we have traced in this chapter, leaving out smaller works, we may add that it was not till 1845 that another ardent worker in the British field of scholarship appeared, John Kitto, with his *Cyclopædia of Biblical Literature*. Five years later he was followed by Samuel Green with a *Biblical and Theological Dictionary*; and by Dr. John Eadie, with *A Dictionary of the Holy Bible for the use of Young Persons*. Dr. Eadie, in the 1868 edition of Brown's Dictionary, which was revised by Brown's youngest son, William, contributed articles on Assyria, Babylonia, Media, Nineveh, Persia, Zidon, etc., in view of the discoveries in these lands since the earlier editions were issued. In 1860, appeared a more ambitious project, *A Dictionary of the Bible*, in three volumes, edited by Dr. William Smith, of classic dictionary fame. Already it has become antiquated. In 1896, Dr. James Hastings sketched his plan for a new dictionary of the Bible and gathered around him an array of brilliant contributors to assist him in issuing a work worthy of the scholarship of the age. In 1898, the first volume appeared, to be followed by three others in quick succession; and a fifth volume, containing articles of first importance that overflowed from the others, and later a one-volume edition. This projected work stirred up others; and step by step with Hastings' monumental production, came the *Encyclopædia Biblica*, edited by Professor T. K. Cheyne. The publishing firm of John Murray also produced a *Dictionary* in one volume, of

E

which the main commendation was its illustrations. Messrs. Dent, in 1910, brought out the latest standard work in English under the capable editorship of William Ewing, D.D., and J. E. H. Thomson, D.D., both of whom, in addition to their scholarship, had personal experience of life in Palestine. In addition to these must be mentioned the Schaff-Herzog *Encyclopædia of Religious Knowledge*, embracing Biblical, Historical, Doctrinal and Practical Theology, and Biblical, Theological, and Ecclesiastical Biography, in thirteen volumes, including the Index. The peril is now of the field being over-tilled.

CHAPTER 15

The Professor

We have been anticipating our story. While the labours in the little square room in the manse of Haddington were being devoted to the *Dictionary* and other works, the eyes of his Church were being directed to the student pastor. Suddenly in 1767, a vacancy occurred in its one professorship. From the first the men of the Secession recognized the supreme value of an educated ministry. The Universities of the country, Edinburgh, Glasgow, St. Andrews, and Aberdeen, trained their students in a full Arts curriculum. Yet the young Church did not bar the door to every one who did not tread that avenue to the ministry. Brown himself was a notable exception. But the exceptions only 'proved the rule'. When, however, it came to the subjects of divinity, the Church claimed its own teachers, and provided for the instruction of its own candidates for the ministry. The arrangement at this period was for one professor to undertake the work for two months in the year under a curriculum extending at first over four and later over five years; and for presbyteries to superintend the students' further studies in theology during the other ten months. As the Church grew in numbers and the number of students increased, the professoriate was enlarged, and four or five professors conducted the classes instead of one.

Since Brown sat in Glasgow at the feet of James Fisher, who held office till his death in 1763, the Church had had only one occupant of the chair, John Swanston of Kinross, who was appointed in 1764. Swanston was a man of handsome appearance, and acknowledged powers, and had the gift of enkindling a love for learning in his students. For only three brief sessions was he permitted to serve his Church in this capacity. In the summer of 1767, while at Perth, he was suddenly seized with an inflammatory illness, and died ere he could be removed to his home at Kinross, in the forty-sixth year of his age. One of his students was the young poet, Michael Bruce, who succumbed to his malady only three weeks after the Professor.

Swanston's widow had troubled waters to pass through after this loss, and two letters of Brown's have been preserved which he wrote to her in her period of sorrow. They have the warm touch of a sympathetic heart, and a delicacy of expression that unobtrusively links life, with its shortcomings and its sufferings, to the central source of all.

To Mrs. Swanston, Kinross

'DEAR MADAM,

'Partly forgetfulness, partly want of time, has occasioned my not writing till now; but how delightful that Jesus never forgets to show kindness, never wants time! How proper He to supply the place of a husband! no breach deserves the name, if it be filled up with Christ. Few women have had a larger breach made on them than you; yet there is more than enough in Isaiah 54. 5, Hos. 2. 19, 20, Jer. 49. 11, and Phil. 4. 19, to fill it up. O were your heart and mind filled to the brim with these! with Christ and His redeeming love! That would sweeten all the waters of Marah to us. It would make us always triumph in Christ, and make us think how good and wise a God, that took a husband, took children, took a brother from us, and out of our heart, that God Himself might fill ALL, AND BE ALL IN ALL, and leave us no room for an idol. If God dry up the streams of our comfort, let us have recourse to Him, the fountain of living waters. Here we, though like wild asses' colts, may drink our fill; and here let all your consolation be. Into His bosom pour every complaint, every request. With Him talk on your solitary case, of Him ask counsel in every perplexity. Lay the great burden of the education of the children on Him.

This in haste, wishing the Lord Jesus may support you under your present load, and make what no doubt you reckon a heavy affliction work for you and yours a far more exceeding and eternal weight of glory. My wife joins in compliments to you and children.

Yours affectionately,

JOHN BROWN.'

HADDINGTON,
April 18th, 1768.

'P.S. – I am glad to see you have a son that is likely to have so much of his father, and I hope he will be a comfort to you. However, let your great comfort be placed in God. All created comforts may soon turn crosses, but Jesus will never turn a cross. O essay to suck comfort out of His fulness and His promises. – J.B.'

Seventeen months later another bereavement befell her, and again his busy pen brought her the tender sympathy of a loyal friend.

'DEAR MADAM,

'I would desire to sympathize with you in your late, and I may say mournful repetition of a former trial. God, I see, is trysting you with death after death, to wean your affections from all creatures to Himself. Not long ago you had, as it were, one on every hand of you, betwixt you and death; now you, as it were, stand alone, without either parent or husband. The only safe course now, and I hope the Lord determines your heart to take it, is to press near and keep near the Lord Jesus to supply all wants, that when parents, husbands, and all have forsaken you, He may take you up. I beseech you, try to support a sinking heart with *that*, "The Lord liveth, and blessed be my rock, and let the God of my salvation be exalted"; and, "Fear not, I am with thee; be not dismayed, I am thy God." Promises are sweet morsels at any time, but especially in a day of trouble. The more credit you give God with respect to His promises, the better it will fare with you and your seed. None perish that trust Him. Let, therefore, the motto of your life be, *Looking unto Jesus* for all you can need. With Him it is more blessed to give than to receive. Though indeed avoiding of proper company is wrong in one that is oppressed with grief, yet there is no companion for a broken heart like Jesus Christ. May your soul now use Him in place of parents and husband, and as your all and in all; for the small remains of children you retain, however agreeable, are but vanity and vexation of spirit, in comparison with Him. This in haste from yours affectionately,

JOHN BROWN.'

HADDINGTON,
September 18th, 1769.'

The question of a successor to Swanston in the professorship of the Church was eagerly canvassed. But only one man in the Church seemed deserving of the honour – John Brown of Haddington. He might have been placed in the chair on receiving licence, such was his mastery of Scripture tongues, and the vast amount of varied erudition he had even then acquired. But the intervening years had added immensely to his stock of knowledge, and he was forging his way bravely toward the height of his ambition, to become 'a universal scholar,' a height he was later sorrowfully to confess receded the higher he ascended. The specializing age was then on the distant horizon; it was the age of pluralists; and a 'pluralist' in learning the young Church had in its widely-informed minister of Haddington – a man to whom the Scriptures in their original tongues were as familiar as his own, and theology a well-tilled field, and church history a well-known story.

He was requested by the Synod to do duty for the Session of 1767, as there was scarcely time to make a formal appointment. In the following year, at the meeting of the Synod in May, the regular official at the clerk's table, Andrew Cock of

Greenock, asked to be relieved of duty as a case was impending in which he was one of the principal parties, and Brown was chosen to act as his substitute. When the subject of the appointment of the Professor of Divinity was reached, three Johns were 'put on the leet for said office' – John Smith of Dunfermline, John Brown of Haddington, and John Belfrage of Falkirk, all strong, capable men. But, as the record runs, 'the roll being called and votes marked, it was carried unanimously for Mr. Brown.' The post to which he was appointed with such acclamation he held with universal confidence for twenty years, to the day of his death.

The students always assembled where, for the time being, the Professor was located. The two months in which they met were August and September. To Haddington accordingly the young men gathered in these autumn days, meeting in the Professor's church.

If Haddington were 'the dimmest, deadest spot in the Creator's universe . . . the very air one breathed impregnated with stupidity,'[1] as Jane Welsh Carlyle depicted it a few decades later, it would be enlivened by the incursion of this youthful band of students. Lying in a hollow at the foot of the southern slopes of the Garleton Hills, it enjoys an air of repose. Pleasant walks for the students abounded, and places to stir the historic imagination. The old church, with its massive central tower, spoke of a thrilling past. To the east were Stenton, Whittinghame, and Hailes Castle, where the ill-starred Mary, Queen of Scots, took temporary refuge with her third husband, after spending the night at Bothwell House, Haddington. Not far off to the south-west was the ancient fortalice of Lethington, once the home of the astute Maitland, the adviser and Secretary of Queen Mary, with its 'Political's Walk.' To the west, in the richly wooded fertile valley, was Saltoun, once the seat of Andrew Fletcher, the famous Scottish patriot, who died a little more than half a century before (1716), and who had left the oft-quoted saying, 'that he believed if a man were per-

---

[1] *Early Letters of Jane Welsh Carlyle*, edited by David G. Ritchie.

mitted to make the ballads, he need not care who should make the laws of a nation.' From the heights of the Garleton Hills extensive views could be obtained of the rich agricultural lands of East Lothian, and with the heights breaking the horizon of Traprain Law, the Bass Rock, North Berwick Law, and Arthur's Seat, couching like a lion watching over the metropolis, and the Lammermuirs in the south, and the Firth of Forth in the north, and beyond the blue hills of Fife. Haddington, therefore, was a centre that had much to interest and delight the student.

During the period of his professorship, Brown had about thirty students each year in attendance. They were, of course, at different stages in study; but he adapted his work to cover the whole course deemed essential for their equipment. The presence of these young men was a fresh stimulus to the eager learner. It evoked the best he had to impart, and provided him with the opportunity of reaping a harvest in the various fields which he had so assiduously cultivated. He entertained a high ideal of the work to which these students were called, and was fired with a glowing passion to inspire them to attain.

The session was a brief but crowded one. The Professor met with his students every morning at ten o'clock. Punctual to the minute, he was in his chair, and all required to be in their places. The same punctuality did not attend the closing hour—it might be eleven, or twelve, or even one o'clock and after, ere they separated; the work mapped out for the morning had to be completed. On four days in the week—Monday, Tuesday, Thursday, and Friday—they assembled in the afternoon to hear students' sermons and lectures. A first-year student had a discourse to give, the text of which was assigned him on the opening day of the Hall, and which had to be delivered ere the brief session closed; the second-year student had to deliver a lecture on a portion of Scripture, and an exercise with additions (a passage in Hebrew, with its meaning and message) from the Old Testament; the third, fourth, and fifth years' students had apportioned them three discourses each – a lecture, a thesis, and a popular sermon. Outsiders were free to attend the afternoon sessions, when these sermons or lectures were delivered. The students were at liberty to criticize one another's productions – a privilege of which they freely availed themselves, the Professor meanwhile guarding the gates of honour, and himself closing with his criticism.[1] It required tact and firmness, kindliness and sympathy to manage this part of the curriculum. And it is recorded as a proof of the geniality which was infused into his strict management of the Hall, that more of Brown's students regularly stood forth as critics than under any former Professor. On Wednesday afternoons the students met by themselves for debate and discussion. On Saturdays they assembled with the Professor for prayer. In the evenings a session was usually held, when lectures were delivered on Church History. About 160 hours per session were thus crowded in.

For the more efficient study of Hebrew, the Professor prepared a short grammar and vocabulary of his own. In Divinity he struck out a path for himself, and discarded what was generally taught in the theological classes of Scotland at the time, the *Medulla* of the Dutch theologian, Marckius, or the *Institutes* of the Genevan Professor, Turretin. He produced a *System* of his own, which he eventually published in 1782. In Church History he mapped out no less a field than one covering the whole course of the Church, from the birth of Christ to his own day, and its conquests in various lands. Lectures on Practical Training were also delivered, bearing on style, delivery, conduct as a pastor, and on examples worthy of imitation.

From time to time, especially when 'the System of Christian doctrine' was under consideration, there would spring from his glowing heart an impassioned soliloquy, suggested by the theme that was being discussed. This culminated in the closing address of the session, when men were leaving the student life proper and commencing the ministerial career. He was anxious

[1] *Cf.* J. L. Paton, *John Brown Paton, a Biography* (1914), pp. 98 ff.

to guard against the peril of divorcing theology from religion, of separating the speculative from the practical side of the faith. The danger was by no means an unreal one, and has often been painfully felt. But if any were disposed to disjoin the dogmatic from the homiletic among Brown's students, his searching queries, delivered with marked intensity of feeling, could not but startle them out of their danger. One student[1] has preserved notes of one of these appeals, which were made on this fateful day.

'Thinking this morning on your departure, two passages of Scripture came to my mind, and you would do well to take them into your serious consideration. "Have not I chosen you twelve, and one of you is a devil?" One may be called to special service, may fill a public station in the Church, may be a preacher, may go abroad into the world and address people on things of deep and everlasting importance, and yet be a devil; may be under the power of Satan, in a state of enmity against God, may be a traitor at heart, and act the part of an open traitor at last, may betray the Master he professed to serve, and come to shame and disgrace. Jesus knows all things. "He searches the heart, and tries the reins of the children of men"; what state you are in, what are the reigning principles in your breasts, what are the motives you are influenced by, and what the ends you have in view, whether you are indeed what you profess and what your outward appearance would indicate – all is known to Him. To commend a Saviour one has no love for; to preach a Gospel one does not believe; to point out the way to heaven, and never to have taken one step that way; to enforce a saving acquaintance with religion and to be an entire stranger to it oneself, how sad, how preposterous! Tremble, O my soul, at the thought, still more at the thing! Better follow the meanest occupation, than enter into the holy ministry solely or chiefly to serve some secular, some selfish design.

[1] Rev. David Carruthers, South Queensferry. John MacFarlane, *The Life and Times of George Lawson*, p. 351.

While I would be far from setting limits to the divine sovereignty, I am afraid it but seldom happens that a person is converted after he has become a preacher. Was there a Judas, a devil among the twelve? – what if there should be one for every twelve among you? "Lord, is it I? is it I? is it I?"

'The other passage comes more closely home, and is still more alarming. "And five of them were wise and five were foolish." It is one half of the number here present that are wise, that are truly serious, prudent, and thoughtful, and wise unto salvation, that are savingly instructed in the mysteries of salvation, in the mysteries of the kingdom, in whom Christ is found, and in whose hearts He dwells by faith, who have felt His Gospel to be the power of God, and the wisdom of God, who have taken Him for their only Lord and King, and have given themselves unto Him. Are there so many of an opposite character, foolish, mere nominal Christians, in the same state in which you were born; who, whatever light you may have in your heads, have no saving grace in your hearts? And is the Bridegroom coming? will He come quickly, come at the hour that ye think not? And shall they that are ready enter in and the door be shut, and you stand without and cry for admittance, but cry in vain? How dreadful the thought, how fearful the issue! I would be far, very far, from judging uncharitably of you; but I know the deceitfulness of the human heart. Surely they who propose to undertake an office, the design of which is to win souls, had need to be convinced, deeply convinced, about their own souls.'[1]

These addresses, spoken with deep feeling at the close of the Session, culminated in a powerful and searching allocution, which was delivered in 1782, and which has been many times reprinted. Brown was then in his sixtieth year, and the vision of the end was breaking upon him; 'when I am gradually slipping into the eternal state' were his own words. He took the consciences of his students to bear him witness that 'my prin-

[1] *Memoir of Waugh*, op. cit., pp. 48-50.

cipal concern was to impress your minds with the great things of God.' There is an intense spirituality and a consecrated earnestness visible in every sentence and paragraph of the address, while, for directness of speech and conscientious fervour of appeal, it is not inferior to that masterpiece of Pastoral Theology, *The Reformed Pastor* of Richard Baxter. Real Christians and real Christianity, he pleads for, and with tremendous passion the reverse he depicts in words that scorch with lightning fire. The ideal of the ministry and the work of the ministry are set forth in language that loses none of its point by being expressed in the apt, telling words of Scripture; and the perils and temptations that beset the ministerial career are outlined under searching interrogatories, that, piled the one upon the other, startle and arouse. The message which the minister should deliver is expressed in a few massive, comprehensive sentences, clinched with Scripture. The duties are cogently summed up; and, in the event of conflicts arising, a warning is sounded out of the mistakes in past controversies. He frankly tells his students, in regard to those which brought his own Church into being:

'I look upon the Secession as indeed the cause of God, but sorely mismanaged and dishonoured by myself and others. Alas! for that pride, passion, selfishness, and unconcern for the glory of Christ, and spiritual edification of souls, which has so often prevailed. Alas! for our want of due meekness, gentleness, holy zeal, self-denial, hearty grief for sin, compassion to souls in immediate connection with us, or left in the Established Church, which become distinguished witnesses for Christ. Alas! that we did not chiefly strive to *pray* better, *preach* better, and *live* better than our neighbours.'

On a tender note the great address closes, dwelling on the encouragements and rich rewards in such service, and concludes with a touching personal testimony.

'Believe this on the testimony of God Himself; believe it on the testimony of all His faithful servants; and, if mine were of any avail, I should add it, that there is no *Master* so kind as Christ, no *service* so pleasant and profitable as that of Christ, and no *reward* so full, satisfying, and permanent as that of Christ. Let us, therefore, begin all things from Christ; carry on all things with and through Christ; and let all things aim at, and end, in Christ. "Christ is all in all." [1]

We can well understand the universal testimony borne by his students that the most profound silence reigned while he thus addressed them, some of whom would not return, their feet being now at the entrance to their life task. Such addresses, delivered with his characteristic energy, fervour, and solemnity, moved many of them to tears, and left a profound and an abiding impression.

His grandson, Professor John Brown, D.D., of Edinburgh, holding an office in the Secession and the United Presbyterian Church of his day, similar to his own, but with three colleagues to assist, reproduced the address of his sainted predecessor frequently and issued large editions of it.

But it must not be thought that the human element did not play a lively part in the Institution of Haddington. The Professor had a humour glinting in his soul and flashing from his eye that charmed his students. His learning and zeal, and manifest, heart-whole interest in them won their esteem and confidence. For the testimony they bear is, 'He was among them as a father among his children; he loved them and studied their good; and they loved him, and regarded his counsel. No time of the year was so pleasant either to the Professor or the students, as the two months of their attendance at the Divinity Hall.' [2]

[1] His successor, George Lawson, Selkirk, on one occasion, instead of giving a 'Valedictory,' read 'a few passages out of his venerable predecessor's address. He took up the book and began to read. So affecting, however, were the ideas that he could not proceed. The tears flowed down his cheeks. The students caught the infection, and the Hall, for the nonce, became a Bochim.' (*Life of Lawson*, op. cit., p. 351.)

[2] *Memoir of Waugh*, op. cit., p. 48.

So we read in the life of Dr. Alexander Waugh of London, one of the founders of the London Missionary Society. Yet Waugh himself came under his lash. He entered the Divinity Hall fresh from Edinburgh University, and still under the spell of that philosophical master, Samuel Fergusson. Brown assigned him a text on which to prepare a sermon, Romans 8. 2. Here was a chance for a philosophic flight, of which, like a young student, he availed himself. The Professor listened patiently to his discourse, to the end; and, after the students had passed their criticism, he brushed the whole production aside with a withering sentence and a flash of his dark, kindling eye. 'I hope I shall never hear such a discourse again in this place.' It so shook the brilliant young student that it well-nigh pitched him out of the ministerial career altogether. A friend wisely counselled Waugh as to the folly of such procedure. The cloud passed, Professor and student recognized each other's character and aims; and no stronger bond of friendship existed between teacher and taught than between these two. Gently did the Professor lead the sensitive and aspiring student into his confidence. On one occasion he recognized he must speak to him as to some delinquency. He did not summon him before the class, 'to meet with me at the end of the hour.' He said he wished to meet with the students from the border district (Waugh was from Kelso). When they assembled, 'Oh!' he said, 'Sandy Waugh will do,' and dismissed the others.

The Professor carried his supervision further than the studies of his students. When he saw apparent cause, he deliberately inquired into their financial circumstances, and, though his own finances were not abundant, he assisted those who through poverty would have been unable to continue all the session.[1]

Their general conduct he considered it necessary also to

[1] Lauchlan MacLean Watt, *Scottish Life and Poetry*, p. 339, speaks of them as 'poor struggling students of a poor Church.' They were far from this description; most of them were sons of those in comfortable positions. A few came from homes where the shoe pinched; but their poverty was no dishonour.

superintend. He was, we have seen, a firm believer in the virtues of early rising. A succession of students he was wont to visit at their lodgings between the hours of six and eight in the morning.[1] He was not concerned about the lateness of the hour of retiring, believing that the candle could not burn at both ends, and early to rise implied early to bed. The houses in which the students lodged were mostly those of members of his own congregation, so that he had practically free access to their rooms. Not a few were startled out of their slumbers by a loud and peremptory challenge, that was occasionally helped by a poke from the pastoral staff. On looking up they saw the grave Professor, who sternly rebuked them forthwith as sluggards. But the student brain was quick to devise devices against such unexpected professorial visits. Plans were arranged with the landlady to apprise the slumberer, when she heard the approach of the Professor's step. She was to burst the door suddenly open, and immediately the student leapt to the floor, dropped into a chair, and pored over a divinity tome, lying conveniently open. The Professor, when he beheld the figure in undress so assiduously studying, complimented him on his devotion to his work, but cautioned him against the peril of sitting in his night garments in the early morning. Sometimes the signal was too late in being recognized, and the slumberer would slip out of his bed-clothes, and underneath the bed; and was comforted by hearing the retreating Professor say to the landlady, 'Ah, he's up, good lad, and out for an early walk.'

At other times than in the early morning, he was wont to drop in upon his students. One day he entered a room where a number were assembled. A hot discussion was absorbing their attention, and every tongue was asserting itself. Amid the din, the knock unheard, the door was opened and the

[1] Does the practice still continue? 'The Principal had been round to some of the lodgings; the first thing he did was to thrust his walking-stick up the chimney to see if it was stuffed with newspapers. "I won't have my men working in poisoned air," he said.' *John Brown Paton*, op. cit., p. 95. Nottingham College.

Professor stood on the threshold. 'Gentlemen,' he said, with a merry twinkle in his eye, 'the *Spectator* says never more than six should speak at once.' Silence fell in a moment; but the roguish laughter of the Professor restored good-humour among the too ardent disputants.

He was quick in seizing a situation and summing it up in a few crisp words. A youth called on him, expressing his desire to become a preacher of the Gospel. He rapidly sized him up, as strong in conceit and weak in intellect, and advised him to continue at his present occupation. 'But I wish to preach and glorify God,' the youth protested. 'My young friend,' replied the Professor, 'a man may glorify God making broom besoms; stick to your trade, and glorify God by your walk and conversation.'

Among his students was George Lawson, of Selkirk, the Scottish 'Socrates,' as Carlyle called him. Lawson, who hailed from Hallmyre, West Linton, Peeblesshire, was gifted with extraordinary powers of memory. He came to Haddington one session without his Hebrew Bible, which was too bulky to be packed. Several long passages had been prescribed to be read that year. Lawson not only read them, but stored them in his memory, and left the ponderous tomes behind. When called to read in the class, the Professor observed that he had no Bible in his hand, and requested an explanation. "I could not conveniently bring my Hebrew Bible,' he said, 'but I do not require one. I have committed it all to memory and can repeat it all.' With his memory ran his humour, which brought a kindly retort from his Professor, who had high appreciation of his talents. On one occasion Brown left the room for a few minutes; Lawson mounted the Professor's chair, and commenced to address the students in the professorial tone. On returning, the Professor, hearing ominous sounds from within, listened for a few moments at the door, till the voice ceased. On taking the chair again, he very good-naturedly remarked, to the delight of the astounded class, 'I perceive I have already got a successor.' As a matter of fact, Lawson did succeed him in the professorship, and, in honour of his remarkable gifts, was the first in the Secession ministry to receive the degree of D.D. from a Scottish University – Aberdeen.

Another of his students was Dr. James Husband of Dunfermline. When at the Hall, he called upon the Professor as he was setting out for Gifford, a few miles from Haddington, in order to clear up some perplexity regarding the doctrines of grace, on which that week Brown had been lecturing. 'Come awa' wi' me, and I'll expound that; but when I'm speaking, look you after my feet.' They passed through the town, and on to a rough bit of common. The eager, full-minded man was in the midst of the unfolding of the divine scheme, and his student was intensely drinking in his words, but forgetting his part of the bargain. Suddenly his master stumbled and fell. On getting up he somewhat sharply said, 'James, the grace of God can do much; but it cannot gi'e a man common sense,' which is as good theology as sense, says his great-grandson in relating the story.

Among the early students of his professoriate was the Professor's eldest son, John, who was settled ultimately at Whitburn. He was followed three years later by his brother Ebenezer, who received the appointment to the church at Inverkeithing. The elder brother was staid and sober, the younger full of animal spirits in those early days, and his bright twinkling eyes were usually on the lookout for the amusing and unexpected, though in after-years he became one of Scotland's greatest preachers, admired of Lord Brougham and Lord Jeffrey. But now the gay vivacity and flash of youth throbbed in his soul.

In the afternoons, as has been stated, it was customary to hear the students' discourses in the church. It occurred to young Ebenezer that, as tremblingly man after man took his stand for twenty minutes or so in the boxed-in pulpit, he might there hide himself and enjoy helping the preacher in his anxious task. He selected the afternoon on which his brother was to preach. When John had commenced his sermon, he was seen to be much agitated. Occasionally he turned round and appeared to be remonstrating with somebody beneath the pulpit seat. The Professor took in the situation at once, and a stern 'Come down, sir,' brought Ebenezer out of his lurking-place where he had secreted himself that he might 'jag' his brother's legs with a pin while he was holding forth.

A human atmosphere was redolent of the Hall, and its varied experiences were a treasured memory. The foundations of a ministerial career were carefully and prayerfully laid; and a stimulus was imparted to build the edifice with a joyous enthusiasm. Throughout the work of the sessions there breathed a kindliness and a sympathy with young minds that after-years more clearly revealed. It made Haddington a green spot in the retrospect of memory, and the Professor a friend in whose eyes lethargy and indifference were a heinous sin, and loyalty to the Cross, love to the Master, and devotion to His cause a first and a consuming passion.

CHAPTER 16

The Professor and his Students

About one hundred and eighty students in all passed through the Theological Institution of Haddington. Though in the five years which their training demanded, it was only ten months that really were spent under the immediate supervision of the Professor, the period left its deep impress upon them. A few turned out failures, and a few succumbed, like Michael Bruce, to the maladies that cut down our youth; but the vast majority entered the ministry, some going as missionaries to America, then opening its wonders to the nations of Europe. Not a few reached high distinction in the Church, and became leaders in the religious life and activities of the country. 'A giant himself,' says Dr. MacFarlane, 'Brown gave birth to giants. The piety, learning, and soundness in the faith, for which the Haddington students were justly esteemed, greatly contributed to the influence and usefulness of the young Secession.'[1]

Besides those already referred to, Dr. George Lawson of Selkirk, Dr. James Husband of Dunfermline, and Dr. Alexander Waugh of London, there were men of the stamp of David Greig of Lochgelly, Fife, strong as a theologian, and spoken of in his day and long after as 'Greig, the Divine,' the presiding Moderator at the union of the two branches of the Secession in 1820; Dr. James Hall of Cumnock and first minister of Broughton Place Church, Edinburgh, one of the foremost champions in the Old Light controversy; Dr. Robert Jack of Greenock, and afterwards of Manchester, noted for his remarkable pulpit gifts, and invariably described as 'silver-tongued';

[1] *Life of Lawson*, op. cit., p. 272.

Dr. John Dick, of Slateford, and afterwards of Greyfriars Church, Glasgow, first Professor of the United Secession Church, whose lectures in Theology had a wide reputation; Dr. John Smart of Stirling, a successor of Ebenezer Erskine, a commanding figure in the midlands of Scotland; Dr. William Kidston of Kennoway, Fife, and first minister of Sydney Place Church, Glasgow, widely known for his varied services, a Clerk of Synod, and Moderator at the union of the Secession and Relief Churches in 1847; Dr. John Jamieson of Scone, Perthshire, spared to serve his congregation and Church for sixty-two years, a man of high attainment and broad outlook; Dr. James Peddie of Bristo Church, Edinburgh, who spoke of his Professor as that 'venerable man whom may skill part from my right hand if I ever forget, a man to whose learning and piety, and indefatigable diligence the Secession entrusted the care of training her young men for the ministry; and to whose instruction, counsels, and prayers I ascribe, under God, much of what little usefulness I may have attained during a long period of ministration in the Church.'

The list might be easily increased; but two others may be mentioned. One was Andrew Swanston, a son of Brown's predecessor. His remarkably brilliant powers were overshadowed by a conscience of extreme sensitiveness. He was greatly beloved and held in highest esteem by all who knew him. Dr. Peddie acknowledged that it was Andrew Swanston who gave him an idea of what an exposition should be. But the Secession Church, which his father adorned, had defects that cost it his allegiance. Other denominations he tried, one after another, but they all failed to reach his standard. When he died, his old Professor said, 'Well, Andrew has got a Church now that will please him!' Another of his men was William Skirving, one of the political martyrs of the age. After a few sessions at the Hall, he turned aside to the pursuit of farming on his estate of Strathruddrie in Fife. He was author of a work on agriculture, and became a candidate for the Professorship of Agriculture in the University of Edinburgh. He joined the

'British Convention,' or 'The General Association of the Friends of the People,' a society whose aim was to secure greater political freedom, but which, under the Dundas 'despotism,' was repressed with a ruthless hand. He was appointed secretary to the movement, but for his active propaganda he was condemned in 1794 to transportation for fourteen years. While undergoing this sentence, he died of dysentery at Botany Bay. His name is inscribed on the monument to the 'Political Martyrs,' in the Calton burying-ground, Edinburgh.[1]

It was an unvarying habit of the Professor to follow his students with a kindly letter when they began their ministerial career. He had individual knowledge of them, and could lay his finger on their weakness and on their strength. Their master's greeting was welcome, because it was personal and sincere. Sometimes when there were competing calls, and the Supreme Court of the Church despatched them to one sphere, while they had strong preference for another, the sense of justice was offended. Sometimes the task in front of them filled them with dismay, before which they were disposed to shrink. The Professor had a word in season for each.

To Alexander Waugh, his keenly intellectual student, hesitating to proceed to 'licence' by his Presbytery, he addressed a letter affectionate but faithful. When a student had completed all the studies preparatory to the ministry, his next duty was to obtain licence to preach from the Presbytery within whose bounds he resided. Waugh dreaded taking this step. He was slow in composition, doubted his ability to produce sermons acceptable or profitable, and was afraid his lot might be that of a 'stickit minister.' In addition, the responsibilities of the office seemed to weigh heavily upon him. Thus he drifted into great uneasiness and perplexity. Friends tendered affectionate counsels of encouragement. There came a letter from the

---

Along with four others, Thomas Muir, Thomas Fyshe Palmer, Maurice Margarot, and Joseph Gerrald. On the base of the monument is inscribed a sentence from Skirving's speech in the Court of Justiciary, January 7th, 1794: 'I know what has been done these two days will be rejudged.'

warm heart at Haddington, a letter that breathed of that tender interest and faithful freedom so characteristic of its author in his intercourse with his students.[1]

To Alexander Waugh

'The hint I heard concerning Mr. Blackhall[2] vexed me. I have written to him, and I hope he will be up at the Presbytery. I beg you will have all your trials ready. Cast your burdens on the Lord; but beware of any attempt to slight what in Providence you are called to, otherwise the Lord may avenge it on you while you live. God makes our strength as our days are. Cast all your care on Him. I am far from thinking it a token that a man is not called, that he, when it comes near to the point, is terrified. Christ got forty days of sad temptation, before He was licensed to preach the Gospel (Matt. 4). But if we will sit God's time, the consequences are apt to be dangerous. My advice to you is, to make a solemn surrender of yourself to God, before coming to the Presbytery. I hope the Lord has let some of the wind out of you, that I thought was in you when first I knew you. Beg of Him to fill its room with Himself and His grace.

Yours affectionately,
JOHN BROWN.'

HADDINGTON,
February 13th, 1779.'

Waugh, happily for the Church, was amenable to the advice of his Professor and friends, and soon justified their decision by proving an able and acceptable preacher. In a short time he was called to minister to a newly-formed congregation in Newton St. Boswells, that is today an important centre on the

---

[1] *Memoir of Waugh*, op. cit., p. 75.
[2] John Blackhall, a fellow student of Waugh's, from Selkirk; called to School Wynd Church, Dundee, which he refused to accept because there seemed to be some fatality that hung over the lives of its ministers: afterwards to Berwick (now Wallace Green, where Principal Cairns ministered, 1845-76); ordained, January 5th, 1782; laboured for thirty-one years; died March 5th, 1813.

railway system of the Border countries, but was then a struggling village. It was hardly worthy of his talents – it only numbered some thirty members; and it seemed like wasting his sweetness on the desert air to minister to such a handful. But a letter[1] from his watchful and faithful Professor placed matters in a different light, and enabled him to see larger possibilities than he imagined in so small a sphere.

'I know the vanity of your heart,' wrote the Professor, 'and that you will feel mortified that your congregation is very small in comparison with those of your brethren around you; but assure yourself, on the word of an old man, that when you come to give an account of them to the Lord Christ, at His judgment-seat, you will think you have had enough.' The appeal of the brief letter to the sensitive and diffident preacher sank deep into his susceptible mind, and he accepted the charge. He was only privileged to labour in it for two years, when, after three successive calls, he responded to the invitation to go to Wells Street, now Oxendon Church, London; and often in his crowded ministry in the metropolis he recalled gratefully the sharp reminder of his Professor concerning the heavy responsibility of fulfilling his trust.

This instance of affectionate interest in the young men that left the Divinity Hall at Haddington, withal so frank and candid, was typical of his dealings with them. Brown possessed the happy gift of blending the dignity of the teacher with the affection of the friend; and he was repaid with the treasured homage of attachment and esteem.

In the course of a few years he issued a series of letters on *Gospel Preaching*, and on *Behaviour of Ministers*, which, when he delivered their substance at the Hall, he was wont to cause his students to transcribe. The letters on *Gospel Preaching* number six; they express the characteristic thought of the time, but are direct, concise, and vigorous, pressing home the individual aspect of salvation. In the first, he dwells on the peril of presenting the Gospel without any definite and distinct

[1] *Memoir of Waugh*, op. cit., p. 91.

message; it is possible to preach 'a multitude of the precious truths of Christ, without ever preaching the Gospel of Christ,' and then he follows with examples. In the second he shows, in brief compass, what is needed to 'hold forth Christ as God's free gift' and our all and in all. The third carries him to an earnest appeal for a personal experience of the truths declared, that thereby the whole message may be rightly communicated, every truth in its order, for 'the misplacing of a single truth, like the misplacement of a single wheel in a clock, may derange the whole sermon.' The next letter is an exhortation to show the two sides of the shield in preaching, not dwelling always, or even long, on such cutting, alarming subjects, as man's sin and suffering in consequence, and to make certain that the Gospel is 'held forth in its suitableness, amiableness, and love, in order to encourage, captivate, melt, and draw the sinner's heart.' The fifth letter leads him to an earnest appeal to see that first things come first in the great news; and the last exhibits, in nine brief paragraphs, what union with Christ, the very essence of the Gospel, implies.

But the Haddington Professor was not oblivious to the practical aspects of the work his men had to do. He was equally solicitous that, along with sound preaching, there should be exemplary living. He was deeply conscious of the unspeakable harm done to religion through lowering the standard of life required of those in the ministry, and as convinced of the immense service rendered to the cause by lives that sparkled in the sunshine, wherever cast. He reminded his students, therefore, of the necessity of 'Exemplary Behaviour' on their part, in a series of ten letters. They are epistles that bathe the reader in the white light of noonday, and are starred with Scripture citations, and this N.B.: 'It is earnestly requested of the Reader of these Letters, that he will, as he proceeds, turn up and muse on the passages of Scripture cited in them, as the means of shedding light on the reasoning, and of imparting divine force to the exhortations contained in them.'

In the first, he directs attention to the preacher's call, and to his personal character, which must be above suspicion, whatever eloquence or eminence in learning may be his. In the second, he cautions him not to envy the fame or success of others, to avoid contentions, to restrain all tendencies to anger, and to 'shun every appearance of, or approach to, intemperance in eating and drinking, and all temptation thereto.' In the next, he turns to the Christian graces that ought to be cultivated, and to the claims and obligations of the home, in the choice of a helpmeet, the education of the children, and the attitude toward servants in respect to their 'proper work and wages and careful instruction.' The fourth letter portrays the becoming conduct in relation to those outside, 'mankind in general.' Replete with judicious hints, it urges, among other things, that 'prudence is necessary in guarding against the advances of designing men, who hypocritically pretend to esteem and love you; in avoiding the unbridled rage of enemies; in attending not only to that which is lawful, but also to that which is expedient; in keeping within the limits of your station, while you are endeavouring to extirpate evil, and promote what is good; in never correcting evils by that which will prove as hurtful. or more so; in studying to suppress the fame of your good deeds, if it be likely that it will be perverted to a bad use; and in never meddling with, or even inquiring into, those things which do not concern you.'

The succeeding letter is an inculcation of the duty of maintaining habits of study, with special emphasis on the value of an intimate acquaintance with the 'oracles of God, especially in their original languages, which, to the public disgrace of even Protestant Churches, are but too little known,' from which he passes to the spirit of dependence, and devotion to ministerial work, and the relation of such workers to their hearers – an affectionate interest, a tender sympathy, and a broad tolerance with them. This leads in the sixth letter to the manner and method of preaching, in which he utters a warning to 'avoid everything which tends to darken or disgrace your discourses; or which tends to provoke or prejudice any of your hearers; such as a hurried, indistinct, or drawling pronunciation, awkward gestures, wild or tedious wanderings from the subject, curious and useless questions,' followed by suggestions on visiting and catechizing. In the next three letters, he directs attention to the different classes of hearers, and the message that is suitable to their peculiar needs. While commending fidelity, he at the same time urges sympathy with them in their varied and peculiar circumstances, so as to win them for the kingdom. The last letter is devoted to the spirit in which the sacraments of the Church are to be observed; and to the dignity and responsibilities of the office which a minister of the Gospel has to fill.

Wide and valuable are the suggestions made throughout these letters, not one sentence of which is without a Biblical reference. They reveal keen sympathy with the perils and temptations that beset the ministerial office, and provide a stimulus to the hearty discharge of the duties it imposes. The glowing heart behind them is as manifest as their saneness and sagacity. They are a compendium of pastoral theology as complete as many of the elaborate treatises on the subject which later times have produced, while none of these equal them in the wealth of Scripture that is employed to substantiate every statement made.

CHAPTER 17

The Home at Haddington

The home at Haddington was brightened by the presence of the Divinity students, assembling for their two months of arduous training. But the presiding genius was not long spared to give welcome to the successive bands of young men. Mrs. Brown had only seen her husband honoured with the Professorship of his Church for three years when she was called away. Often had the angel of death visited her roof during the years of her married life, and had borne away six of her children in their infancy. Only two were left – John, the elder, born in 1754, and Ebenezer, born in 1758. John entered the University of Edinburgh at an early age, as was common in those days. Like a youth, he was sometimes forgetful of his home obligations; and the following motherly letter shows the watchful, generous, anxious heart, careful of all that concerns her boy:

Mrs. Brown to her Son

'DEAR JOHNY,

'I received yours this day by Mrs. Lowney. I was wearying very much to hear from you. Your father and I were in full expectation to have heard from you last week, and, when no word came, we were somewhat uneasy. I think you have only written to us once since you went last from us. You should never let two weeks pass without writing us. We are all pretty well. Be sure to send out your foull (soiled) clothes this week. And I suppose you will be needing money: write us, and not straiten yourself; only do not buy books foolishly that you have no need of. . . . Little Janey Hunter died of the small-pox yesterday. We have great need to improve the present moments we enjoy for eternity; we know not how few they may be. Dear Johny, youth is a precious time; lett it not slip without being concerned that Christ be yours and you be His.

Yours affectly,

JANET BROWN.

HADDINGTON,
February 14th, 1771.'

On May 10th, 1771, Mrs. Brown passed to her rest, at the age of thirty-eight, and was buried at Haddington.

Speaking of her death, the bereaved pastor said: 'I confidently trust she went to her first and best husband.' He wrote to an old friend regarding his loss, expressing himself somewhat severely, as was characteristic of the period, on his own shortcomings in view of the passage of time and its missed opportunities.

'I am the old man still, sinning over the belly of troubles, convictions, and everything else. Only God can tell how inconsistent my sermons and inward life before God are; and yet, after all, I cannot say He is "a barren wilderness or land of drought." Even yesterday He seemed to smile, and enable my soul to say, Amen, to the last clause of Zech. 13. 9. In short, my life is and has been a kind of almost perpetual strife between God and my soul. He strives to overcome my enmity and wickedness with His mercies, and I strive to overcome His mercy with my enmity and wickedness. Astonishingly kind on His side, but worse than diabolically wicked on mine! After all, I wish and hope that He, not I, may obtain the victory at last. Time not allowing me to enlarge, I conclude requesting your earnest prayers for me, and my congregation and students. One thing galls me with respect to my departed consort: that I did so little for the furtherance of her spiritual comfort and eternal salvation, and profited so little by her. Take heed, you and J—, and play not the fool as I did.'

But though shadowed days fell on the Manse household from time to time, the two boys were lively in their moods, and were in the heart of many a frolic. Ebenezer kept the times merry, and was heedless of the consequences of his pranks. On a sacramental occasion at Haddington, a meat pie had been prepared for dinner in the manse. There was a gathering of ministers, and the services were long for a hungry boy. Ebenezer obtained his chance, and carefully removed the crust of the pie, and abstracted the meat. He as carefully filled the pie-dish with grass, and replaced the crust. When the party gathered round the festive board, and the crust was broken, to the amazement of the host and his friends, the green herb appeared, with a card on which was inscribed, 'All flesh is grass.'

In the garden behind the manse, well stocked with its fruit-trees, there was a jargonelle pear-tree whose produce the master strictly guarded. The apples, pears, gooseberries, and other fruit might be taken at liberty; but the Professor considered this as his specialty, and prohibition was laid on its luscious fruit. This scarcely coincided with Ebenezer's idea of the fitness of things. He saw the last of the tempting pears in the late autumn; and, throwing a sop to Cerberus, he donned the parental boots and captured the prize. The pears were missed, but the footprints of the culprit were distinctly visible. Suspicion fell on Ebenezer, and his boots were tried – in vain. 'Suppose we try your boots, father,' suggested Ebenezer. They were tried and fitted exactly. 'How did you know, Eben, my boots would fit?' at once queried the parent with a significant lifting of the eyebrows.

But Ebenezer had his thoughtful moments; and the death of his mother profoundly touched him. He was then little more than twelve years of age, and with this sad event his mind sought the deeper channels. Not long after his mother was laid to rest, he was prostrated with fever. His father tenderly nursed him. As he sat by his bedside one day reading a newspaper, the youth turned his eager eyes upon him and startled him by saying, 'Father, you are reading the account of my death.' 'No, my man, you are not dead.' 'Oh, yes, I am, but in the papers it does not give my name; it only says "A Young Man."' From the fever he rose a new man, not sombre or austere, but with life tingling with higher things.

In the year 1771, with its sad memories, there began an active correspondence between the pastor at Haddington and the Countess of Huntingdon, a correspondence about which the Professor, in his modesty, never spoke to any one in his lifetime. Selina Hastings, Countess of Huntingdon,[1] was one of the most remarkable women in England in the eighteenth century. Born in 1707, daughter of the ancient and honourable house of Shirley, married to the Earl of Huntingdon, she evinced from her earliest years an interest in spiritual things, and throughout her long life (she died in 1795) her heart glowed with a passion for the spiritual uplift of her country. She lost her husband in 1746, but, possessed of considerable means, she used it with a lavish hand to further the work of Whitefield and Wesley. Claiming the privileges of a peer, or rather peeress, she employed chaplains of her own, who had access at first to many Church of England pulpits. To equip men of the right stamp for the ministry, she founded a college at Trevecca, in Breconshire, in 1768, over which the saintly Fletcher of Madeley for a time presided. From it went forth a constant stream of men fired with a holy zeal to preach the Gospel. Many of them were admitted into the Church of England ministry, but by and by the Bishops resented their admission, as they were wandering preachers, and barred the door against them. Very unwillingly, but of necessity, the Countess consented to her students being ordained by men in her connexion, as it was called, who had episcopal ordination. This led to exclusion from the Church of England; and thus the community which her efforts gathered came to lead a separate existence. Today it is practically absorbed in the Congregational Church.

[1] *The Life and Times of Selina, the Countess of Huntingdon*, by a member of the Houses of Shirley and Hastings. Two vols., 1839-40.

The early years of the college at Trevecca[1] had its difficulties in obtaining men of evangelical spirit and the necessary learning, to teach the youths who came up with untutored minds, but with fervent, Christ-filled hearts, to prepare for the ministry. The Countess was anxious also about the doctrines taught to the rising youth. The old controversy between free-will and free grace began to show its ugly teeth in the rising time of evangelical fervour. The Wesleys took a strong stand for the former; the Countess and her supporters, such as Toplady and Whitefield, championed the supremacy of the latter. John Wesley and the Countess parted at this crisis, although one aim animated both, and directed and inspired all their energies, to win the nation and the world to a living faith. John Wesley at the time was preparing to conduct the second anniversary of the new college; but the controversy, though then in its infancy, blocked the way. Already had the Countess determined on her course, and with that course the Haddington Professor was in fullest sympathy.

By the works he had issued, and especially by his *Bible Dictionary*, Brown's name was being carried far beyond his own denomination. The views he had enunciated in the Dictionary on the burning questions of the hour were clear and concise; and his work proved an armoury for weapons in the controversy. His opinions commended themselves to the Countess; and she was desirous to know at greater length his mind on the great subject of justification by faith. This led to a series of articles from his pen, which appeared from time to time in the *Gospel Magazine and Theological Miscellany*, between the years 1770 and 1776. Most of the letters that passed between the Countess and the Professor have been lost, but one or two have been preserved. In the following, the writer gets away from the commonplaces of life and into the higher regions, where he expresses himself with a fulness that is amazing.

Trevecca was given up for Cheshunt, a few miles from London, shortly after the Countess's death. In 1905, the college was transferred to Cambridge to breathe more freely of the academic air that pervades that ancient home of learning.

'MADAM,

'In consequence of a message from the Rev. Mr. Shirley[1] I have, so far as the late death of a dear consort, and penury of time permitted, thrown together a few thoughts upon the doctrine of justification through Jesus' blood, that great foundation of all our holiness and comfort, and transmitted them to your care. But, since the High and Lofty One that inhabits eternity appears to have singled you out as one of the not many that are called, has espoused you to His Son, and rendered you an eternal, a distinguished debtor to the exceeding riches of His grace, and a zealous contender for the leading points once delivered to the saints, might not I, an unknown and inconsiderable friend of the Bridegroom, for your encouragement, speak a word in His behalf?

'Truly, Noble Lady, let your life have Christ for its all and in all (Phil. 1. 21). Let it be a looking to Christ, a coming to Christ, a receiving out of Christ's fulness, a resting on, and rejoicing in Christ; and, in fine, a worshipping and serving of the Lord Christ. Amidst all the temptations of a high life, let your meditation on Him be sweet. When you awake, may you still be with Him!

'What are all the dignities, the glories of creation, in respect of Him, the brightness of His Father's glory, the King, the God of glory? O! sweet to us! the man, God's fellow! the Word made flesh! God bone of our bone, and flesh of our flesh! Our Brother born for adversity! Our Friend that sticketh closer than a brother! Immanuel, God with us! Our Mediator between God and us! Thrice blessed, thrice wondrous, and effectual means of reconcilement! Blessed surety of the better testament, that undertook and paid our infinite debt, till God

---

[1] Walter Shirley (1725-86), fourth son of the Hon. Laurence Shirley, and first cousin to the Countess of Huntingdon, rector of Loughrea, Co. Galway. He was in full sympathy with the Countess in her work, and sided with her in the above controversy. He adhered to the Established Church to the end. He was the author of some hymns. His portrait hangs in the library of Cheshunt College, Cambridge, in the founding of which college at Trevecca he took an active part.

could take no more! Powerful Redeemer, that takes us a prey from the mighty, and delivers us, the lawful captives! Blessed Prophet, to whom God hath given the tongue of the learned to speak words in season to our weary souls, and whose words are spirit and life, and like new wine that goes down sweetly – they cause our dull and dumb hearts to sing! Great High-Priest of things to come, that loved us and gave Himself for us! All-prevailing Advocate with the Father, that welcomes us, with all our perplexed cases, and desperate-like cases! Our Prince of Peace, to command deliverance for us, subdue our mighty lusts, defend and support us against every foe!

'Behold, Madam, what the Son of God, in our nature, is to you! Your Shepherd to support you against want, to lead you beside the still waters of His everlasting love, His redeeming blood, His new-covenant promise, to restore your soul again, and make you walk in the paths of righteousness, for His name's sake. Your Father that has begotten you to a lively hope, to be an heir of God, a joint-heir with Christ; your divine Husband that rejoices over you with singing, and rests in His love; your boast, your bliss, your rock, your refuge, your comforter and comfort; in fine, your God and your all. Methinks your ravished heart criest out, "Is the Son of God so much to me, and, ah! do I regard Him so little? Has He so little room in my heart? and am I of so little use, so little service to Him?"

'Think again. Did the eternal God pass by lofty angels, pass by millions of men, pass by multitudes of my fellow-nobles, and think of me, no better than the worst? engage for me? obey the rigid law, and bear infinite wrath for me? rise and ascend for me? pour forth unceasing prayers for me? send His word to heal me? and, at last, in a pang of almighty love, break in, notwithstanding all that the world from around, hell from beneath, inexpressible guilt and raging corruptions from within, could do to oppose Him, and fix His eternal residence in that hidden hell, my heart? O day of power, indeed, in which He made me, so outrageous an enemy, willing to be

F

what He pleased; when my haughtiness was brought down, when all the unnumbered idols of my heart were tumbled headlong, and the Lord alone was exalted! O time of love, when Jesus came to me in my blood, and said to me, Live; when my soul was courted with the words, the sighs, the bloody tears, dying groans, of an incarnate God! How my heart burned within me while He talked with me, and opened the Scriptures! when He rehearsed, in the manner of the Godhead, the story of His everlasting love to me! when He showed me His pierced hands, His wounded side, His melted heart! How was my soul then all captivated, all inflamed with His love! If I love not the Lord Jesus let me be anathema maranatha. Blessed day of espousals, when He betrothed me to Himself in righteousness and in judgment, and in loving-kindness and in mercies; yea, even betrothed me to Him in faithfulness, and made me know the Lord! when He made stupid, obstinate, and unreasonable me, to reason together with Him, till He washed me in His blood, clothed me in His righteousness, made my scarlet, my crimson transgressions white as wool and snow! when He testified against me, I am God, even thy God, and, with overpowering evidence, made my careless and unbelieving heart cry out, Amen, so be it, Lord, my Lord and my God! when He put to me the everlasting covenant, well ordered in all things and sure, which is all my salvation and all my desire! when Christ was effectually made of God to me wisdom, righteousness, sanctification, and redemption! Birthday, indeed, when it pleased God to reveal His Son in me! when Christ was formed in my heart! when I was made God's workmanship, created in Christ Jesus unto good works! when He that sat on the throne made all things new!

'Think, further, what is in reserve for you – a going to God, your exceeding joy; an eternal, an immediate vision and fellowship with the Three-one God, as your all in all; a sitting with Christ on His throne; a being for ever with the Lord; a being for ever like Him by seeing Him as He is, and knowing Him even as we are known. Ah! puny joys of earth, when compared with the rivers, the oceans the fulness of joy that is at His right hand. But whence spring these living waters? Not from works, lest any man should boast, but from the free, the abundant, the exceeding abundant grace of God. What is their price? Not human works, but the works, the blood, the death of God!

'Once more, think what is my charter of rights to this inheritance of grace, of glory, of salvation, of God Himself? It is the new covenant, the New Testament in Christ's blood. How much more firm than all thy claims on the estate of Huntingdon! O blessed charter, planned by God, written by God, confirmed by His oath, and ratified by His blood! May I pore much on it! May His word be found of me, and I eat it, and it be to me the joy and rejoicing of my heart! May I esteem the words of His mouth more than my necessary food! When He has so framed His promises that I cannot but see my own shameful name – sinner, rebellious, stout-hearted, and far from righteousness – marked in them: and, when He so points His blessings to my case, and urges them on my soul, that I cannot shift them, without blasphemous reproaches of God, as a liar, a perjured person, without desperate fighting against His grace: What am I, that I should withstand God? Lord, I believe; help Thou mine unbelief.

'May your life be the life of faith on the Son of God, Who loved you and gave Himself for you. May God enable you to adorn your station, not only with the reality of religion, but with a liveliness in it, successful in winning many to Christ, as your accounts at Jesus' tribunal cannot fail to be very extensive and important. May He Himself enable you so to act in all your ways that you may give them in with joy, and not with grief. Thus wishing the choicest blessings of time and eternity to you and family, I am, Madam,

Your most humble servant,

HADDINGTON,
    July 25th, 1771.'   JOHN BROWN.

The heart-to-heart intimacy of correspondence between the Professor and the Countess encouraged and strengthened the latter in the course she pursued at that critical period, when brought into sharp conflict on matters of doctrine with friends whose labours she prized. She acknowledged the value of his services. It is manifest that it was his teaching on the subjects of justification and other cognate doctrines that was taught at Trevecca; later on we shall see how his whole lectures on theology were asked for, and used at this seminary. Brown thus shared in giving the impress to the work of this college, that has sent forth so many young men into England and to the colonies and the foreign field with the stewardship of a vision there caught of the rich fulness of Gospel truth and the great opportunities in a Gospel ministry.

The Professor came into contact with others upon whom he left an abiding mark. In 1772,[1] he had an unexpected interview with Robert Fergusson, Edinburgh's youthful poet, Burns's 'master,' that has occasioned a good deal of controversy. Brown was passing through the churchyard of Haddington, when he came across the poet in one of his dark moods. He hailed the youth, then only in his twenty-second year, but with a reputation already established of being in poetic succession to Allan Ramsay, through the verses which he had been contributing weekly for the past two years to Ruddiman's *Weekly Magazine*. Life had dealt hardly with the author of 'Auld Reekie,' and the 'Farmer's Ingle.' Born in a dingy house in the Gap and Feather close in Edinburgh, educated at the High School there, and, through a Fergusson scholarship, at Dundee Grammar School, and St. Andrews University, he had turned aside from the clerical life, to which he was destined, to a clerkship in the Commissary office in Edinburgh. His poetical effusions, vivacious, pungent, and arresting, especially when he clung to his native Doric, drew around him a convivial crew. They led him into excesses that soon told upon his none too robust constitution. Friendly voices besought him to be careful of the perils thronging his path. But the vision of the pinched home and the toiling

[1] A. B. Grosart, *Robert Fergusson*, p. 124.

mother rose before him; and, covering his face with his hands, he would sob and say, 'Oh, sirs, anything to forget my poor mother, and those aching fingers!' Yet withal, regular as the Tron Kirk bell he would be seen rounding the corner to proceed to what Charles Lamb called 'the daily drudgery of the desk's dead wood.' A county parliamentary election in which he was taking part exposed him to the keen winds and the violent excesses that usually accompany such contests; and the reaction took the form of a brooding melancholy. Shortly after this he was in Haddington, where the Professor happened upon him. They entered into conversation, and Brown tendered him counsel that awoke the spiritual fires, for which the youth was grateful. He did not pester him with his 'damnatory creed,' as Stevenson crudely assumes,[1] nor terrify him with Calvinist doctrines, as some of his biographers[2] have alleged. The Professor, though ever on serious purpose bent, had too much geniality and kindliness in his nature, and quickness to understand and sympathize with sensitive minds thus to worry him. But he opened his eyes to the spiritual side of life to which the poet was keenly alive, and regretted so largely ignoring; and Fergusson went back to Edinburgh with a blither and braver heart. Unhappily, his boon companions lured him again, in his own pathetic phrase, to 'the baneful pleasures of the time,' with 'their delusive mirth,' and the melancholy returned. Insanity began to dim the brilliant brain. Two months before the end, he stumbled at the top of a stair in a friend's house, and fell to the bottom. Concussion of the brain followed, which by no means helped his malady; and in a public madhouse, the brief tragic life ended on October 16th, 1774, two years after Brown's interview with him.

In the beginning of the year 1773, John Brown brought a second mother to his desolate home, in Violet Croumbie, daughter of William Croumbie, merchant in Stenton, a townlet a few miles from Haddington. In one of his famous letters on

---

[1] R. L. Stevenson, *Edinburgh: Picturesque Notes.*
[2] *Fergusson's Poems, with Life,* 1807, p. 56.

the *Exemplary Behaviour of Ministers*, he offers some shrewd advice to his students, or to any one, on the choice of a wife. He urges much circumspection and gracious direction from God as 'necessary in the choice of a pious, prudent, active, frugal, kind, and affable wife, who may be an help and ornament to you and your family; not an hurt, hindrance, reproach, and grief.' Such was the happy selection he made himself. Violet Croumbie was noted for being frugal and industrious, clear-headed and clever, a superior, and even a remarkable woman, and one who had the charm of a stored and cultured mind. She was evidently as devoted to books as her husband. She would have immensely gratified Jane Austen, who was vehement in her contention that women should read; but her grandson, Dr. Samuel Brown, was rather dubious of this excellent trait in his progenitor, for he records, 'She was especially voracious of books, a thing not to be commended perhaps; and literally read the libraries dry."

The Croumbies of Stenton were a noteworthy family. They had for generations supplied the travelling dealers of the district with their miscellaneous wares. These travellers went all over the south of Scotland, and into the northern counties of England. Though the Croumbies did not mount the pack themselves, they belonged to the Chapmen Guild, which in those days was an influential body, with its centre in East Lothian. They met annually in general assembly at Preston Tower, elected their king and his lords depute, and made laws for their realm of trade. One of the Croumbies was a lord of this estate. With the changed conditions of trade, the Guild was dissolved; and the Croumbies began to make Haddington, the more populous community, their centre.

John Croumbie, a brother of Mrs. Brown, was the first to come to Haddington, a man of high integrity, open-handedness, and devout spirit. He had it in his mind to purchase the birthplace of John Knox, and give it to the community, which Thomas Carlyle did at a later date; but he deemed the money might be more profitably devoted to a religious purpose. He had a remarkable escape in the course of his business career. He stored gunpowder in a cellar beneath his shop. One summer evening, as he sat at the shop window over his ledger, an apprentice went down to the cellar with a lighted candle. A spark from the spluttering candle fell on the exposed barrel. Immediately a terrific explosion occurred. The lad was killed instantaneously; his master was shot into the air, and carried up the street about thirty yards, where he was deposited among the debris without a scratch. It was a never-to-be-forgotten experience. The good man, while he lived, scrupulously observed its anniversary, shutting himself within his bedchamber the whole day long, pouring out his thanksgivings for his preservation. He firmly declined the amount for which he was insured, as he could not forgive himself for his gross carelessness in giving the charge of the cellar with such combustibles to an inexperienced youth. The Insurance Company acknowledged such unheard-of delicacy of conscience by the presentation of plate, which is still in the possession of the Brown family.

On January 19th, 1773, John Brown and Violet Croumbie were married. On the day after the wedding, a friend of the bride's, daughter of one of the elders of the congregation, called at the manse with her congratulations. She was informed that it was not a day for receiving – the day was being spent in fasting and prayer.

In this home it was not unusual for its master to observe days of fasting and thanksgiving with his family. As circumstances seemed to call for it, he gathered his household together for this purpose. Prayer was to him the very necessity, and at the same time the delight, of his life. He frequently set apart a morning for extraordinary devotions. Often he appeared to engage in pious ejaculations. When, in the last months of his life, he began to reveal the hidden depths from which he drew his strength, he pointed out to his sons various places in the field behind his house where he often stood and mused, till 'the fire burned.'

CHAPTER 18

The Church Historian

The mind of this master of Divinity had frequently been traversing the long, winding road in which the Church worked out and applied its great principles. He was keenly alive to the value of history, and was specially concerned at this time with the need for prominence being given to the history of the Christian Church. He was jealous of her honour, and anxious that her record should not escape attention. He brought his eager and inquiring mind to survey the vast field, and orientate its leading features.

As it happened, never were there so many historians in Scotland, busily educating the public, as during the later half of the eighteenth century. The literary bent of Scotsmen now largely turned into this channel. David Hume published his *History of the Stuarts* in 1754, and completed his whole *History of England*, from the Roman period downwards, in 1762. William Robertson, Principal of Edinburgh University, was gathering fame among the learned by the issue of his *History of Scotland* in 1758-9, to be followed by histories of the reign of the Emperor Charles V, and of America, and by his *View of the State of Europe*. Adam Fergusson published his *History of the Roman Republic* in 1782, a work that Carlyle recommended in his famous Edinburgh Rectorial Address as 'particularly well worth reading.' William Tytler of Woodhouselee produced his defence of *Mary, Queen of Scots*, in 1759, vindicating her from the charges brought by Robertson and Hume, by which he so angered the latter portly historian that thenceforth he could not bear his presence. Lord

Hailes began the output of his Histories in 1762, and continued issuing, till 1777, volumes of his *Annals* of Scottish history, beginning with the accession of Malcolm Canmore. 'Dry, deplorably dry,' they are acknowledged to be, but contain an amount of matter-of-fact history of great value. The Principal of St. Andrews University, Robert Watson (1730-81), like his brother Principal of Edinburgh, was also a student of history, and like him also a clergyman, and issued a *History of Philip II of Spain* in 1777, which enjoyed great temporary popularity, and was translated into French, German, and Dutch, and which gained for its author the approbation of the arch-critic of the day, Dr. Samuel Johnson.

The activity on the part of churchmen in the field of secular history seemed to Brown to be an unworthy and unfair neglect of their own special domain. The Church, with its epoch-marking episodes, and its epoch-marking men, afforded ample scope for the historian's gifts, and its rich and thrilling story was not too well known. He concludes his preface to his *History of the British Churches* with an expression of regret at the ignoring of this department of research by those so well qualified to investigate it. 'It is not, perhaps, to the clerical honour, that so many of them labour in civil histories, while that of the Church of Christ is so much neglected.'

For himself, with his usual encyclopædic survey, no limited section of the Church's labours, and no single period could suffice. He must trace its course from earliest times, and its progress in every country, with special fulness from the period when liberation from the thrall of Romanism enabled the Church to raise the flag of civil and religious freedom. Accordingly he plans out a History that shall '*first*, comprehend a general view of transactions relating to the Church, from the birth of our Saviour, till this present time; *second*, contain more fully the histories of the Reformed British churches, in England, Scotland, Ireland, and America; *third*, comprehend the histories of the Waldenses, and of the Protestant Churches of Switzerland, France, Holland, Germany, Denmark, Sweden,

Poland, and Hungary.' He had even a larger vision that captivated his imagination, the history of the world from the birth of time. But Nature's time limit narrowed his execution to the first two projects, with the addition of a *History of the Waldenses*. When, in 1784, he issued his *History of the British Churches*, he had regretfully to acknowledge that the two volumes more, in which he hoped to record the history of the Continental Churches, had to be abandoned. 'Want of access to many necessary vouchers, together with the increasing infirmities of old age, oblige me to drop the design.'

The besetting difficulty of Church historians is the impartial setting out of the plain facts without prejudice. The dominant figures cast their spell on the writers; and their actions in the cold light of the past are portrayed either with the glow of noontide or the gloom of night upon them. Brown was fully conscious of this peril. His wide reading broadened his vision, and his mental equipment enabled him to seize the salient features of a period, and delineate them succinctly and clearly. But he was aware of the pitfalls by the way, and resolved, if possible, to avoid them.

'I have aimed at impartiality in my narrative, but dare not pretend that I have attained this rare historical excellency. That I might not be tempted to impose my own convictions instead of facts, I have seldom dipt into the secret springs of men's actions, or made reflections on them. Freedoms of this kind too often render histories little better than well-written romances.'

In 1771, he issued his *General History of the Christian Church*, in two volumes. He terms it 'A succinct Account of external Events, prosperous or calamitous; the State of Learning, the State of Practical Religion; and the Disputes, Heresies and Sects, that have troubled the Christian Church in each century.' There is an Appendix, containing the 'History of Philosophers, Deists, Socinians, Arminians, Anabaptists,

Quakers, Moravians, etc., to which is subjoined a List of Errors, especially since the Reformation.' He relates the history according to the centuries. He acknowledges his indebtedness to 'the celebrated Mosheim, chancellor of the Hanoverian University of Gottingen; but along with him I have consulted all the valuable church histories, whether Popish or Protestant, that lay in my power.' He submits an extraordinary list of writers, 240 in all, British and Continental, who have treated of the subjects bearing on the sixteen centuries with which he deals. He will not pledge his credit upon the excellency of these productions. Some are fabulous or partial, he knows; but he affirms that it is necessary for one who desires a true acquaintance with history to peruse what is said on both sides.

The history of the centuries of Christendom which he presents is not a bare mass of details crowded on the canvas: there is a warmth of colour added that makes the period live before the mind of the reader. The method he adopts of apportioning to each century its own tale has its disadvantages, which he acknowledges, for events have their origin and issue with scant regard to the divisions of time; but it enables the spectator to obtain a bird's-eye view of the leading incidents and the trend of movements over a definite period.

Thirteen years elapsed ere he issued the second part of his great scheme, the *History of the British Churches*. It appeared in two volumes in 1784. *A Compendious History*, he entitled it. The first volume opened with a 'Brief Sketch of the History of the Waldenses.' Nine chapters are allotted to the Church of England, and the two concluding chapters are devoted to the history of the Church of Ireland, and of the Protestant Churches in America. In his Foreword he enumerated his authorities for his English History—Foxe, Fuller, Burnet, Strype, Collier, Warner, Neal, Calamy, Bennet, and Pierce. He makes no further reference to them in the course of his narrative, and without allusion to any authority ploughs his way through the stormy seas from the introduction of Christianity into England down to his own time. With considerable success he disentangles the narrative from the history of the State, and presents the Church at its distinctive work, moulding and making the nation. A touch here and there suffices where Church and State necessarily trench on each other; but the absorbing events occurring in the latter never entice him from the pursuit of the Church and its doings. Graphically and firmly he records its conquest of the country and the development of its polity and doctrine. With a sharp, crisp phrase he sums up a situation or some aspect of life. For example, in the hot but futile contentions that raged in the Universities of Oxford and Cambridge over the *Institutes* of Calvin, he remarks, 'After the disputants had fatigued themselves, the controversies were dropped.' Cromwell's sturdy independency did not altogether meet with his judicious approval, and he dismisses him as 'the bold, and crafty, and perhaps pious Protector'; but he writes that, during the Protectorate, 'which hath been so much reproached as an age of horrid rebellion, the Universities abounded with pious and learned teachers and students. Never did another period produce so many or so remarkable ornaments to the English Church. Better laws were never made in England, nor good laws ever so well executed. The dress, the language, the conversation of the people were sober and virtuous'—a condition of things that was quickly altered when Charles II resumed the reins of monarchical government, and his 'most brutish and infernal example' let 'debauchery and wickedness of every form break forth and overflow all ranks in the kingdom.'

The second volume contained his *Compendious History of the Church of Scotland*, a quarto volume of 439 pages, concluding with 'an Historical Account of the Secession.' The early years are rapidly sketched, and the heralds of the new dawn are soon upon the scene with their martyr witness. He seizes the main episodes of the long story and presents their outstanding features. The Assemblies of the Church after the Reformation that were of historic interest have their decisions fully but tersely recorded. The notorious fifty-five questions of James VI before setting up Episcopacy are related, among which were: What power have the king and clergy in the making of ecclesiastical laws? When is it lawful for ministers to leave their flocks? Whether ministers may from the pulpit point out particular transgressions? For what enormities may they publicly blame magistrates? Whether preachers may wander from their texts in declaiming against vices? If the clergy neglect their duty, may Christian kings rectify their character?

The salient feature of Brown's histories is his power of summarizing. In fewest words, long decrees, canons, and deliverances, are set forth. He goes straight to the heart of the question that has been the centre of controversy in the Church, sifts out its leading points and in one comprehensive sentence masses the whole. The main defect of his work is the lack of references to his authorities. This is a characteristic of Brown's method. He states his authorities at the beginning in his Preface, and troubles the reader with them no more. While his histories enjoyed a reputation in their day, this detracts from their value now. But annals of the past, because of the emergence of new material, demand frequent resetting, if they are not to suffer eclipse. With the single exception of Gibbon's monumental work, *The Decline and Fall of the Roman Empire*, the numerous histories of that time have all shared the fate of Brown's, and find their repose on the dusty shelves of our great libraries.

It requires to be said, however, that a vaster range of history caught and fired the imagination of this historian. He possessed the spirit of a Lord Acton, and beheld how movements were linked the one to the other, that ought to be traced and related, if history were to fulfil its part. The days for specializing in one branch of a great subject had not yet arrived, and men had not learned how to unite in the unfolding of the great drama of the past, though Brown, by offering his help to others, in a measure anticipated such a time. Meantime each writer had to stand alone, and effect his own conquests. The

[173]

historian of Haddington, however, conceived a project of vast proportions with which he regretted that he had neither time nor strength to grapple – a History of Redemption. He long and eagerly canvassed the problem, or rather the double problem, that from another point of view equally fascinates the scientist, as it did the late Lord Kelvin: What have the records of the past got to tell us of this universe in which we live, its beginnings so far as we can reach back, and its end so far as we can look forward? A history from the birth of time to the present hour would reveal, he felt, the Divine hand in the world events. To accomplish such a task would call for careful research, extensive reading, wide vision, and spiritual insight. These requisites would not have daunted him; but his energies were summoned in other directions, and life was advancing at a pace that could not contemplate great schemes. Often he expressed the wish that someone 'able and well-informed' would undertake the work, and show 'how all the great events in the history of nations were calculated to promote the grand design of redemption in its purchase, publication, and application.'

Brown often referred to this vast scheme, and appealed to some eminent men to undertake it, proffering freely his own help. None would venture. He was delighted when he learned that Jonathan Edwards[1] (1703-58) had essayed the task; but he was disappointed when he discovered the meagreness of the scale on which he had planned his work, and was convinced that it demanded a much larger canvas.

It was a bold idea; but the widening horizon of human knowledge has simply appalled the human understanding, and the vastness of the proposal has silenced all attempts to bring it to fruition. In spite of brilliant assaults upon the domains

[1] *A History of the Work of Redemption*, which was published by his son, Dr. Jonathan Edwards (1745-1801), in 1773. Originally the work was a series of sermons preached in 1739. But, says his son, his father's heart 'was so much set on executing this plan that he was considerably averse to accept the presidentship of Princeton College, lest the duties of that office should put it out of his power.'

of history, by men of the first rank combining together, the great plan of John Brown still awaits fulfilment.

What he himself thought might be done is outlined in a tractate he published, with the title, *A Brief Chronology of Redemption*. Brief as it is, it shows the extraordinary range of his knowledge, and the mental outlook that surveyed events from the far-distant dawn right on to a long-distant future. Of course, he wrote in an age that had not unlocked the great treasures of the lands of the East in which civilization had played its part, like Egypt, Assyria, and Babylonia. The chronology of Ussher was accepted without demur; the Scripture records were confined within a too narrow compass of time. In the centre of the vision throughout is the peerless Figure that gathers round Him the homage of the centuries. The marvellous movements that led to the Israelitish nation founding a home in Palestine, a centre from which the radii of its circle could reach to the whole world, and the striking events among other nations that brought them into contact with Israel, are filled with meaning and really become intelligible when light from the Victor of the cross and the grave falls upon them. The onward march of events since 'those blessed feet walked the holy fields' have had as their goal the coming of His kingdom, and the issue cannot be a matter of doubt.

In compact paragraphs with dates definitely assigned, he carries the reader through the thick maze of the centuries, and notes from time to time how Christ's coming is prefigured, and the world prepared for His advent. His reign is being established, and the conquest of the race gradually won. Towards the end of this amazing production, the historian becomes the seer, and attempts to pierce the future and discern the end.

'A.M. 5870, A.D. 1866, or perhaps 150 years later, we expect the Fall of Antichrist, and the beginning of the glorious thousand years' reign of the saints. . . . Perhaps, for the weakening of the kingdom of Satan, punishment of Papists,

Mahometans, and heathens, the world may be for about thirty years or more, fearfully plagued with wars, pestilences, famines, and earthquakes. But, certainly, by the spread of the glorious Gospel, preached with the Holy Ghost sent down from heaven, all nations, Jews and Gentiles, shall be converted to Christ. To manifest His regard to their ancestors, the Jews will probably be reinstated in their ancient country, and many of them made singularly useful in pulling down Antichristian, Mahometan, and heathen delusions, and in converting Gentiles to Christ. For a very long time, perhaps a thousand years' continuance, the Church of Christ in a most peaceful, pure, orderly, lively, and glorious form shall fill the whole earth.'

The 'times and the seasons' it is impossible to foretell; but, whatever may be the procession of events, the triumph of the kingdom is the certain hope of the Christian Church.

CHAPTER 19

The Self-interpreting Bible

No work carried the reputation of the author so far afield as his *Self-interpreting Bible*. It was not issued till 1778, but it cost years in preparation. Brown preceded its coming by bringing out in 1775 an edition of the *Metrical Psalms* with notes intended to shed light on their historical connection and their spiritual significance, and contribute to their devotional value. It was then the custom to sing right through the Psalter from beginning to end in the weekly service of the Church, and to preface the psalms before they were sung with a brief account of their scope and tendency. For this purpose the plan of Brown is well conceived and well carried out. The general substance of each psalm is concisely stated, and its devotional spirit happily caught. The Preface, though commendably short, is an interesting production. It contains a full account of how the psalms in their metrical form came to be produced. He relates the efforts of the various versifiers, from the Wedderburns of Dundee in the days before the Reformation, and their successors throughout the next hundred years, Sternhold and Hopkins, Whittyngham, Norton, James VI, the Earl of Stirling, Sir William More of Rowallan, and Francis Rous, to produce a psalter suitable for the Church's needs. Ultimately, after various revisions by committees of Assembly, the Church in Scotland decided in 1650 upon the form in which we have the Presbyterian Psalter of today, and enjoined its use in the congregation and the family, the 'old paraphrase' of Sternhold to be 'discharged.' Brown admits that 'this metrical version has long been esteemed for the simplicity of its diction and its universal accordance with the original'; but confesses that, in the then refinement of the language, 'the versification, in many instances, is obviously harsh and inharmonious, and even its diction evidently requires considerable improvement.' That was penned one hundred and forty years ago; but the many attempts to comply with his suggestion have been met with a blank, stolid refusal. The words, today, it is felt, have become wedded by the generations with a music that drowns the grating notes, and leaves only a rich and pleasing harmony behind. His edition of the Metrical Psalms was frequently bound up with the *Self-interpreting Bible* in its later issues.

The object Brown had in view in this Bible must be clearly observed in determining its value. There was no lack of commentaries for the learned, but the wants of the multitude had hitherto been entirely overlooked. This vast circle the Haddington Professor was anxious to reach. An intelligent knowledge of the Divine Word would, in his opinion, be one of the most effective instruments in raising them in the intellectual, moral, and spiritual scale. His work, therefore, was planned to be available for devotional use, with just sufficient explanations to make the meaning plain, and sufficient information bearing upon the nature of the Scriptures, their inspiration, and historical setting, to meet the wishes of an intelligent reader. Hence there was no parade of learning, no quoting of authorities, no critical dissertations, no speculative theories. There was the plain word for the plain man, with the resolute purpose to make the passage reflect its light on the heart and conscience of the reader.

'Self-interpreting' his Bible seeks to be, by its use of marginal references,[1] so as to compare one statement of Scripture

[1] 'Canne, the author of the marginal references on the Bible' (Brown's *Church History*, vol. i, p. 235). John Canne, thought to have been born in Bristol, ministered to a congregation of Independents and Pædo-baptists in London in 1621. After two years he left for Amsterdam, where he ministered to English Independents for seventeen years. There he became author and printer, issuing a work of recognized ability, *Necessitie of Separation from the Church of England* (1634), also *A Stay against Straying* (1639). In 1647 his reference Bible with

with another, elicit the development of a subject, or focus the lights that bear upon it. He was among the first to make any extensive use of such references, which today are so common. As a proof of the care with which he sought to verify his citations, no less than five copies of the Scriptures were worn to pieces by the incessant use to which they were put. In a meagre fashion prior to the issue of his work, references had been adopted. But his marvellous and minute knowledge of the Book, coupled with his tenacious memory, enabled him very largely to extend the field.

In addition to the marginal references, at the bottom of each page of the bulky tomes are brief, pithy explanations of any verse that might seem obscure. The author's mastery of the Hebrew and Greek languages enabled him to furnish these. Each book is introduced with a brief account of its scope and purpose. Each chapter has a clear statement of its contents at the beginning; and at the close, under the title of 'Reflections,' a vivid, refreshing summing up of its bearing on the individual life. He never allows it to be forgotten that this book is not meant for mere reading, but casts the very mould for the shaping of conduct and character. With clever ingenuity, he arrests the reader by the appropriateness for him of the message just read, be it psalm or prophecy, argument or history; and in a succession of warm, kindling sentences, not many in number, he presses the truth home.

As an instance, take his reflections upon Ruth, chapter 1, where is related the story of Naomi and her daughters-in-law:

'Numerous and diversified are the arrows in God's quiver for the punishment of men's sins, and often, while His enemies riot in plenty, his people are pinched with scarcity and want. A diligent care to provide for our family is highly commendable; but it is seldom safe to flee from God's land, though

notes, appeared, which refers to an earlier work, which, however, is not known; an extended edition was sent forth in 1664. He is believed to have died in Amsterdam in 1667.

He frown on it, or to suffer scarcity of bread to draw us from the ordinances of God. It is not in fleeing from God's mighty hand, but in humbling ourselves under it, that safety lies. It is not in outrunning crosses, but in taking them up, and following Christ, that true comfort is to be had. Young people often mistake in their marriage, through want or neglect of their parents' advice. But marriages and deaths are near neighbours; and one death in a family is but the forerunner and warning of another. Both comforts and crosses are often nearer us than we suspect; and if we are shut up into the society of the wicked we should escape for our life as soon as our hindrances are removed. It is a mercy when God embitters our condition of distance from Himself, that we may be weaned from it, and hastened to our heavenly home; but yet it is pleasant to see near relations knit together in love and loath to part. With the most strong and fixed resolution should we set out in the Lord's way, as we know not from what repeated and strong temptations we may have to turn back; but the difficulties of the way, which discourage the temporary believer, will but bind the faithful soul the more closely to Jesus Christ. Nothing, no, not death, can separate them from Him and His people. Poverty and age make great alterations on mankind; and it is proper that all around should remark it with solemn awe and cordial sympathy; for surely it is but madness to set our heart on that comeliness and wealth which so quickly fade. Let us, therefore, keep waiting on God in the way of His judgments; in patience possessing our souls; eyeing the Lord's hand in all that we meet with; humbling ourselves under humbling providences; mourning, but never murmuring, under His hand; and ever remarking how the minutest circumstances of our lives are directed by the overruling providence of God.'

The Introduction to the *Self-interpreting Bible* is as elaborate and crowded with solid information as that of any learned commentary. In the original edition it covered 118 compact, double-columned quarto pages. The author's aim is to provide 'a right understanding of the oracles of God.' It is characteristic of his invariable habit of getting to the heart of a question, and patiently setting it forth for the benefit of his readers. To deal with the Scripture problems meant extensive research and a close and comprehensive study of the Word; but these to him were as the sniff of battle to the war-horse. His Introduction he divides into five chapters. In the first he discusses the question of inspiration – 'the Divine authority of the Scriptures of the Old and New Testaments.' Human reason, he points out, could never unaided have furnished this revelation. 'The penmen of the Scriptures exercised their own reason and judgment; but they were stirred to write, given their part, guided to select, used their illustrations, by the Holy Spirit.' 'Many of the sentences recorded are not inspired of themselves, being the words of Satan, or of wicked men; but the Scripture relative to these expressions is directed by divine inspiration.' The subject-matter and manner, the scope, the purpose, the preservation of the Scriptures, as well as the character of the promises, are irrefragable proofs of the 'divine original.' The question, so bristling with difficulty, is sanely handled, and, as becomes his manner, is clinched in its conclusions with scriptural citations.

The second chapter of the Prolegomena is upon 'Rules for understanding the Scriptures.' He lays down no less than fourteen admirable rules, beginning with a request for the help of the 'Enlightener,' and ending with a call for 'humility of mind.' The rules indicate what experience had taught and good common sense would inculcate. The twelfth rule would have saved many a commentator and critic from pitfalls.

'Where Scriptures at first sight seem to contradict one another, we must, by a serious consideration of them, labour to discover their harmony. But if we should not be able to reconcile them, we ought not to pronounce them irreconcilable, but rather attribute a deficiency to our own understanding.'

'Jewish Laws and Types' form the subject of the succeeding chapter—a lucid and comprehensive study. After an explanation of Jewish civil government, he expounds the Jewish sects, and then enters upon a favourite study of the time, 'Typical Representations,' maintaining as his plea the Apostle's description of the Jewish ordinances, as 'shadows of good things to come.' He gives examples of typical persons, 30 being enumerated; typical classes, 15 in all; typical events, 17 detailed; typical places, 6 referred to; typical utensils, 8 described; typical oblations, 10 given; typical seasons, 7 specified; typical purifications, 8 set forth. It is a cleverly compacted bit of work, showing a perfect mastery of the subject.

The fourth chapter is a monument to the author's wide and extensive reading: 'The Geography and History of the Nations' that come under the cognizance of Scripture. It is called a 'short view,' but it is a *multum in parvo*. The history is naturally limited by the view of the age, but it is succinctly and graphically related. His object is to throw light on the historical and prophetical parts of Scripture, 'the correspondent texts of which,' he says, 'are all along generally quoted, and ought to be carefully compared.' There is a fine directness in the narrative of the history of the hazy dawn of the ages, where, in spite of the mists of antiquity, its course is threaded with confidence, and the peopling of the earth is described with singular felicity. The degree of the latitude from London is stated where stood the garden of Eden, 'about the 32nd degree of north latitude,' a spot 'not only extremely delightful in itself, but adapted for the spread of mankind from thence into the rest of the world.' But the histories that recorded all that could then be told of Chaldea and Canaan, of Egypt and Ethiopia, of the Assyrians, Medes and Persians, of Greece and Rome, of the rise and advance of the Mohammedans, of the Jewish people and the Christian Church, were laid under contribution, to furnish material for this great chapter. Not content with a calm unravelling of prehistoric times, as a man with a vision who would search the future, he dares to adumbrate, as in his

History of Redemption, its onward course. Seasons of peace and prosperity, and of peril, will befall the Church and the world – 'then cometh the end of the world, *at what distance we know not.*' Historians have neglected the faculty of outlining the future. The commentator of Haddington, with an outlook that embraced the universe, and sustained by Scripture warrant, hesitated not to look down the files of time; and, as ever with him, he defends his position with a bristling array of Biblical references.

In a concluding chapter he provides a 'Chronological Harmony of Scripture Histories and the Fulfilment of its Predictions.' It reveals his patient and painstaking investigation, and love for detail, as well as his passionate interest in the correlation of the great movements of the world. The Ussher reckoning is the guide throughout the Biblical part, and the dating of events is carried from creation's beginning down to his own time and beyond.

It will be evident that an extraordinary amount of valuable material was thus placed at the command of the ordinary reader. It was the information that a student of the Scriptures hungered for, who had not access to the learned works dealing with such subjects.

There were difficulties in getting the elaborate work issued to the public. The expense awakened fears in the minds of the ordinary publisher. Brown himself had to lend pecuniary aid, in the first instance. At last, in 1778, it was sent forth in two volumes and immediately secured a place in the households of the reading public. Although the two bulky volumes were issued at a price that was costly, £1 2s., they were rapidly disposed of. Unfortunately for its author, the publisher of the first edition failed, and the money Brown had advanced towards its production was lost. But new editions were called for, and were sent forth with fresh material added. Brown extended his Introduction, supplying a chapter containing an 'Alphabetical Table of Proper Names, and their Meanings,' and another on 'Measures, Weights, Monies and Times, mentioned in Scripture, and their equivalent carefully wrought out in English terms.' These were succeeded by a brief but amazing statement on the 'Number of books, chapters, verses, etc., in the Holy Bible,' the fruit of leisure moments and passionate love for the very letter of Scripture:

'The Old and New Testaments contain:

Books in the Old, 39; in the New, 27. Total, 66.

Chapters in the Old, 929; in the New, 260. Total, 1,189.

Verses in the Old, 23,214; in the New, 7,959. Total 31,173.

Words in the Old, 592,439; in the New, 181,253. Total 773,692.

Letters in the Old, 2,728,100; in the New, 838,380. Total 3,566,480.

The middle chapter, and the least in the Bible, is Psalm 117.

The middle verse is the 8th of the 118th Psalm.

The middle time is 2 Chron. 4. 16.

The word *and* occurs in the Old Testament 35,543 times.

The same word in the New Testament occurs 10,684 times.

The word JEHOVAH occurs in the Bible 6,885 times.

'In the Old Testament:

The middle book of the Old Testament is Proverbs.

The middle chapter is Job 29.

The middle of the verses is 2 Chron. 20, between the 17th and 18th verses.

The least verse is 1 Chron. 1. 25.

The 21st verse of the 7th chapter of Ezra has all the letters of the alphabet.

The 19th chapter of 2 Kings and 37th of Isaiah are alike.

'In the New Testament:

The middle book of the New Testament is 2 Thessalonians.

The middle of the chapters is between the 13th and 14th of Romans.

The middle verse is the 17th of the 17th of the Acts of Apostles.

The least verse is the 35th of the 11th of John.'

The publication of this work brought the author his world-wide reputation. Its success from the first was extraordinary. It met the requirement of the times, and led to imitators.[1] It would be difficult to say how many editions of it were issued,[2] sometimes in one volume, sometimes in two. After his death publishers summoned the help of others, to add to its notes, to improve – if that were possible – its reflections, while the pages were brightened by illustrations. Issue after issue went forth till it traversed the English-speaking world.

The last edition of Brown's Bible is undoubtedly the best. It was issued in America, in 1897, and a new edition followed in 1909. It is Brown's idea brought up to date. The editor is the Rev. James W. Lee, D.D., St. Louis, U.S.A. Bishop H. Vincent, D.D., LL.D., contributes an Introduction. In order to bring the Land and the Book closely together, advantage is taken of the investigations by the late L. Porter, D.D., LL.D., who spent many years in Palestine, while dissertations and side-lights are supplied by other writers. There is also an admirable article by William Blackwood, D.D., on 'Aids to the Study of the Holy Bible.' Not the least interesting and valuable feature of the issue is the 448 half-tone engravings specially taken for the work by R. E. M. Bain of St. Louis. The artist and Dr. Lee went specially to the East to obtain these and other material for this sumptuous edition. But it is a tribute to the solid learning and sane experimental knowledge on which Brown's Introduction, Notes, and Reflections were based that they are left practically untouched. The work con-

[1] Thomas Scott (1747-1821) acknowledges in his *Commentary* that Brown gave him the hint as to the plan on which it was best to work.
[2] In the British Museum there are twenty-six editions of Brown's *Self-interpreting Bible*, the first dated 1778, the last, 1909.

tains a brief sketch of Brown's life, not free from errors, in which he is credited with being not only a D.D. but an LL.D.! It is in four large volumes, and carries out to the full the conception of a Self-interpreting Bible.

Spurgeon, in his *Commenting and Commentaries*,[1] says, in reference to Brown's *Self-interpreting Bible*, 'Useful in its day, and still popular. Notes on New Testament are undisguised plagiarism from Guyse.' There is little foundation for such a sweeping indictment. John Guyse (1680-1761) published his *Exposition of the New Testament* in three volumes in 1739-42, and again in 1752 in six volumes. His work is mainly a paraphrase, somewhat ponderous in style, with occasional notes. It was exceedingly popular in its day, and went through six editions. But not a single note from it has Brown adopted. Brown, in his Foreword to his Commentary, refers to those who had preceded him in interpreting the Scriptures – Poole, Patrick, Clarke, Henry, Burkitt, Gill, Doddridge, and Guyse, 'judicious Guyse,' as he calls him here in his *Journal*. He states that his avowed aim in his publication is not to depreciate the valuable commentaries of these writers, but 'to exhibit their principal substance with all possible advantage, in a manner that might best comport with the ability and leisure of the poorer and labouring part of mankind'; and, in referring particularly to the New Testament, he adds that 'there the explication is peculiarly extensive, and attempts to exhibit the substance of many learned and expensive commentaries.' He thus frankly acknowledged his indebtedness to other authors. The influence of Guyse, as of the other commentators mentioned, may be traced in his work, in the same way as commentaries of today represent the views of other writers than their authors, the difference being that they supply the references as they pass from verse to verse, whereas Brown, as was his wont, records the references at the beginning, and suffers no further interruption to occur. Spurgeon's assertion is therefore very misleading. He also adds, 'not a students'

[1] C. H. Spurgeon, *Commenting and Commentaries*, 1887, p. 36.

book.' Brown had not students in view in preparing his work, but in his Introduction, References, and Reflections students will find today what is not likely to be found in similar productions.

The issue of this Bible Commentary brought Brown into correspondence with many notable persons, among them the saintly Charles Simeon of Cambridge. Simeon prized the *Self-interpreting Bible* above all others, and made acknowledgment of the spiritual enlightenment and quickening which he received from its daily perusal. Simeon was born at Reading in 1759, and passed from Eton to Cambridge when he was nineteen years of age. He never left the famous University seat. He secured a Fellowship in King's College, which he held throughout his life, and became, in 1782, minister or perpetual curate of the Church of Holy Trinity. He was a man with a new voice in the dark religious days of Cambridge, a voice that rang out with vehement earnestness in the midst of violent opposition and fierce obloquy. In the opening years of his ministry, parishioners and undergraduates bitterly resented his preaching. The former not only abstained from attending his church, but locked their pews and locked the church doors, and the latter caused many a riotous scene in the streets adjoining the building. But, by his tact and singular gentleness, Simeon gradually wore down opposition, and turned the prejudice against him into profound reverence and regard. Even the unsympathetic were compelled to listen to him. 'Well, Simeon is no fool,' said an undergraduate to his companion on leaving the church. 'Fool!' was the answer, 'did you ever listen to a sermon like that?'[1] In later life, his rooms in Gibb's building at the top of the second staircase from the chapel, were the resort of many pilgrims, and prominent on his table lay the Bible of the minister of Haddington. When his day closed in 1836, 800 University men paid tribute to his work by their presence at the interment of his body in the famous Chapel of King's.

[1] Arthur Gray, *Cambridge and Its Story*, p. 272.

It was Simeon's habit, summer and winter, to rise every morning at four o'clock. After lighting his fire, he devoted the first four hours of the day to private prayer and the devotional study of the Scriptures. The favourite companion of these devotional hours was Brown's *Self-interpreting Bible* in one volume. Says the Bishop of Durham in his *Life of Charles Simeon*:

'There lies before me, as I write, the massive volume of *The Self-interpreting Bible*, with explanatory Contents, parallel Scriptures, large Notes, and practical Observations, by John Brown, Minister at Haddington; printed in 1778, and bought by "C. Simeon, King's College, Cambridge, March 24, 1785." This Bible was his life-long companion, and is inscribed with many notes from his pen.'[1]

The correspondence between Brown and Simeon began toward the end of the former's career, but only one letter of Simeon to Brown has been preserved. So much, however, did he prize this commentary, which to the end of his life, says Carus,[2] he was continually enriching with valuable notes of his own, that he wrote to the author at Haddington as follows:

Rev. Charles Simeon to John Brown

'CAMBRIDGE,
January 19th, 1787.

'DEAR SIR,

'Your *Self-interpreting Bible* seems to stand in lieu of all other comments; and I am daily receiving so much edification and instruction from it, that I would wish it in the hands of all serious ministers. I have conceived a thought of purchasing a few to give to those godly ministers who would find it very inconvenient to purchase it for themselves. But, having no very great affluence myself, it is needful that I should

---

[1] H. G. Moule, *Charles Simeon*, p. 16.
[2] William Carus, *Memoir of the Life of the Rev. Charles Simeon, M.A.*, p. 68.

proceed upon the most saving plan. I take the liberty, therefore, of asking whether you (whose heart seems to be much set upon forwarding the cause of Christ), could procure me forty at the booksellers' price for *that purpose alone*; and to inform me whether there will be a new edition soon.

Yours sincerely,

CHARLES SIMEON.'

The date, it will be observed, is January 19th, 1787. At that time the Professor was at the beginning of the end of his mortal journey. He evidently was unable to reply to Simeon's interesting request. His sons found the letter among his papers, after he passed away, and Ebenezer replied in the following terms:

Rev. Ebenezer Brown, Inverkeithing, to Rev. Charles Simeon

'HADDINGTON,
June 26th, 1787.

'REV. SIR,

'My Father, Mr. John Brown of Haddington, fell asleep in Jesus on Tuesday last. Looking through his papers I observe a letter from you. By its date, I see that it came here about the beginning of his distress. This being the case, I am afraid that it never yet received an answer. You mention a wish that my father would procure for you 40 copies of the *Self-interpreting Bible* at prime cost. Had it been in his power I know that he would cheerfully have served you, and now, were it in mine, you should have them conveyed to you without delay; but the truth is that in Scotland there are few copies to be found. A new and more correct edition is intended. Very probably it will be printed in London, and then I hope you shall have as many as you please. I rejoice to hear that the Doctrines of the Gospel are so highly esteemed in England. May the whole earth be filled with the glory of the Lord!

'My Dear Sir, there is a small catechism published by my Father some time ago: it contains a summary of the principles of religion, and is used in the Schools for the instruction of thousands. As in your letter you manifest an uncommon regard for men's spiritual welfare, would you be so condescending as to accept Two or Three hundred of these Catechisms to be distributed among poor children? Believe me, if I know my own heart, had I ability I would make you a present of as many *Self-interpreting Bibles*. Oh what should we not do for the salvation of souls, when the Son of God *died* for sinners!

'If you please to return an answer, you will do a singular pleasure to one who would wish to be numbered among the servants of Jesus Christ.

'EBENEZER BROWN.

'Direct to me, Minister at Inverkeithing, Fifeshire.

'P.S. – Perhaps it will delight you to hear that my revd. Father died testifying his faith in the Doctrines which he preached and expressing earnest desires to be with Christ.'

Brown's Bible was treasured in the homes of the people with all the reverence and care enjoyed by Bunyan's *Pilgrim's Progress* and Boston's *Fourfold State*. It supplied what was lacking in these great soul classics, providing a clear path to the fount from which they derived their vitality and strength. The three were considered the necessary literary and religious equipment of the household. They furnished pabulum for serious reading; and they produced strong men. Burns linked them together in a manner that showed the popular reading of the time:

> For now I'm grown sae cursed douce,
> I pray and ponder butt the house;
> My shins, my lane, I there sit roastin'.
> Perusing Bunyan, Brown, an' Boston.[1]

The grandson of the author, Dr. John Croumbie Brown[2] (1805-95), relates that in distant lands, where it had been his lot to travel, the reputation of the *Bible* had gone before him,

---

Epistle to *James Tennant, the Miller of Glenconner*.
[2] J. C. Brown, *Centenary Memorial*, p. 163.

and the bulky volume, or volumes, as the case might be, would be produced as forming a connecting link between the host or hostess and himself, and that they were still appealed to as an authority on doctrinal and ecclesiastical subjects. He also recounts that, one one occasion, travelling from Perth to Dundee, he had his attention directed by a farmer in the compartment to the site of Abernethy sheltering so sweetly under the hills across the Tay. To the farmer's surprise, he seemed to know more about Abernethy than he himself did, though he was a native of the neighbourhood. His companion was curious to know how this happened; and he told him of his grandfather having been born at Carpow and lived at Abernethy. This led to inquiry as to his name. On hearing it, his questioner replied with great relish: 'Eh! that's wonderful; I belong to the Parish Kirk, and nae further gane than last Sunday, we had an ordination o' elders in the Kirk; and the minister spak o' elders as if they were mair like angels than men. That wasna my experience o' them; and says I tae mysel', When I get hame, I'll rax doon the *Bible*, and see what John Brown says; and here I've met wi' his grandson.'

The great-grandson, Dr. John Brown, the author of the immortal *Rab*, began his professional career in Chatham, where he fought the cholera that then raged in the town, with singular self-sacrifice and heroic courage. Into a house which he entered on his professional duties, a woman, on learning that his name was Dr. John Brown, asked in all sincerity, 'if he was the son of the *Self-interpreting Bible*!'

The labour expended by the author on this work overflowed in other directions. It led to the preparation of a *Concordance of the Scriptures*, which was published in 1783. Alexander Cruden, the pioneer of this work in the English language, produced his third and final edition in 1769. Brown added very considerably to his stock of references; and his work was issued with considerable frequency, until it was superseded by larger works that aimed at including every word of Scripture.

CHAPTER 20

The Lives of the Saints

John Brown was convinced of the great value that biographies of men eminent for their piety and usefulness possess in quickening and developing the interest of the people in things spiritual. He was an intense reader of this kind of literature himself, and felt its stimulus. Unlike George Borrow, who had a great passion at one stage of his career for the lives of criminals, Brown preferred the other side of the shield, and reckoned the world needed the example of good men to spur it on to high endeavour, rather than the ingenious deviations from rectitude that captivated the imagination of the brilliant devotee of gipsy lore.

In this respect Brown was in accord with a later historic figure in the Church Catholic, John Henry Newman. Before his exit from Protestantism, he took an active part in issuing a series of *The Saints of England*; and after it, in his enthusiasm for his new faith, he, in conjunction with a fellow pervert, Frederick Faber, began the issue of *The Lives of the Saints*—whom Romanists hold in favour—which enterprise, however, had an abrupt ending.

Newman's *Lives* were more than even Roman Catholics could tolerate. 'Some features in them scandalized,' says his biographer, 'many English readers.' The abundance of imperfectly proved miracles was objected to, and some of the stories of scandals within the Church were considered unsuitable for Protestant England. The series had to be stopped, for two reasons, says Newman in a letter to a fellow Oratorian: 'The first great fault was *dryness*. . . . Next that, the feeling of

Catholics about them might be summed up in these two objections, that the miracles *need* not be believed (and were difficult), secondly that they would *prejudice Protestants*. Some Catholics or Protestants (I forget which) scrupled at receiving the account of St. Winifred carrying her head – that Bacci was dry.' The future Cardinal felt the snub keenly. 'Why,' he continued in his wrath, 'are they [the Roman Catholic clergy] jealous? *What* have we done? Since the day we were Catholics, they have been bursting with "jealousy" – and we are on every occasion to give way to this indefinite terror.' But he was severely called in question for his sensitiveness and pugnacity, and taught that it was only his to obey.

Brown's *Lives* had no such flaming sword drawn over them. They had the hearty approval of his Church, and were read by increasing multitudes. Long after he had passed to his rest they continued to be issued, and might with profit be issued still. Of course, the so-called miracles that Newman and Faber delighted to serve up with their chosen saints find no place in the lives of the men that Brown set before the public. He was content to allow the story of their experiences and activities, their defeats and triumphs, to carry its own testimony.

In issuing them, he said, his aim was 'to disparage the fashionable but soul-ruining flimsiness in religion' that prevailed, and 'promote a distinct, deep, and heart-captivating experience of the gracious working of the Spirit of God, issuing in a devout, active, and orderly practice.' He appealed in particular to his students to gather from these *Lives*, so as to 'lay deep the foundations of their professed religion, if they wished the ravishing delights of it.' In characteristic fashion he goes on to say:

'For real gnawings of the shell will but render it disgustful to you, and make your ministrations of the Gospel a task, a burden to yourselves, and a curse to your hearers. None that know how long and how eagerly I have hunted after human literature, as my circumstances permitted, will readily suspect

G

me as an enthusiastic contemner of it. But as, on the brink of eternity (he was then in his 59th year), I dare pronounce it all "vanity and vexation of spirit," when compared with, or not subordinated to, the experimental knowledge of Jesus Christ, as "made of God unto us, wisdom, and righteousness, and sanctification, and redemption." There is no language, ancient or modern, like that of the Gospel of the grace of God, pronounced by the Holy Ghost to one's heart, and of heaven-born souls to God, under His influence; no history like that of Jesus Christ, redemption through His blood, and effectual application of His grace; no science like that of beholding the Word made flesh, and beholding the infinite perfections of Jehovah in Him and through Him, in every creature; no pleasure like that of fellowship with the Father and with His Son Jesus Christ.'

The first series of Brown's Lives appeared in 1781, and bore the title, *The Christian, the Student, and the Pastor.* The saintly men whom he portrayed were James Fraser of Brea, Thomas Halyburton, the seraphic Professor of Divinity of St. Andrews, Owen Stockton, a minister of Colchester, Matthew Henry, of Commentary fame, and Philip Doddridge, eminent as a preacher, scholar, and Christian poet, and, in brief compass, three American writers, Thomas Sheridan, Cotton Mather, and Jonathan Edwards. The men are allowed mostly to relate their own story, and to concentrate on their spiritual conflicts, with the result that the impression deepens with every page. The call of the inner life and the necessity for its thoughtful culture, are what concerns the editor. Newman declares that 'The *Lives of the Saints* were one of the main and special instruments, to which, under God, we may look for the conversion of our countrymen at this time' to Roman Catholicism. Brown's was a much truer and loftier conception, the conversion of his countrymen to the Lord Christ.

The reception accorded the publication was exceedingly cordial. The Professor, much in advance of his time in his care for the rising generation, proceeded in the following year (1782) with a second series, entitled *The Young Christian; or, the Pleasantness of Early Piety*. Eleven Lives are given, in order to –

'Encourage all concerned, to their utmost, to study, or promote an early fear of God. . . . How delightful to have our children, servants, scholars, or young hearers living or dying in the manner these young ones did! How delightful to have them, on their death-beds, blessing God, and thanking us for the pains we took in their Christian education! – Why do we complain of the ignorance, folly, pride, prodigality, and profaneness of the rising generation, if our neglect of their souls, or our encouragement of them in fashionable conformity to the world, be the cause? If any of them be a burden or a reproach to us, doth not our own wickedness correct us, and our backslidings reprove us?'

To his young readers he addresses the appeal:

'In these little histories which I now present to you, behold what your lives ought to be! Behold what, by the grace of God, they might be! Behold what they would be, were it not for your own sloth, folly, and wickedness! Behold what an honour and comfort you might be to your parents, masters, teachers, and ministers! and what a mercy to your families and country! and what a joy and crown to Jesus Christ, that loved you and gave Himself for you!'

The examples given are certainly remarkable; they illustrate, however, the surface meaning of the classic proverb, 'Whom the gods love, die young.' One or two reach the age of twenty-two, but most are of tender years. The precocity of youth on its religious side is strikingly manifest, but the editor himself, in a footnote, makes the assertion, 'I myself once saw a child dying in a cradle that appeared to have more knowledge of the principles of religion than some who apply for admission to the Lord's table.' The study of child life has revived in recent years; and the results tend to support the contested utterance of Wordsworth, 'Heaven lies about us in our infancy.' The series closes curiously with the 'dying sentences of some great, learned, or godly men.' They are aptly chosen, and culled from a wide field – Cardinal Richelieu, John Knox, Archbishop Ussher, Hugh Grotius, John Selden, Dr. John Donne, Hugh McKail, and others.

In the year following, 1783, Brown completed his series of *Lives*, in a work entitled *Practical Piety, exemplified in the Lives of Thirteen Eminent Christians*. These 'complete my intended exemplification of Practical Religion, in which, I hope, believers of every age and station may find somewhat for their own reproof, correction, and instruction in righteousness.' These thirteen consist of eight men and five women. Among them were Joseph Williams, a rich merchant in Kidderminster, Sergeant James Nisbet, son of John Nisbet of Hardhill, one of the Scottish covenanters, Margaret Abercrombie near Alloa, Elizabeth Cairns, whose family suffered from 'the fury of the Highland rebels,' James Barry, who, as a boy, passed through the Irish massacres of 1641, a nephew of the Lord Chief Justice of Ireland. Most of his list had gone through the sifting fires of persecution. When the torch is lit, the truth burns. Those whose souls hungered for the light, and at last were satisfied, felt that they had a stand to make which called both for a reason to support it, and for a record to preserve it. It was such that this indefatigable worker in the rich field of Christian biography brought before men.

The fact that the saints selected were from the quieter walks of life was the more effective, in Newman's phrase, as 'the popular evidence of Christianity.' There is nothing so striking about them as the varied nature of their personalities. Such dwelling upon the inward moods might lead to monotony and morbidity. But there is a refreshing note in the testimony of each, as they severally relate how, like Dante, 'they climbed

[196]

the mountain.' The times also reveal themselves in their narrative with an intimacy that brings the reader into closer touch with the realities of the period than is depicted by the painstaking historian. The narratives are to a large extent the personal histories of the writers, and two of them are direct from their manuscripts. They show how deep the roots were planted in an age that rang with controversy in Church and State, and what rich fruits were garnered in spite of the prolonged and fierce storms of contention.

The series was followed by *Casuistical Hints, or Cases of Conscience*. These hints were 'originally formed for my own use; and may now be considered,' says the author, 'as an appended illustration of the *Lives*, or as an appendix to my system on the head of Sanctification.' They afford a glimpse into his mind and method of dealing with the practical problems of life. Brown's difficulties were not specially of an intellectual nature, they were rather of an ethical and spiritual type. His faith mounted over the perplexities of the mind facing the mysteries of the universe. It steadied itself on the sunlit heights of God's sovereignty and His revelation in Jesus Christ, and accepted what was in the shadow as beyond human power, and rejoiced, and was content to rejoice, in the vast region where the light fell. But when it came to the region of character and conduct, it made him agonize in his endeavours to reach the lofty altitudes of rectitude and holiness, and he was deeply humbled that the ascent was so slow.

The problems of conduct therefore concerned him greatly. Here he centres his inquiry round five important spheres, in which action is difficult to determine – temptation, indwelling sin, spiritual experiences, the Christian walk, and errors and divisions in the Church. Both the examples and the experiences of the saints whose lives he had been detailing, as well as the great doctrine of Sanctification that he was fond of emphasizing, opened up fields where the path safely to pursue was not the easiest found. While the main route was plain, there was soon reached a doubtful belt, where right and wrong, good and evil, truth and error, appear to meet and merge Brown set himself to act as guide and interpreter, and would –

> Like a trumpet . . . rouse
> Those who with half-open eyes
> Tread the border-land dim
> 'Twixt vice and virtue.

He discusses the 'Temptations' that beset men of all ages, in all ranks and professions. He deals with each in detail, and pursues, with the scent of a sleuth-hound, the tempter in all the twists and turnings he takes to capture his prey. Then, in a few vigorous sentences, he furnishes the weapons which grace and Scripture provide to meet the foe. He thereafter turns to 'Indwelling Sin,' whose two leading properties are deceitfulness and power. In this chapter he displays his analytical faculty in tracking evil to its hidden depths, and dragging it to the light. 'Spiritual Experiences,' he next examines in their varied character, in regard to conviction, conversion, inward feelings, doubts and fears. This is followed by a chapter on the Christian life, with its roots in faith, its fellowship in God, its safeguards in spiritual-mindedness and a conscience void of offence, and its fruits in the hours of trouble and sorrow. The concluding chapter is concerned with 'Casuistical Hints relative to Scandalous Practices, Errors, and Divisions.' He himself, in his early days, was the occasion of a good deal of offence, by the malicious slander foisted upon him by unthinking comrades, and was ministering in a Church that caused the first rent in the fabric of the Scottish Church. He could view this grave matter, therefore, from a standpoint that had been reached by a rugged route of personal experience. In a sane and temperate manner he subjects to examination scandalous practices, pointing out the pitfalls, and how they are to be avoided. 'Errors' are to be repudiated, albeit the greatest care is to be exercised in defining and determining what is 'error.'

'Divisions' in the Church are considered under a profound sense of the grievous disasters they may produce on the spiritual life of the individual and the community. In all cases, they are, if possible, to be avoided, and much is to be allowed for imperfections in this imperfect world. He will only allow that 'heresy in doctrine, idolatry in worship, tyranny in government, habitual intrusion of ministers, progressive indulgence of manifest scandals, imposition of sinful terms of communion by requiring any omission or commission which as circumstantiated is sinful, are sufficient grounds of withdrawment from a Church, with some of whose members left behind Christ holds spiritual fellowship.' And separation is only justifiable if the Church is 'obstinate in holding fast to her evils.' Providence often points out 'the duty of separation by permitting some faithful ministers to be tyrannously thrust out of her communion.'

When he turns to the means to heal the divisions in the Church, he has much wise and sensible advice to offer. In view of the special circumstances of the Church today, not only in Scotland but elsewhere, the wisdom of his words may well find a place in the thoughts of men. Discordant parties are warned against any attempt to crush each other, or 'one party be shy in their condescensions because the other appears sinfully stiff.' 'When meetings for promoting union are held, the most sensible, peaceable, prudent and humble ought to be the only managers, or at least the principal speakers.' The first thing to be considered is how far there is agreement, in order to 'conciliate affection and manifest that the real differences are but few and comparatively of smaller importance, if anything at all but words – and the most ticklish points ought to be last considered.' The differences that arise on doctrinal points not fundamental, manner of worship, personal faults, authority of certain courts, and practices of courts, are handled with consummate sense; and again he insists on separation being a necessity only when every method of reaching common ground without a betrayal of the highest principles is exhausted. It is interesting to see how the author who himself toiled along the thorny and difficult path that clave the Church of his land, deemed secession or separation no light thing, but the very last to be resorted to, and to what lengths he would go to have the breaches healed. The union among Christians ought specially to be studied and promoted 'in face of the perils threatening the Church, the inability of the State to help, the weakening caused by divisions,' and, above all, 'when God in His providence offers any remarkable opportunities of a happy conjunction.'

The discussion of these grave problems affecting conduct appropriately closed the remarkable series of *Lives* which Brown issued. The situation disclosed of difficulty or peril was courageously faced; and he hesitated not to furnish a solution, whether it might commend itself to the perplexed reader or not. He had the faculty not only of diagnosing a condition, but also of discovering a remedy. The value of his 'Hints' was their honest and sincere attempt to provide guidance in regions of conduct where cross-roads meet at almost every turn.

Here it may be fitting to record an experience which he himself had, in a situation equally difficult and delicate. He had a particularly strong aversion to what in those days was termed the 'transportation of ministers,' that is their being called from one sphere to another. In 1779, the pastorate of the great congregation of Bristo Church, Edinburgh, became vacant through the death of the minister, the Rev. John Patison. Five calls were presented to ministers, which were in turn unsuccessful. Brown was appointed moderator (to take temporary charge) in 1782. Many of the people were bent on having the Rev. James Hall (afterwards Dr. James Hall) of Cumnock, Ayrshire, as the minister. Others favoured a brilliant student of Brown's (both were his students), newly licensed, James Peddie (afterwards Dr. James Peddie). The long vacancy had created adverse currents in the congregation. At the moderation for a call, Brown preached a sermon on Acts 1. 24, that had its application to the circumstances, and, while not advising the calling of the settled minister, steered strongly in that direction. When the vote was taken, Peddie had a bare majority. The other side raised a clamour about the unfairness of the sermon, which Brown immediately published, under the title, *The Necessity and Advantage of Special Prayer for the Lord's Special Direction in the Choice of a Pastor*. It was correct to the last particular; but it was followed *With an Appendix of Free Thoughts on the Transportation of Ministers*, in which he deprecated strongly the translation of ministers except under the very highest necessity. This *Appendix* did not soothe matters, and involved the author in a controversy which, he says, 'occasioned me many sleepless and thoughtful hours,' and in which he had vigorously to defend his principles.

The issue in the congregational struggle was an endeavour to make the charge a collegiate one, and both candidates were requested to preach on alternate Sundays. This, however, did not conduce to harmony. Ultimately Mr. Peddie was ordained to the charge on April 3rd, 1783, in which he was succeeded by his son, William, and the two ministered to the same congregation for the long period of 110 years till 1893. Mr. Hall and his party withdrew, and formed the congregation of Rose Street Church, in the new part of Edinburgh that was rapidly rising. The numbers in both congregations quickly increased, in Rose Street Church so greatly that in 1821 Dr. Hall and a part of his congregation moved to a larger church in Broughton Place, on the opening day of which the rival candidates of Bristo forty years before, Dr. Peddie and Dr. Hall, both preached. In both these charges, in Rose Street, and Broughton Place, Dr. Hall was succeeded by the grandson of John Brown.

CHAPTER 21

Letters and Tracts for the Times

The correspondence that Brown maintained in his lifetime came as a marvel to his friends after he had passed away. His epistolary intercourse extended to all classes. Unhappily, such fugitive material is not generally treasured, a fault more pertinent to the eighteenth century than to this; and a large part of his correspondence has been lost. A few letters to the Countess of Huntingdon have been preserved, showing the intimacy of his fellowship with that remarkable woman. He had also frequent communication with John Mason[1] of New York, Annan of Boston, Philips of Sarum, and others. The letters that have survived show that it was not the dash of a pen over a few lines of commonplace that satisfied him, but talk on the highest themes. So refreshing were these letters in their wise counsel and comfort, so brightening and stimulating, that many of them were sent to his sons after his death, and published. They may not have the touch and insight, the charm and vivacity of his distinguished great-grandson, the author of *Rab*; but they possess a character and an individuality of their own that made them welcome to that age, and called for their frequent publication.

The extracts we furnish will enable us to enjoy a closer view of the man, and the burning passion that ever animated him.

Here is one dated August 20th, 1765:

John Mason, D.D. (1731-92), belonged to Midcalder, Midlothian. The Secession Churches sent out a number of missionaries to the United States, and he went as one in 1761. He became minister in New York, and a distinguished leader in the Dutch Reformed Church.

'You ask me concerning marks of fellowship with our Lord Jesus. Alas! that I should know so little about that happiness. How easy to talk about spiritual things, when we feel not their power; but, without doubt, our communion with Christ is real, if it make us lie in the dust before Him, and cause us to loathe and abhor ourselves in His presence. . . . Real communion, too, melts the heart with love to God, and to His laws, ordinances, and people, and renders us vexed and shamed that we cannot love Him to purpose. But it is one thing to know these matters in our head, and another thing to feel them in our heart. Ah! how many of us called Christians are led like beasts by the *head*; and how few, like saints indeed, are led by the *heart*.'

To a correspondent engaged in trade, he penned a letter that made his occupation a source of daily instruction. The date is, Haddington, 1769.

'Yours I received. Oh that we had learned Christ to any purpose! It were well to have learned but as much of Him as to convince us that He is far above our comprehension. There is nothing in creation, but the more acquaintance we have with it, the more spots and blemishes we shall see; but Christ, the more He is seen and known, appears so much the more comely. . . . As all lawful business is full of Christ and of eternal things, yours is so in a peculiar manner. Your asking of persons what they desire, as they come in, is an emblem of Christ saying, "What will ye that I shall do unto you? Buy of Me gold tried in the fire, that thou mayest be rich." Your arranging of goods on shelves, puts me in mind of Christ arranging His blessings in the ordinances of the Gospel, and in the various promises. Often you let people see things, and they refuse to buy them at all, or at least to take them at your price – a sad emblem of our conduct toward Christ! Ah! how often do we come to His ordinances and buy nothing, view His covenant in a careless manner, and refuse to have any of

[203]

His special benefits! We reason with Christ; not to have His blessings cheaper – that cannot be, but to have them at a higher rate than that at which Christ offers them. Is not this madness with a witness? . . . Perhaps you sometimes exchange goods; but no exchange is like that which Christ made. He took our curse, and gives us His blessings; He took our sorrows, and gives us His joys; He takes our old heart, which is little worth, and gives us a new one; He takes away our filthy garments, and clothes us with a change of raiment! You get your own share of slack trade on some days; but if you could learn the way of trading quick with Christ, if bad debtors make you rightly consider what you owe to Christ and how poorly you pay, you might make the worst part of your business the most profitable.'

Out of the anguish of a sorrow-riven heart another wrote him, making a request at the same time for the illustration he had used at the Communion Table.

'I desire to sympathize with you in your affliction. Experience hath made me know how hard it is to part with a pleasant child. God hath in His dispensation shown you that "vanity of vanities, all that cometh is vanity." There is no certain source of pleasure besides Christ. When we come into life, we are much in the same situation as you were when you got home – we find created joys on their death-bed. May we put as little trust in them as they deserve! In this stroke, I am sure God is righteous. Think if your tender little one did not twine about your heart, and draw it off from God. Is it not, then, just that God abolish the idol? But, methinks, this stroke is not only just, but it is good also, both to you and to your child. What you have met with on this occasion appears to me an evidence, so far as I can see into the secrets of Jehovah, that God has at once taken your child to Himself, and, in some measure, taken your child's room in your heart. If, when young ones are in such danger here, God hath taken your daughter to educate her in heaven, if she is gone to Christ, your best Friend above, is she any worse? rather, is she not far better? Do you well to be angry that God has dealt so graciously with her? Learn from the death of children to pant for the ever-living God; to consider them, and all created things, as mere loans, which God may recall at pleasure. Esteem nothing but Christ your proper possession; all things beside Him give us the slip.

'As to the note at the service of the table, of which you spoke, it was to this purpose: "When the savages of Louisiana were going to murder Lasale,[1] or his Italian friend, he told them that, such was his regard for them, that he had them all in his heart; and would they murder a man who loved them so well? At the same time applying a small looking-glass to his breast, he desired them to look, and see if it was not so. It is said that the poor savages, observing their own image, had their barbarity melted into the most tender compassion and love; they would not for the world have hurt him or suffered him to be hurt by others." Now, believing communicants, Jesus bids you look into His heart, and see yourselves there. "Behold," said He, "you were on my heart from eternity, when I undertook for you; then My delights were with the sons of men, and I rejoiced in the habitable parts of the earth. Lo! you were on my heart on Calvary, when it was melted as the wax with the wrath due to your crimes! Behold you are on my heart, now that I am in the midst of the throne, while I appear in the presence of God for you and prepare a place for you!"'

To a relative on the death of her first-born he wrote:

'God indeed has manifested, in your case, the vanity of all earthly enjoyments, in giving you a child to look about her and die. However, O mind! it is the Lord; let Him do what seemeth to Him good. She was not given, but lent you. Grudge not the recall of the loan. I am sure He did not recall it till He saw it proper and necessary. In plenty of wisdom, as well

[1] Robert Cavelier La Salle (1643-87), a great French explorer in North America.

as justice, He doth afflict. Nay, in plenty of mercy too. . . . I beseech you, beware of immoderate sorrow for the loss of your only child. If you do not, it may break your own delicate constitution, and quickly hurry you to the grave. You have not reason to sorrow as those who have no hope. . . . Indulge not the mind in recalling her agreeable looks and the like, but turn aside, looking unto Jesus, the Child, the Son of God. Fellowship, close fellowship with Him, can allay the bitterest griefs, and make up the greatest losses on earth.'

In these letters are occasional glimpses of his own personal life. To a mother who had lost her husband he sent a heartening message for herself and children:

'I am essaying to weep with you that weep. . . . The Lord hath now an opportunity of giving you an experience of Himself as the widow's husband, the widow's judge, and the widow's stay. Stir up your soul and cry, "I know that my Redeemer liveth"; 'my Lord and my God'; yea, mine own God is He." Permit me to say a few things to the children. Remember your father hath often and solemnly devoted you to the Lord. O! for the Lord's sake, never give yourselves to Satan, or to your own lusts! If you cast yourselves on the God of your father, I dare foretell that God will take care of you all, both of soul, and of body. I myself was thrown to the wide world when young, and yet to this moment I never was in a strait as to outward things; nor as to inward things either, unless when my unbelieving heart was the cause.'

Writing from Stow, June 6th, 1769, to a friend tried in the furnace, he sought to sustain him with views of 'our liberal Jesus, Who seeing our need, doth grant unto us His gracious promises.' He makes appeal for his friend's sympathy, in view of his own shortcomings. 'Dear friend, pity me, and cry mightily to God on my behalf. It is shocking, if you knew it, to think what difference there is betwixt my sermons and my own inward life.'

[206]

To Miss Christian Scott, Edinburgh, battling with mental depression, he brought the solace of a wise comforter:

'I would not have you to sink under your burdens: Christ says to you, "Cast thy burden on the Lord, and He shall sustain thee." What, though you be weak, is Christ not strong enough to help you? And is He not willing enough? is He not a tender-hearted brother and friend? Was He not manifested for this end, that He might destroy the works of the devil? And is not that hardness of your heart, that stupidity and carelessness about divine things, that inability to apply divine promises, that unfitness for prayer, that you are plagued with, a work of the devil? Surely it is; oh then give it up to Christ, that He may destroy it in you and for you. . . . Do not be afraid at every blast, but essay to grip to the promise of Christ to encourage you. . . . It is true, God has said, "Thou shalt call me, My Father, and shalt not turn away from Me"; what more could you desire God to engage for you? Oh! hold Him at His word, essay to plead it in prayer, and though, for a hundred times on end, you should be so straitened in essaying to plead it, plead on; God waits to be gracious—and will you not wait till He be gracious? . . . Is it not very pleasant, that where sin abounds, grace, sovereign grace much more abounds? I hope that God will bring you to a wealthy heritage, though He draws you through fire and water to it. Oh! my dear young friend, when your feet are in the net, let your eyes be toward Jesus, the conqueror of sin, death, and hell; and by looking to Him you shall be lightened. Whenever you ponder your own dismal case, be sure to ponder the sure grace, mercy, and saving power of the Redeemer, and ponder how many claims you have on Christ. . . . It is the faith of Christ's love, saving power, and infinite righteousness that must melt your heart; think on it night and day; try to get that text pressed on your heart, "He loved me, and gave Himself for me." '

The letters overflow with profound sympathy for those who

'bear the whips and scorns of time.' He himself had tasted the bitterness that life can offer in some of its moods, but had drunk yet more deeply of the streams that flow from the crystal fountain. The sorrows and sufferings of men and women touched a responsive chord in his heart, and he was eager to help them to reach the refreshing waters. In this way he exercised a wider ministry than he contemplated, as the recipients carried his messages to others in like perplexity. A demand arose in time for their publication, with which his sons complied; and thus, that which was meant to be the enlightening help of one became the comfort and stay of many.

His letters were only one feature of his crowded life; 'tracts for the times' poured forth from his busy pen. These were Tracts that had a special appeal to their day before those that with momentous consequences to the Church of England originated the Tractarian movement in the 'thirties' of last century. Many of Brown's were afterwards collected and published. Some of them take the form of Meditations, musing soliloquies, especially where some enkindling aspect of revealed truth enthralled the vision, *Christ being made of God to us Sanctification, The Grace of God as manifested in Redemption, The Purchase and the Application of Redemption, A Soul shut up to Faith, Spiritual Elevation and Dejection.* The style is simple but incisive, and the language vibrates with the passion of a man in tune with the Infinite. 'Redemption! thou eternal excellency, the joy of many generations, return, return, that I may look upon Thee! How my heart is amazed, is ravished with the view of what my adored Jesus hath done for me in the purchase of redemption, and doth to me in the everlasting application of it to my soul!' Then the great theme unfolds itself, discovering fresh beauties to the ardent spirit; and he concludes, 'What melting views are these! How my heart heaves with joy, flames with love, would burst with praise, if wonder would allow!' (Tract III, *A Contrast of the Purchase and Application of Redemption.*)

Other tracts have more specific reference to the events and

controversies of the day that were engrossing the minds of the people. These he utilized to wing a message for his Master. The contention between Arminians and Calvinists then raged fiercely, and a tract entitled *Conditional Election and Free-will* set forth his views with conspicuous clearness, where the Arminian theory is described as 'a miserable comforter and physician of no value.' In 1775 came a dissolution of Parliament, with a general election and all the orgies that then gathered round such an event in those pre-ballot days, when bribery and corruption flourished. He sees in it another 'Dissolution,' and it impels his pen to quicken to a better life his fellows in the muddy whirl of politics.

'The late dissolution of Parliament in no way that I know of affects my private interest.[1] Scarce any, such as I could have freedom to choose for my representative, viz. "able men, fearing God, and hating covetousness," will be turned out, and perhaps as few brought in, by the change. But when I consider the terrible scenes of deceit, bribery, drunkenness, ignorant and profane swearing or perjury, that will be thereby occasioned, it sinks my spirits, and I look on the dissolution as a means of hastening our ruin. Alas! what numerous, what heavy curses of Jehovah, the King of nations, the wickedness committed in the electioneering work will draw down! And what court, what kingdom, can prosper under so many fearful curses of Almighty God! It is neither N. nor F. nor P. that I either fear or trust, but a long-provoked and exceedingly angry God. Till our madness and profligacy in diversions, elections, and many things else, and the fearful murder, deceit, and robbery, committed in our East Indian trade, and our hatred and contempt of Christ and His Gospel, be turned into weeping and mourning and girding with sackcloth, I cannot expect any blessed prosperity for Britain. Nay, I am astonished that God,

[1] He was not an elector. A very limited franchise then obtained. The electors of Haddingtonshire, whose member was James Hamilton of Pencaitland, numbered only 75 (Sir C. E. Adam, *Political State of Scotland in the Last Century*, 1887, pp. 160-71).

in His infinite patience, hath borne so long with us, and hath not dissolved us from being a nation. But, turn thine eyes, O my soul! to a much more solemn scene. In a little our lower world shall be dissolved.'

And then the scene is depicted that shows 'the vast assembly of mankind dissolved'; and it furnishes an armoury to press home a vigorous message.

This Tract was followed by another on *The Grand Poll*. The candidates make their appeal to the electors.

'Terrible confusion having happened among mankind, their original state was totally dissolved by the great King, the Lord of hosts. It was, therefore, necessary that they should be represented and directed by a new head. Two candidates, of very different characters, appeared to solicit their votes. Beelzebub – a prodigal rake, who, in a few days of his youth, had spent his large patrimony, and rendered himself and many millions of his friends absolutely bankrupt and miserable; but who, nevertheless, became more and more proud, and, by his impudence, flattery, falsehood, and other arts, gained the character of a most fashionable and prevalent orator – was the one. Jesus Christ – the only begotten Son of the Most High God, whose abilities for management, and whose fidelity, as well as His true love to God and men, were absolutely infinite; and who had the tongue of the learned to speak words that are spirit and life to every attentive hearer – was the other.'

Beelzebub had the presumption first to ascend the hustings, and, with a fawning smile and loud cry, called for attention. Into his mouth is put an ingenious and eloquent harangue, flattering human weaknesses, which in the end gained the loud and prolonged huzzas of the assembled hosts, 'No Jesus Christ, but Beelzebub for ever! Beelzebub for ever! Beelzebub for ever!' When Jesus Christ, in infinite compassion to the multitude, mounted the hustings, with difficulty He obtained a hearing. Many turned away; to those that remained is delivered a powerful plea, throbbing with tenderness and love, exhibiting the greatness of the divine compassion, and the dignity of the divine calling, so that multitudes, even of those that had most heartily voted with Beelzebub, with great melting of heart, cried out. 'Behold, we come unto Thee, for Thou art the Lord our God,' 'God my Saviour, my Master, my Lord and my God.'

In 1782 there was a change of Government. The death of Rockingham led to a new Ministry being formed under Shelburne. Some members retained their posts, among them being the Lord Advocate for Scotland, Henry Dundas, who was then entering upon his thirty years' term of office, which became known as the period of 'The Dundas Despotism.' A peace had just been concluded after what had been 'a most ruinous, perhaps on all hands a most unnecessary and sinful war,' according to John Brown; and there was loud talk among politicians about the British constitution, and the perilous state of the nation, owing to the immense debt the war had incurred. To the eager-eyed patriot of Haddington, there was too little recognition of the King of nations in the national councils, and in a tract on *The State of Britain's Debt to God*, he enforced this with uncommon spirit. 'Amidst all their pretensions of regard to the British constitution, and concern for the indebted and dangerous state of the nation, neither the old nor the new Ministry had in the least adverted to the extensive accounts between us and God.' He proceeds to enumerate the blessings the nation had enjoyed, the priceless blessings of redemption, and personal, family, and national mercies, and, to enforce his plea, contrasts these with a 'few of the leading articles of Britain's debt to God.'

The country was deeply concerned with its enormous burdens. The political horizon was lowering. France was on the eve of its revolution. Measures were anxiously discussed to avert catastrophe in our sea-girt isles, and to bring the ship of state into smoother waters. In a further tract on *Britain's*

Sole Preservative, he discusses this, and the proposals for remedy.

'Let our political managers project what schemes they will for the reformation and salvation of our nation, they will but issue in vanity and vexation of spirit. Nothing but a remarkable outpouring of the Spirit of God can prevent our superlative miseries, answerable to our heaven-daring national iniquities. As no civil societies have any existence in the future state, national sins must of necessity be punished with national judgments in this world.'

He proceeds to elaborate, with a wealth of Scripture incident and citation, the nation's best asset, and highest defence, and calls upon –

'Every Briton that wishes well to his country, to cease from trusting in men, and their carnal and selfish politics, and to cry mightily to God, that He may think on us, that we perish not; that He may plentifully pour out His Spirit from on high upon all ranks.'

In 1783 there came the accession of William Pitt to power as Prime Minister, at the early age of twenty-four. The period was critical, and the appointment struck the imagination of the country. Hearty approval was met by violent disapproval. John Brown beheld the matter in a different light, and he sent forth Tract xvii, *Christ the Best Minister of State*, in the spirit of Savonarola, who hung out the scroll over the doorway of the Senate Hall of Florence, 'Christ the King of Florence.'

'Upon our sovereign's advancing his present young Minister, while multitudes strive who shall most condemn or defend the British Premier, let me turn mine eyes, my heart, and my tongue towards Jesus Christ, to whom the Majesty of heaven hath committed all judgment, and given all power and fulness in heaven and on earth. Unless for an introduction to a better subject, it is not much worth my while to think or speak of British managers of State. Grey hairs assure me that I shall soon be put out of their reach, with respect to both their good and their evil. But, blessed be God, I hope never to be out of the beneficent reach of the Administrator of the new covenant.'

With Jesus Christ as ruler, he shows what blessings befall both the individual and the nation.

From the watch-tower in Haddington the Professor eagerly scanned the horizon, and allowed few occasions to pass without attempting to lift men's minds by means of the flitting events to higher altitudes. He dwelt there himself, but kept in touch with all that was occurring on the plains below. He did not withdraw from mundane things, as if it mattered not what befell his country. He was alive to the surpassing importance of the movements of the time, and was too observant a student of history not to know that whatever did not make for righteousness in a people was to their peril. 'The truest patriot,' said Adam Smith, 'is the man who has the keenest conscience of the nation's sins.' By the Tracts he issued, with their extensive circulation, and by other efforts of his pen, he strove to enkindle in the hearts of his fellows a real patriotic love for their country, fearlessly exposing the evils that preyed on its vitals, and stirring them up to loftier ideals. In this way he became one of the silent forces that contribute to the making of a nation, the modelling of its character, and the shaping of its destiny.

CHAPTER 22

Incidents of the Home, and Minor Works

The years that slipped past found the Professor, with his widening reputation, pursuing his course steadily in Haddington in the work of his congregation, the duties of the professoriate, and abundant service to his Church. The incessant labours of the study went on, and issued in a constant stream of works for the press. Some of the original manuscripts have been preserved. They are crowded pages, written on both sides of the paper, with scarcely an erasion or correction, for before they were allowed to proceed to the printer's table they had to submit to two or three revisions.

Two of his sons were now preparing for the ministry. They had passed through the curriculum of the University of Edinburgh, and received their training in divinity in the Haddington Hall.

Regarding the elder one, John, a somewhat amusing incident occurred as he crossed the threshold of his career. In 1776 he completed his studies. Before he was called to Whitburn in Linlithgowshire, he undertook the charge of a congregation in London, ministered to by the Rev. Archibald Hall, who had been a pupil of his father's while schoolmastering at Spittal near Penicuik. Mr. Hall's health had broken down, and he was obliged to rest for six months. During this period, John Brown the younger discharged the pastoral work. While in London, a young lady in humble position, but of excellent gifts, hailing from the borders of Scotland and residing with an aunt in the city, working as a dressmaker, captivated his affections. The commentator, when he heard of his leanings, was gravely dubious if she were a suitable helpmeet for his son, and if her position in the social scale was sufficient for her to be a daughter-in-law in his household, who himself was a weaver's boy. He despatched Ebenezer to London to play the part of Major Pendennis. When he returned, he was eagerly questioned if he had met the young maiden. Ebenezer gave the overwhelming reply, 'Father, if John does not marry her, I am going to marry her myself.' Isabella Cranstoun,[1] with her noted personal beauty, and meditative turn of character, became the spouse of John, and she more than fulfilled the standard which the Professor laid down for his students in the choice of 'a help and an ornament to themselves and their family.'

On May 22nd, 1777, John was ordained at Whitburn, and his father introduced him to his flock on the following Sunday with a sermon on religious steadfastness, that was published and extensively circulated. John, also, was the author of numerous works, and the editor of considerably more.

Among the few letters to his own family that have been preserved, there is one written by Brown in 1782 to this son, which reveals the simple homely touch, and how all life to him was transfused with the unsetting light. It was no jar for him to pass from the mundane and the commonplace to the supreme heights. He had been at Stow on Gala water, a congregation that elected him to its pastorate in his student days, and for such confidence enjoyed a warm place in his affections. He paid it an almost yearly visit – it was only about thirty miles from Haddington. On this occasion, with the snows of sixty years upon him, his health had been impaired. His town also was threatened with the ravages of a cholera that was playing havoc among the dwellers in the metropolis.

> *To the Rev. John Brown, Whitburn*
> 'DEAR SON,
>   'At present we are all moderately well. My illness at Stow, I suppose, was entirely owing to want of cold meat and

[1] John Cairns, *Memoir of the Rev. John Brown*, pp. 13-15.

good porter, in consequence of which I was obliged to take as little meat as I could. I now experience the truth of the proverb, Home is home, though never so homely. Oh to be ready for that eternal home from which we shall go no more out!

'I intend to be with you at your sacrament, if the Lord will, providing you could persuade Mr. Dick [South Queensferry] to come east and see his friends, and we should some of us supply Queensferry for him that day. I ever blush to desire brethren to take this trouble for me, but I suppose all these things will soon be over with me; and I would like to be once more in your country.

'The trouble that is raging in Edinburgh appears to have entered our place. Oh to hate sin, the cause of it!

'The books were sent off to you last week. This with our compliments to Bell [John's wife] and to Brother [John Primrose] at East Calder. I received Mr. Low's [minister at Biggar] letter too late, but sent off to Mr. Thorburn [South Shields] to go to Biggar on 4th Sabbath, but know not yet whether he is to come or not. Had I but got Mr. Low's letter at the Presbytery, I could easily have supplied him on the 4th Sabbath of June. May the Lord learn us all to look beforehand to the concerns of our souls!

HADDINGTON,
June, 1782.

'Our sacrament is on the 5th Sabbath of June. Pray for our withered corner.'

A short time after this, the home at Longridge was deeply shadowed by the death of the firstborn; and from the sympathizing heart at Haddington came a letter addressed to 'Dear Bell,' making anxious inquiries regarding herself and Johnny, as no message had been received in answer to a former communication. With the warm sympathy again expressed there is affectionate counsel 'to eye the hand of God in this dispensation,' and 'recommending a moderate freedom' in visiting some of the kindly-hearted neighbours, 'as too much lone-liness may do you hurt.'

On May 24th, 1780, the Professor had the pleasure of seeing his second son, Ebenezer, ordained to a charge at Inverkeithing, Fifeshire. Ebenezer, full of boyish spirits in his youth, the hero of many a rollicking story, became in process of years one of the most eloquent preachers in the country. His saintly character was as noted as his rare oratorical powers. From far and near men came to listen to the sublime eloquence of the brilliant son of Haddington. Lord Brougham and Lord Jeffrey sought him out and declared that he was the greatest natural orator that they had ever heard. The Professor felt that neither himself nor his eldest son at Whitburn could stand alongside the preacher of Inverkeithing. 'You and I,' said the Teacher of Preachers, '*try* to preach; but Eben *can* preach.'

In introducing Ebenezer to his congregation he chose as his subject 'the duty of raising up Spiritual Children.' The sermon was afterwards published. The full title of it had the flavour of the age, 'The Fearful Shame and Contempt of those Professed Christians who neglect to raise up Spiritual Children to Jesus Christ.' The text was a 'corner' one, Deut. 25. 5-10. In the spirit of the homiletics of the time, he regarded the people for whom the law was intended as typical, and the body as that of the Church.

'Jesus Christ, our glorious Elder Brother, died, and went to His Father, leaving the New Testament Church a *widow* deprived of His bodily presence, and childless without any remarkable increase to God. It therefore becomes His professed younger brethren, particularly Christian parents, masters, and ministers, in their holding fellowship with His Church, to exert themselves to the uttermost for raising up spiritual seed to Him.'

In the year 1780 a vigorous pamphlet came from the Professor's pen, vindicating the stand his Church had taken in the conflict for the rights and liberties of the Church of Christ.

A new generation was rising that heard as afar off the battle-cries of the first half of the century. The human memory is proverbially short; the present is ever recording its exciting passages across the deep dark lines of the past. The Established Church was learning little wisdom from the results of its high-handed action in the settlement of its ministers; and the three streams that separated from it were rapidly gaining in depth and volume at its expense. But those who championed the honour and purity of the Church had time and again to justify their position, sometimes against those with whom they had a good deal in common. In the other branch of the Secession was a protagonist of restless energy, Adam Gib, whose undoubted powers were limited by his keen partisanship. He was scathing in his denunciation of the followers of the Erskines, and, as usual, misrepresented their attitude.

In 1774 Gib produced two ponderous volumes, *The Present Truth: A Display of the Secession Testimony; in the Three Periods of the Rise, State, and Maintenance of that Testimony.* He traversed with great fulness of detail the whole secession controversy; and somewhat cavalierly dismissed Brown's account of the numbers present at the momentous Synod of April 1747, which witnessed the unhappy schism. Brown wrote him two letters,[1] giving his authority for his statement and pointing out other mistakes in his elaborate *Display.* He affirmed:

'I took my information from the minutes of the meeting; which, I daresay, you will own to be an authority superior to the assertion of twenty members of it, on that point. When you had no such voucher, and accordingly have been exceedingly varied in your accounts, was it not rash in you, to represent me as guilty of falsehood, without once inquiring for my authority to say so?'

After giving the names of the thirty-two that took the broader

[1] The letters are to be found at the close of the second volume in one of the issues of the *Display of the Secession Testimony.*

view of the burgess-oath, as against the twenty-three led by Moncrieff and Gib who opposed it, he adds:

'Now, as you have sent abroad perhaps some thousands of copies, to spread this false reproach against me, and to perpetuate the same, I hope regard to truth, as well as to your own honour, will induce you to make your acknowledgment of your mistake as wide as you have made your groundless reproach. Nothing more becomes ministers of Christ than a due regard to integrity and truth.'

He had just posted this letter on the morning of June 17th, 1774, from Haddington, to his correspondent in Edinburgh, when he recalled other notable mistakes, and wrote immediately in the hope that the letters might 'come to your hand this day, and not disturb you on the Saturday.' This was to correct Gib's designating the first Testimony of 1734 of the Secession Presbytery, an *extra-judicial deed*. Brown shows from the original minutes that it was drawn up by presbyterial appointment, and was judicially approved at subsequent meetings of the Presbytery. A like assertion had been made by Rev. A. Moncrieff of Abernethy twenty years before. Brown had called his attention to the error, which Moncrieff ignored. After relating this, Brown proceeds:

'If, sir, you as publicly acknowledge your mistake on this point, and in the other as to the number of members at the Sederunt of the Breach, it will both prevent sin, do honour to truth, and to yourself; and make such hints as we have only your word for, better credited. These are not all, nor near all the mistakes, I think I see in your performance. But what I intend is not to dispute with you, but to give you friendly information from better vouchers than you had to go upon. And if you make such an use thereof as will testify your impartial regard to truth, perhaps I may be encouraged to give you some other hints, which I long ago learned from the minutes or original papers.'

Adam Gib, in his reply, declared his two letters did not reach him till the evening of Saturday the 18th, discounted the value of the minutes as containing an accurate record, and preferred to lean on the rather precarious testimony of the recollection of those present at the historic Synod of nearly thirty years before. He held by his contention on the other points, and closed by saying, 'To conclude, I know myself to be a hearty well-wisher to you—with all those you are in connection with.'

The controversy was engaged in by others, and ultimately the Professor intervened in 1780 with a pamphlet on *The Re-Exhibition of the Testimony, vindicated in Opposition to the Unfair Account of it by the Rev. Mr. Adam Gib*. He kept by authoritative documents bearing on the discussion, and from this armoury of facts was able to make a trenchant reply.

Into a wider controversy than this, however, was Brown allured. A new political question was at this time rising on the national horizon, the question of Catholic emancipation. It was stirring the passions of men profoundly; and it came too near the Church of Christ not to draw him into its zone of fire. So deep were the wounds inflicted on the body politic in the eyes of some by Roman Catholicism, when in power, that any opening of the doors that barred its freedom awakened a sense of dread in many hearts. The latter decades of the Stuart dynasty were not forgotten; and the late attempt of the 'Bonnie Prince,' backed by Catholic Powers, was a vivid memory. For England, Parliament had passed a measure in 1778, relieving Roman Catholics from the disabilities imposed by the Act of William III for the further preventing of the growth of Popery. By that Act Catholics were prohibited from teaching their own youth, from purchasing or inheriting a single acre of land, even from becoming domestic servants. The disqualifications indeed were so drastic that the Act was more honoured in the breach than in the observance.

The whole story of these penal laws is no doubt a painful

puzzle to those in our time who know little of history, and regard religious toleration as an unquestioned principle. The state of mind that passed these acts with such disabilities is inconceivable to us. Yet the people who passed them, and those who were averse to repealing them, were not fools, nor, speaking generally, fanatics. To understand their point of view, we have only to remember that the Papacy claimed to be a world-power, a spiritual empire, with the right itself (its own) to define the boundaries of the spiritual world, and the further right to enforce its claims, where possible, by the temporal arm. Before the Reformation, this claim, with certain modifications and occasional protests, was admitted in the British Isles; and the series of Acts by which the Papal jurisdiction was transferred to the Crown, henceforth to be supreme in all causes, temporal and spiritual, meant an important stage in the development of the national consciousness. The interference of a foreign Power, whether in Church or State, was naturally suspected and resented; and when the Papal pretensions were backed by the Spain of Philip II, and the France of Louis XIV, it aroused feelings which grew to a passionate hatred. Those, therefore, that clung to the 'old religion' were regarded not so much as heretics as prospective traitors.

It was proposed to apply the repealing Acts that had been passed in England to Scotland; but the dread and hatred of Rome were more intense in Scotland than in England; and the proposal aroused such fierce opposition that the measure was for the time withdrawn. The opposition sprang from all classes and shades of religious and political creed. The first, indeed, to sound the alarm was an Episcopalian clergyman, Dr. Abernethy Drummond, who afterwards became Bishop of Edinburgh. Dr. John Erskine, one of the most influential ministers in the Church of Scotland, wrote a severe pamphlet in which he held that such an act would be disastrous both to religion and liberty, and maintained a spirited correspondence with Edmund Burke on the question. John Brown pub-

[221]

lished two pamphlets, one in 1779, and another in the following year. The two together make a fair-sized volume. Their titles speak for themselves. The earlier one is designated *The Oracles of Christ and the Abominations of Anti-Christ compared; or, a Brief View of the Errors, Impurities, and Inhumanities of Popery;* the other appeared as two Letters to a Friend, and was written in the form of question and answer, *The Absurdity and Perfidy of all Authoritative Toleration of Gross Heresy, Blasphemy, Idolatry, and Popery in Britain.* These pamphlets show the hatred which John Brown entertained for the erroneous doctrines of Rome, and his unwillingness to have affairs of state entrusted to those who held them.

The next few years must have kept the minister of Haddington and his publishers busy. Not a few of the works already referred to, on which he had been engaged for a considerable period, emerged from his pen. In 1781, 1782, and 1783 were issued his three series of *Lives.* In 1781 appeared in bulky volume his *Types and Figures of the Old Testament Dispensation,* and in the year following his *System of Christian Doctrine* was published. In 1784 two other works appeared: a *Compendious History of the Church in Scotland,* in two volumes, and *The Harmony of Scripture Prophecies, and History of their Fulfilment,* in one. Another work of his had great popularity, *Devout Breathings,* in which room was given for expanse of soul and lofty vision; by 1784, it had already passed through sixteen editions. A small volume, sometimes bound up with it, was extensively circulated, *The Awakening Call: Four Solemn Addresses, to Sinners, to Children, to Young Men and Women, and to Aged Persons.*

These productions, along with the other works that laid the foundation of his enduring fame, carried his name to distant shores. In 1784 a signal honour was paid to him who had been a herd-boy at Abernethy, and sat on the benches of no University, but who, by his untiring industry and indomitable spirit, had climbed into the ranks of Christian scholarship. America was commencing its great and prosperous career, and was anxious to fill its rising colleges with strong men. The Dutch Reformed Church invited John Brown to accept a professorship in its new college. It was an honour that was a tribute to his fame and learning, but he declined it, never mentioning to any one what had been proffered him. It might have savoured of egotism, and that he detested. Had he seen fewer years it might have received a favourable answer, but he was in his sixty-second year, and he felt Time's strong hand stealing over him. If the proposal had been accepted, and he had migrated to the new world with his numerous family, that have left such deep marks on various departments of learning, it would have meant a loss of no mean kind to Scotland, and without doubt a great gain to America.

Written in this same year 1784, moved thereto, perhaps, by this honour, there was found among his papers when he died a calm dedication of himself to God in which the true spirit of the man appears. His professorship had now continued for seventeen years; twenty-seven books had proceeded from his pen, most of them demanding extensive reading, protracted study, and careful regard to minute detail. His name was a household word in Scotland, and was known to many far beyond its shores. His books, pamphlets, tracts and catechisms were being read by increasing numbers. It can scarcely be denied that he was the most voluminous religious writer of his day. It is true that his writings may lack the magic style, and while some live and others are dead beyond hope of resurrection, yet they won extraordinary success. No more potent force for the furtherance of evangelical truth existed in the land. And if that bright flame could be kept burning, until others caught it up and turned it round to suit the needs of their age, he was content; fame might do what it chose with its crown. In this fervent nature there was manifest a deep sense of self-subordination, and an intense desire that the glory should not be unto himself. Here he unveils the hidden sources:

'Lord! I am now entering upon the 34th year of my ministry, an amazing instance of sovereign mercy and patience to a cumberer of the ground! How strange that Thou shouldst have, for more than sixty years, continued striving to exercise mercy and lovingkindness upon a wretch that hath all along spoken and done all the evil that I could; nor ever would yield, but when the almighty influence of free grace put it out of my power to oppose it. Lord! how often have I vowed, but never grown better; confessed, but never amended! Often Thou hast challenged and corrected me, and yet I have gone on frowardly in the way of my heart. As an "evil man and seducer," I have grown worse and worse. But where should a sinner flee but to the Saviour? Lord! all refuge faileth me; no man can help my soul. Nothing will do for me but an uncommon stretch of Thy Almighty grace. To Thee, O Jesus, I give up myself, as a foolish, guilty, polluted, and enslaved sinner; and I hereby solemnly take Thee as mine, as "made of God to me wisdom, righteousness, sanctification, and redemption." I give up myself as a poor, ignorant, careless, and wicked creature, who hath been "ever learning, and yet never able to come to the knowledge of the truth," to Thee, O Lord, that Thou mayest bestow gifts on the rebellious, and exalt Thy grace, in showing kindness to the unworthy. O Saviour! come down, and do something for me before I die. I give up myself and family, wife and children, and servant, to Thee, encouraged by Thy promises: Gen. 17. 7; Jer. 31. 1; Isa. 44. 3; 59. 21. I commit my poor, weak, withered congregation, deprived by death of its pillars, that Thou mayest strengthen, refresh, and govern it. I commit all my students unto Thee, that Thou, O Lord, mayest train them up for the ministry. May never one of them be so unfit as I have been, Lord! I desire to take hold of Thy new covenant, "well ordered in all things and sure. This is all my salvation, and all my desire."

JOHN BROWN.'

One must allow due weight to the sense of shortcoming when the full blaze is turned inwards, but there rings out the true man.

The immense labours of the study were solely intended to benefit his fellows. Pecuniarily his works profited him little; but that concerned him as little. He stood absolutely clear of the witchery of the purse. 'I would not wish,' he said to his sons at the end of his days, 'that there should be the least appearance of avarice in me.' He was utterly devoid of it. He might well stand for Goldsmith's well-known couplet:

> A man he was to all the country dear,
> And passing rich on forty pounds a year.

His stipend never exceeded £50 per annum, and for a considerable time was only £40. His professional work was done without fee or reward, as was also his clerkship of Presbytery and Synod. While his writings circulated widely, and new editions were called for, the profits did not find their way to his coffers. In the publisher's hands he placed his works, in the hope that they might be sold more cheaply for the sake of the poor. As already mentioned, one of his publishers, of his own good will, presented him with a sum variably mentioned from £25 to £40. But this sum he lent to the publisher of the first edition of his *Bible*, inasmuch as it was an expensive book to print. Unfortunately this publisher failed, and the money was lost. After his death, his widow received £90 for several of his works which he had prepared for the press, and some of his MSS.

When one remembers the very numerous editions of his *Christian Journal* that were called for, and the wide circulation enjoyed by his *Catechisms*, *Dictionary*, and *Self-interpreting Bible*, not to mention his other productions, it is evident that others reaped a harvest where he had so diligently sown. His son maintains —

'Though, in regard to his writings, it must be admitted he acted disinterestedly, it cannot be said that he acted wisely. He

H

himself and his family would have been much the better of receiving a fair portion of the fruits of his labour. Nor can it be alleged that, in receiving this, he would have been less "serving the Lord Christ." He might, on the contrary, have served Him more effectually, and been useful in ways in which he was not otherwise able to be.'[1]

Be it deemed wisely or unwisely, the Professor's dominating idea, it is apparent, was to promote the highest and best interests of all whom he could reach by voice or pen. If he could accomplish that, his chief end was served. Although his means were, as we shall see, a little augmented in a private manner, how he acquired the numerous tomes in his library in so many languages, and kept the wolf from the door, behind which was a young and growing family, is a mystery. He held strongly that every man was bound to devote at least a tenth of his income to pious and charitable purposes. Whoever lays that down as a principle, and acts upon it, invariably surpasses it—he comes to learn what is meant by the 'luxury of giving.' Though Brown had a large family, he often, we are told, exceeded this proportion. He carried the limits of the necessaries for his own person to the extreme; but the comforts that he denied himself were that he might the more liberally supply the wants of others. Congregations that were springing up invariably appealed to the older ones to assist in the erection of their churches; but, rather than burden his own congregation, whose resources were not abundant, he contributed considerable sums out of his own pocket.

One instance might be mentioned. He was mainly instrumental in forming a new congregation at North Berwick. As his son, Ebenezer, and he were riding to the ordination of the first minister, James Scrimgeour,[2] he said, 'Eben, this is a poor congregation, and you should be as liberal as you can on

---

[1] William Brown, op cit., 1856, p. 54.
[2] Ordained April 21st, 1784; demitted, 1799; went to America; died minister of Little Britain, February 4th, 1825.

this occasion. Once I gave them five pounds – perhaps it was more than I could well afford, but the Lord soon repaid me by inducing a Mrs. – to leave me a legacy of £20, the only one I ever received.'[1] He deprecated ostentation of any kind in the bestowal of his goods, and took special pains that the left hand never knew what the right hand did. A minister in the other branch of the Secession, who had spoken of him in severe and scathing language, was overtaken by misfortune, and, in a way that concealed the source from which it came, he helped him in his necessities. When he died, Brown generously offered to take one of his destitute children and bring him up with his own family. The kind offer was declined, but that it was made showed the thoughtful generosity of the heart that prompted it.

---

[1] *Memoir of Ebenezer Brown*, pp. 71, 72. It is added: 'Ebenezer was led by this recommendation to contribute perhaps more than he was easily able, but in a few days afterwards, as he was riding through Musselburgh, he heard one calling after him, when a Mr. Thomson, a relative of his mother's, informed him that a sum of money had been left for him – and this was for a debt never expected to be paid.'

CHAPTER 23

The Churchman

Brown was not only a studious bookman and a busy writer, but also a practical man of affairs. He threw himself into the work of his Church with great ardour, and, were it not that his Church throughout its history never recognized leaders, he would have been an acknowledged guide and pillar in his day. As we have seen, he was early summoned to the Moderatorial chair; but his business qualities were as early recognized, and he was called to the clerk's table, first of his Presbytery, and then of the Synod, which latter post he held from the year he became Professor, 1768, to the year of his death. The Presbytery met about a dozen times in the year, mostly in Edinburgh; and the Synod assembled twice in the year – when special business pressed, three times. The Presbytery included all the congregations within a certain area, the Synod embraced all the congregations within the denomination. The meetings of the supreme court were held at first in various centres, Stirling, Falkirk, Dunfermline, Glasgow, and Edinburgh; later they alternated between Glasgow and Edinburgh, and ultimately were confined to Edinburgh, taking place in the Bristo Church. They lasted usually three or four days. One period of assembling was in May, the other in the end of August or beginning of September. Attendance upon them was not so easily effected as today, with its speedy railway communication; then it was the slow process of walking, riding, or stage coach.

Of the forty meetings of Synod before Brown was appointed clerk, he was absent from only eight. Of the next forty-one that were held, he was absent only from two – the May meeting in

1786, when the Synod, after meeting for eighteen years in Edinburgh, was on that occasion convened in Glasgow, in order to get into closer touch with the growing section of the Church located in Ireland, and the May meeting prior to his death.

In the varied and anxious work of his Church, which, being a self-subsisting and self-governing body, required counsel and prudence of the first order, Brown was frequently summoned to serve on committees appointed to adjust matters and direct lines of procedure. Questions that are easily solved today, by the application of rules laid down, were thrashed out then; and in most cases the action then determined on forms the rules of today. In one instance it is departed from, where ministers, demitting their charge, are allowed to retain their seats in the supreme courts. In 1768, two instances arose of this nature, John McAra of Burntshields (near Kilbarchan, Renfrewshire), and David Horn of Cambusnethan (Lanarkshire), having resigned their ministry in these places, were anxious to retain their seats in Presbytery and Synod. Their plea was that, by laying down the key of doctrine, they had not surrendered their right to the key of government and discipline. Brown was a member of the committee that reported on the subject, and the decision, supported by eight weighty reasons, scriptural, historical, and practical, was adverse to the claim. The practice, however, in course of time was altered and the concession agreed to, more on the ground of expediency and courtesy toward the servant who had served the Church so long than from compliance with strict ecclesiastical procedure. In other matters during these formative years of the Church, it is noteworthy to find such sane lines of action adopted as have stood the test of the changes of succeeding periods even unto this day.

The question of extending the praise of the Church beyond the psalter was favourably entertained, and the selection of suitable 'spiritual songs' with which the Christian Church had been enriched was entrusted (1750) to Ralph Erskine, Dunfermline, whose poetic gifts eminently fitted him for such a task. Unhappily, his death supervened at the beginning of the movement, and, as no one else possessed to such a degree similar tastes and aptitudes, and as other subjects of immediate importance were pressing upon the Church, the matter was allowed to drop for the time. There were those in the membership, like Michael Bruce, who could have produced material for such a collection. Many of Bruce's productions found their way into the first hymnary of the Scottish Church, the 'Paraphrases,' as they were termed, which are as dear to the hearts of many as the metrical psalms themselves.[1]

Schemes were inaugurated for the support of widows and orphans of deceased ministers, and for the assistance of weaker congregations. The appointment of days for fasting and thanksgiving was then a common act of Synod. The reasons that called for such days were carefully detailed. Occasionally days for fasting were ordered by the Government in the name of the King; and the question was seriously discussed whether such intervention was not an intrusion upon the rights and liberties of the Church that must be jealous for the honour of its Lord and His place in matters appertaining to His kingdom. But loyalty to the reigning sovereign always won its acquiescence.

Brown's minutes of the Presbytery, and of the Synod, are clear and concise, the business stated and the decisions recorded in succinct terms. The records sometimes are of extreme length, when matters of importance necessitated a full statement. This is the case with the Testimony, which the Church felt itself impelled to state in order to account for the position it occupied in the country, or when it was considering new developments of any kind.

---

[1] James Mackenzie, *Life and Works of Michael Bruce*, 1914, pp. 333-71. Paraphrases 8, 9, 10, 11, 53, and 58 are acknowledged, on well-grounded authority, to be Bruce's. Bruce unfortunately had, as first editor of his works, John Logan, a notable literary brigand. A college comrade of Bruce's, he obtained possession of his MSS., and never returned them; he became minister of South Leith, was dismissed for drunkenness and immorality, and died a literary hack in London in 1788 at the age fo fifty-one.

Not a little time of the various Synod meetings was given up to devising how best to respond to the call from the colonists in America and Nova Scotia pleading with the young Church to come over and help them. Their appeals were sympathetically received, and, though the demand for preachers in the homeland was most urgent, ministers were loosed from their charges and probationers despatched to assist the brethren on a distant shore to build up their Church.

The rapid progress of the young Church at home was taxing the energies of its guides to the utmost. At every Synod meeting there were intimations of new congregations being formed and urgent requests from various centres for supply of sermon. Had there been preachers available, the advance would have been greater. In many instances vacant and newly-formed congregations had to wait for a long period before a fixed ministry could be granted; and the same reason prevented the Secession undertaking missions to distant lands, although it was eager to do so. As it was, such activity prevailed that in the course of Brown's ministry his own Church more than quadrupled the number of its congregations. In 1751 there were about twenty, and, at the time of his death, there were over ninety; and by the end of the century they numbered 169, eight of which were in England, and forty-seven in Ireland. In 1765, the rapid increase of the two Secession Churches and the Relief Church throughout the country began to awaken alarm in the Established Church, from which they had been driven out. The latter had cherished the hope when the split of the Secession Church took place in 1747, that their speedy extinction would follow. It thought, therefore, it could look with complacency, if not with contempt, upon its seceding members. But its leaders did not recognize that it was the supreme matters of the faith and the rights of the Church for which these were contending, and that the breach with its unhappy consequences was a mere passing phase. The thoughtful, conscientious religious men of the country recognized that, and from the shores of the Moray Firth to the Solway and beyond they flocked to their standard. In the year mentioned (1765) the Church of Scotland became so impressed with the fact, that their Assembly was overtured to consider the extraordinary circumstance of the astonishing progress of these denominations, and requesting measures to be taken to arrest 'this alarming evil.' This 'schism-overture,' as it was termed, stated, as the ground of its appeal, that there had been 120 meeting-houses erected, to which more than 100,000 persons resorted, who 'were formerly in communion but have now separated themselves from the Church of Scotland.' A large committee considered the overture for a year, and recommended further action, but at next Assembly, by a vote of 98 to 85, it was agreed to take no further steps.

From the *Scots Magazine* it would appear that the real object of those who introduced the overture was to put down the Secession by force. Adam Gib, in a communication to it, referred in straight terms to this alleged intention, and declared that, if such were its purpose, 'it was near seventy-seven years out of time.' He asserted that, according to his information, many in the Assembly did not relish the proposal, but, should it have been tried, 'the Seceders have ground of confidence that a suppressing of the testimony among their hands, whatever might be done with their persons, would prove too hard work for all the people of the earth.' Another writer disclaims, on behalf of the supporters of the overture, the intention to have recourse to violence, but in strong terms urges the necessity of some measures being adopted to arrest the progress of the 'schism,' as 'an established Church, without a general adherence, or from which the body of the people are alienated, appears to be an object not worthy the notice, the care, or the protection of any Government.'

But the men of the Secession repelled the charges made against them that they were schismatics. In the Re-Exhibition of their Testimony they declared that the reason of their continuance in a state of separation from the Established Church was not because they held opinions with regard to doctrine, worship, discipline, or government different from those which she maintained in her subordinate standards, but because they objected to the system of maladministration which that Church was pursuing, and which they considered to be no less opposed to the Word of God than it was inconsistent with the principles of her constitution. 'Their secession is not a schism in the Church, for they never seceded from the principles and constitution professed and established at the Reformation and Revolution; but upon every occasion they have declared their steadfast adherence to these, in opposition to the prevailing party who have receded from them.' But they maintained that the Church of Scotland, since 1733, had deteriorated, and that the grounds of secession were stronger than before; in consequence, they regretted that the prospect of reunion was more remote than ever.

Subsequent events have justified their attitude and action. Yet it is the confident assertion of some writers[1] on the period

---

[1] Sir Henry Craik, *A Century of Scottish History*, vol. ii, p. 107: 'The Church was freed from a party that had been a clog upon her advance and a hindrance to her usefulness, to her dignity, to her self-respect.' William Law Mathieson, *The Awakening of Scotland*, p. 231: 'The student who extends his survey from the Establishment to the Secession will find that he has passed at a step from the eighteenth into the seventeenth century.' Henry Grey Graham, *The Social Life of Scotland in the Eighteenth Century*, p. 380: 'Dissent was not without its advantages to the Established Church. For it carried off the ill-humours of the religious body into congenial sects. If persons with such moods and temperaments had continued in the Church, they would have perpetually disturbed its quiet, and seriously hampered its progress and development.'

It may be as well to hear the other side. Thomas Carlyle (*Reminiscences*, edited by Charles Eliot Norton, vol. ii, pp. 11 ff.), writing of the early days of Edward Irving, says: 'This other fact was visible enough, if you examined: A man who awoke to the belief that he actually had a soul to be saved or lost was apt to be found among the Dissenting people, and to have given up attendance at Kirk. . . . Very venerable are those old Seceder Clergy to me, now when I look back on them. Most of the chief figures among them, in Irving's time and mine, were hoary old men. Men so like what one might call antique "Evangelists in modern vesture, and Poor Scholars and Gentlemen of Christ," I have nowhere met with in Monasteries or Churches, among Protestant or Papal Clergy, in any country of the world.' The Rev. Dr. Candlish, Edinburgh, speaking in the General that theirs was the foolish cry of 'back to the seventeenth century.' This is a strange misreading of history. For what did these men of the Secession and their followers contend? For three things in particular: for the truth and freedom of the Gospel, for liberty of choice to the people in the calling of their ministers, and for the outspreading of Christianity to the ends of the earth. The Church of Scotland was indifferent to the first, she contemptuously rejected the second, and deemed the third a matter of no concern to her. Today, which is right? Is the record of history not conclusive that every one of the principles for which Erskine and his successors fought is emblazoned on the Church's banner in Scotland, established and non-established alike? No one would dream of defending today the positions which Principal Robertson, and Carlyle of Inveresk, and others maintained as being the essentials of a Church.

The contention is laboured that ministerial appointment by a patron, and not by 'an enthusiastic but unlettered mob,'[1] contributed to the learning, the dignity, and the liberal spirit of the clergy. But the stubborn facts began to speak otherwise, and it had to be admitted that nominees too often became the mere tools of those who appointed them, and that the patron-

---

Assembly of the Free Church of Scotland, May 1852, said: 'I am bound to say that at a time when the Church of Scotland was unfaithful, when even evangelical religion was at a great disadvantage within the Establishment, at a time when scriptural truth was not very commonly to be found preached within the walls of parish churches, at a time when the liberties of Christian people were trodden underfoot by the high-handed tyrants of Presbyteries and Commissions of Assembly, backed by the bayonets and swords of the military, at a time when the whole authority of Christ in His own house was compromised, and when there was a tame truckling to Cæsar in all things —at such a time, when there was but little evangelical light in the ministry, little evangelical truth in the pulpit, and little of faithfulness and freedom either in presbyteries or congregations, they (the Secession men) fought the battle outside the Establishment, and maintained the cause of Christ. The Seceders were the men who preached the pure Gospel; the Seceders were the men who diffused the true light and the principles of the Church of Scotland.'
[1] Craik, ibid., vol. i, p. 483.

age of the Crown was frequently made a tool of political jobbery.[1] This reflected itself on the Church, and by no means contributed to its spirituality or power.

It is customary in certain quarters to make merry over the warm discussions of the Secession men in their several courts; and there is the curious episode of one conscience-burdened soul, Smyton of Kilmaurs (1782), who seriously argued as to whether the bread should or should not be lifted before the blessing of the sacramental symbols. The instance was a mere ripple on the surface of the waters. It must not be forgotten that these were men of strong convictions, who took their stand on principle, and sacrificed means, prestige, and preferment for things that were dear to them. They had to devise rules for the guidance of their Church, and men of conviction do not accept with simple stolidity or placidity what those who pose as leaders may dictate. They must and did examine, scrutinize, and canvass every proposal submitted, and determined accordingly. The very life that throbbed within them sought active expression.

But the forces in the country that rallied to the Secession proved that it was the spiritual life of the day which found expression in their assemblies. At their doors was a Church that asked nothing of its members for the erection or the maintenance of its fabrics, or the support of its ministry, or the spread of the Gospel – only a few working expenses. Here, in spite of the acknowledged poverty of the times, these men, because of their hunger for the meat which perisheth not, erected their own buildings, churches, and manses, and bore the burden, on occasion, of being tithed and taxed to erect or repair the churches and manses of the Establishment. They supported their own ministry, and maintained the whole machinery of their organization. This was not done in ill-humour and sourness of spirit. These were men of higher mould. A passion, not of earth, fired their souls. But the task made them self-reliant, tenacious, and resolute. It put iron

[1] Ibid., vol. ii, p. 109.

into their blood. In the community they became the leaders of new movements. They looked at matters for themselves; they took independent views, and were not afraid to declare them. This was unspeakable heresy in the eyes of the proud and arrogant leaders in Church and State; hence the suggestion to suppress them. But as suppression was impossible, to ignore, disown, and defame were the weapons employed. The breath of liberty, however, was too fragrant and too bracing to be affected by the contempt of the haughty. The men who felt the spell of the Master in the dissemination of His truth were indifferent to the specious values placed on position and privilege. They awoke a new spirit among the people, and were the fervent advocates of civil and religious liberty. Far from being laggards in the onward march of the nation, they were the progressive spirits that cared deeply for its moral and spiritual weal, and were leading it out of a morass of indifference and cold morality, into a spiritual freedom and independence that ultimately became its heritage.

Brown, by his pen and many-sided labours, was not a little instrumental in giving impetus to this upward movement in the nation. The betterment of the people in the highest sense was in the background of all his thoughts and supplied the quickening motive in the production of his works. When he stepped into the arena of Church courts, it was the same spirit that animated him. While intent, however, upon such a service for his fellows, and intensely loyal to his convictions and to the Church he espoused, he did not look at others and their labours through a red mist. He was conscious of defects in his own conduct in estimating the viewpoint of others; and one who has attained to such consciousness has climbed a goodly height. He can understand and appreciate the convictions of those from whom he differs. In a letter to his professorial colleague in the other branch of the Secession Church, Alexander Bruce of Whitburn, he put the controversy that had sundered their forces into its true setting:

'Our conduct on both sides of the Secession I have often thought to be like that of travellers, both walking on the same road, not far from one another, but in consequence of a thick mist suddenly coming on they cannot see one another, and can suppose the other to be off the road. After some time the darkness is removed, and they are quite surprised to find that they are both on the road, and had been all along so near one another.'

In his *Historical Account of the Secession*, Brown is eminently fair to both sides in the burgess dispute. But he urges that, in view of their agreement on so many points, they might seriously consider 'what hurt their division and vain jangling have done, and are likely to do, to the honour of Christ, the life of religion, and the souls of men.' If they would entirely lay aside their pride and prejudice, and often meet for mutual prayer and Christian conference, especially in what they agree in, they would certainly, ere it was long, consign their censuring, division, dry or almost unintelligible disputes, to everlasting oblivion, and return as brethren, to join together in the fear and service of God.[1] With the Established Church, also, from which they parted, he hoped they would ere long be able to resume fellowship, once the standards they all professed were really observed. 'They intend to unite with the established judicatures whenever they observe them reforming from the various and growing defections introduced since the Revolution.' But his Church, as it grew with the years, enlarged its vision and was called to bear further testimony to the spiritual freedom of Christ's kingdom; and only now are the happy omens gathering of the fruition of this long-deferred hope.

[1] They were united in 1820.

CHAPTER 24

The Latter Years

The wide field of theological and Biblical literature which Brown traversed enabled him to reap a harvest in many quarters, in pure divinity, Church history, Christian biography, and didactics. In one department his extensive knowledge sought little expression, where it might have exercised itself with freedom, that of translation. As a master of languages he could have submitted to English readers the choice productions of continental writers or the Fathers. But he confined himself, and more for his own perusal, to the translation of one of the smaller books of Drelincourt,[1] a French Protestant divine, some of whose works had a wide reputation in this country. It was long alleged that that masterpiece of plausibility which Defoe wrote, *The True Relation of one Mrs. Veal*, was produced to sell Drelincourt's *Consolations on the Fear of Death*, as an appendix to which it first appeared in print. But Lee, in his life of Defoe,[2] exploded that idea, and showed that Drelincourt's book was already in its third edition, and that it was to the fourth edition that Defoe's pamphlet was attached. It was *The Charitable Visits*, as the book was curiously entitled, that Brown translated. The *Visits* have reference to the presence of the Divine Helper and Comforter in the perplexities and anxieties of life. Sixty-one in all are detailed, showing that the whole circle of life in this aspect is pretty well covered by the study. The paragraphs dealing with each are brief and concise, enriched with Scripture, and illustrated by inci-

[1] Charles Drelincourt (1595-1669), born at Sedan; pastor near Paris for nearly fifty years; an incisive and spiritually minded writer.
[2] William Lee, *Life of Daniel Defoe*, vol. i, p. 127 (1869).

dents, mostly of French history or biography, that give point to the instruction. The translation is so well executed that one feels it to be a pity that Brown did not give more of his attention to this kind of work.

A subject that appeals strongly to sensitive souls in these days is the extent to which ordination vows ought to be adhered to in face of the fluid state of thought. Brown issued a brochure on the question, under the title, *Strictures on Ordination Vows*. As might be expected, he held strongly that this was a matter too serious and far-reaching in its consequences to be lightly regarded, and urged that, on their entrance to office, 'church-officers, particularly ministers, should solemnly declare their real principles and their sincere resolutions with respect to them, as well as the faithful execution of their office.' With that in view he passes through the five important questions of the formula bearing on matters of faith, doctrine, and church government, that are put to office-bearers on accepting office, and examines each with thoroughness to see what they really imply. His historical knowledge and clear insight stand him in good stead in dispelling misconceptions and securing a hearty, intelligent assent to what is required.

From Samuel Rutherford [1] he gathered a number of 'Pleasant and Practical Hints,' as he termed them, especially from the letters that were written to his congregation at Anwoth, when banished for his principles to Aberdeen (September 1636 to February 1638) and sent them forth with his imprimatur to quicken interest in spiritual things. Rutherford left a deep impression upon his country by his pre-eminent abilities and saintly character; but his works, and in particular his letters, were not available to the multitude. Brown, drinking for himself so refreshingly at this fountain, was anxious that others might quench their thirst at a spring to which so many in

---

[1] Samuel Rutherford (1600-61), minister of Anwoth, deprived of office for two years, afterwards Professor and Principal of St. Andrews University, one of the Westminster Assembly Commissioners, whose letters are accounted 'the most seraphic book in our literature.'

succeeding generations have been drawn and been more than satisfied.

The safeguarding of the Day of Rest has been an anxious problem for all who deem its claims paramount for the well-being of the nation. Incessant toil for every day that dawns lowers the vital force physically and saps the spiritual strength. To turn this day into one of manual labour is to tamper with the highest assets of the State. History repeats the warning, which, alas! is so frequently scoffed at. When the State itself submits to the demands of short-visioned minds and selfish clamour, there is need for bold utterance. At this time the question of the mail on Sundays was troubling the community. It was evidently the purpose of the Post Office to have despatches and deliveries of letters on this day as on other days. Brown took pen in hand, and, in the form of a letter to a friend in Edinburgh, he issued a pamphlet on *Free Thoughts upon the late Regulation of the Post*. He deprecated such action on the part of the State, and pleaded with his usual ardour and scriptural fulness for the effectual guarding and sane observance of a day that contributes its by no means unimportant share to the health and wealth, material and spiritual, of the individual and the nation. The force and wisdom of such contentions were in time acknowledged, and the labours in the Post Office on Sundays reduced to a minimum.

Probably the last published work of Brown was a reproduction of the story of a young life that created a stir in certain circles at the time, *The Most Remarkable Passages in the Life and Spiritual Experiences of Elizabeth Wast, a Young Woman, sometime Matron of the Trades Hospital, Edinburgh*. This was issued in 1785. His publications ended where they began, in seeking to inform and stimulate the opening mind of youth, that from earliest days, if possible, first things with it might stand first. He launched upon the sea of literature with his *Help for the Ignorant*, and, after sailing it widely, especially in Biblical latitudes, he returns with the picture of a dedicated young woman, in humble sphere, that might stand beside that of St. Teresa of Spain.

He left, however, other fruits of study and meditation which never were given to the public. Among them was a close examination of the Book of Job, which so fascinates reflective minds, and makes its own special appeal to every age. Here he laid down the sane, guiding principle that 'in attempting to understand this portion of the sacred oracle, it is absolutely necessary not only to know somewhat of the eastern flowers of rhetoric, but especially to attend to the scope of every particular speaker,' and, in compliance therewith, he proceeds to elucidate the teaching of that remarkably living book.

But not the least interesting of his unpublished manuscripts are three letters on style, or what he calls 'The right Method of Preaching,' evidently for the benefit of his students, written with perspicuity and vigour, and that remind one of Gibbon's preparation of his paragraphs, balancing sentences until they satisfied his fastidious taste.[1] He has elaborate notes on Blair's Rhetoric; but here he strikes out for himself, showing how the youth that stammered out so haltingly his apology for his acquisition of Greek became a master in the language of his country, and knew how to wield it with effect. The first letter deals with delivery. And the first point in elocution, he urges, is to observe and correct the faults of pronunciation. An over-strained voice exhausts speaker and hearer; a too low voice shows unconcern, and produces weariness in the listener. Whether the voice be weak or strong, speak on the middle key; and let every word, syllable, and letter be distinctly pronounced. To hem, haw, sneeze, yawn or cough between sentences is altogether intolerable. The unity of a sentence must be studied, parentheses avoided. 'It is common for those who deal in long sentences, as Clarendon and sometimes Temple, Shaftesbury, and Swift, to overcharge them by crowding two

---

[1] 'It has always been my practice to cast a long paragraph in a single mould, to try it by my ear, to deposit it in my memory, but to suspend the action of the pen till I had given the last polish to my work' (*The Autobiography of Edward Gibbon*).

sentences into one.' He deals with figurative style, with emphasis, and with graceful action in delivery, which ought to be easy and to vary with the subject. To acquire all this his advice is, be natural and study examples, but 'in the pulpit be wholly occupied with your subject, leaving it to nature and previously formed habits to prompt and suggest the manner'; and never must it be forgotten that such utterance is only a handmaid to introduce the great gospel truths.

In his second letter he proceeds to the language of preachers. He disapproves of wasting time in smoothing periods, giving delicate touches to definitions, or forming quaint divisions and seeking for antitheses, or straining after finical expressions. 'That is to act the cook, whose sole care is to give high seasoning to his dishes, or to present them in gilded vessels, adorned with fantastical conceits, never regarding whether their matter be unwholesome carrion or not.' Proper language is necessary: on grand subjects, strong and majestic, on subjects affecting the tender passions, tender and wooing, on common subjects plain and familiar, but never coarse or grovelling. Perspicuity and ornament are the two general properties of a good style. 'Weak writers and speakers ordinarily use a loose style, and by their superfluous words confound their readers or hearers.' Though Tillotson and Sir William Temple be perspicuous, they are not precise, but loose and diffuse in their style. And even Addison himself often falls into this fault. By his figures or circumlocutions, Shaftesbury is ordinarily far from being precise, but pours forth a great redundance of words. He agrees with Blair that, to render a sentence perfect, it must have clearness and precision, unity, strength, and harmony. To secure this, however, every word in it ought to be not only strictly answerable to the idea, but properly placed. He proceeds to deal with the characteristics of a sentence, and, turning to the choice of language, asserts that to deck out a puny thought in pompous language is no less fantastic than to deck out a pitiful moth or an ugly spider with broidered hair, or gold or pearls or costly array, or to put a jewel in a swine's snout. In all language, plain or figurative, sublimity, and beauty or sweetness are of prime importance. 'Airy bombast, in which we have a high swell of language, without sentiment, or with very puny and common thoughts, or trivial objects described as if they were grand, or grand ones in an extravagant manner,' is contrary to true sublimity of language. 'Frequently Dryden, Lee, and sometimes Shakespeare thus deal in mere fustian and rant.' Various styles are discussed, a multitude of literary examples being given from Aristotle and Cicero down to the writers of his time, with criticisms as to the style they employ. To acquire the best style, he adds, have clear ideas, compose carefully, read the best authors, no book abounding with a grandeur of language equal to the Bible; and avoid servile imitation of anyone.

In his third letter he discusses the composition of discourses. 'I would have every preacher to possess a solid and extensive acquaintance with learning, his mind dilated by an extensive knowledge of the several parts of philosophy, well instructed in the history of nature, nations and churches, and chiefly mighty in the Scriptures, even in their own original languages.' Then follow a number of judicious hints as to the production of a discourse, with the urgent reminder that the one aim is to 'instruct and persuade men to flee to the Lord Jesus Christ for salvation, fear God, and keep His commandments.'

These letters exhibit Brown's characteristic habit of 'getting to the bottom' of a subject. Though literary composition was one that might have been thought to lie outside the range of his studies, yet it concerned his work both as a writer and a professor; and that was enough to constrain him to probe it to its depths. The letters show him a literary critic of no mean order, with his own clear conceptions of what is best in style, – what should be cultivated and what avoided. The authors he cites to illustrate and enforce his views are taken from a wide field and indicate how diligently this theologian, fired with an early ambition to be a 'universal scholar,' garnered in all literature in order to achieve his lofty purpose.

But the vision left its vast sweep to focus itself on the spiritual betterment of men. Wherever that could be furthered Brown was willing to lend a helping hand. He was eager that his students, wherever they were located, should magnify their profession by their life and service. In October 1786 he addressed a letter to those in Ireland who had been under his tuition; and the whole letter, so warm in its sympathy and tender in its appeals, was ordered to be engrossed in the records of the Associate Synod:

To the Members of the Associate Synod of Ireland

'MY DEAR YOUNGER BRETHREN,

'Though I have no hopes of seeing you any more on earth, yet I continue earnestly desirous to see you, and multitudes by your means, entered on or entering into the joy of your Lord. You cannot but remember, and God is also witness, that with some measure of faithfulness, as the Lord enabled me, I exhibited and urged the great truths of God on your understanding and conscience. God forbid that any of your consciences, or companions, the seats in which you heard them, or the light in which you read them, should have to rise up in judgment against any of you, for setting at nought all my counsels, and hiding your talent in a napkin. . . . As your affectionate teacher, I leave with your consciences the Preface to and Reflections on my *System*, as a kind of last words. Notwithstanding charitable hopes I or others may entertain of your being truly gracious, and called by God to preach the Gospel of His Son, oh! give all diligence to have these points clear to your own consciences; let Matt. 7. 21, 23, Jer. 23. 32, Rom. 10. 14, 15, 1 John 1. 1, 3, be deeply impressed on your heart. . . . Brethren, can any of you think of Jesus' death, of Jehovah's love, of the striving of His Spirit, of the worth and danger of souls, of the last judgment, of an eternity in hell or heaven, and yet be careless, slothful, unfaithful, unexemplary? This, dear Pupils, is my dying word to you, wishing you all supply of grace and glory in Christ Jesus.'

A few years ago there were some keen discussions regarding the date of the founding of Young Men's Christian Associations, when their jubilee was called to be celebrated by the London Association. Scotland claimed a priority for such an organization. It is worthy of remark that the Professor of Haddington drew up *Rules for Fellowship Meetings*, which fact shows that they must have flourished in his day. An association of this kind must, in his eyes, be planted on a sure foundation, and he begins with 'the divine warrant for such meetings, and the ends they seek to serve.' Thereafter he details twelve rules for their guidance – clear, sensible rules, three of which are, that 'to avoid the frequent return of the same subjects of discourse, and in order to extend knowledge, it might be best to proceed orderly through some form of sound words, as the *Shorter* or *Larger Catechism*, or *Confession of Faith*'; 'that no member ought ever to affect a tedious length in prayer, or in answering of questions'; and 'that to render their prayers or speeches more lively and edifying, members ought by meditation and otherwise, to prepare for each meeting.' He closes his memorandum with a statement of the advantages of such meetings for religious fellowship, these being 'great and many.'

His interest in young life found expression in many ways, and not the least in correspondence. The following two letters were addressed to a young man whose health was precarious. In them the writer blends the care of the soul with that of the body. They were sent to James Pierston, a young farmer at Stonypath, near Garvald. The Pierstons were intimate friends, if not relations, of the Croumbies.

To James Pierston

'DEAR SIR,

'As I see you still look poorly, I would earnestly beseech you to make your time of trouble a time of serious consideration of your infinite need of Christ, and of His answerableness to all your needs and of His being freely offered to you in the Gospel, and a time of prayer for the effectual work of God's Spirit in your heart, in convincing you of your sinfulness and misery, and enlightening your mind in the knowledge of Christ, and renewing your will and thereby persuading and enabling you to embrace Jesus Christ as freely offered to you in the Gospel. That, to be sure, ought to be your principal care, as your soul's eternal salvation is of more value than the whole world.

As to your body, I beseech you, do not put off riding on any account. I am persuaded that, under God, the preservation of your natural life depends on it, and that all delay of it tends to fix the disease on you; and I am the more earnest with you as to this as persons in your way often through a light sense of their trouble, or a sluggish inclination to sit or lie in the house, shift off their riding till it be too late, and so rendered useless.

'Believe me that I give you both these advices in good earnest and in real friendship,

Yours affectly.,
JOHN BROWN.'

He was anxious about the welfare of this youth, especially with the ominous autumn approaching, and he wrote him again a short time after.

'DEAR FRIEND,

'As this is a most critical season for your health, I beseech you to do everything in your power, by riding when the weather permits, etc., for the preservation of what health you have, and recovery of what you have lost. Not only does the law of God peremptorily require us to use all lawful endeavours to preserve our own health and life, and holds us guilty of destroying our lives if we do not, but our life on earth is of great importance, as it is our only season of preparation for eternity, and therefore concern for our eternal welfare ought to make us as careful about our natural life and health as we can. And while God is shaking your natural constitution in the days of your youth, see that your soul be deeply concerned to receive Jesus Christ into your heart as the free gift of God. Without this there can be no solid happiness in this world, and nothing but inexpressible misery in the eternal state hereafter. This is ever an excellent mean of health (Job 33. 19-28). Please read the passage along with Lamentations 3. 22-29, and ponder both as before God in order to experience and practise them.

Yours affectly.,

JOHN BROWN.'

HADDINGTON,
September 8th, 1786.'

There are two delightful pictures of the Professor in his old age that reveal the child-love in his nature. In his house on Saturday evenings was wont to gather a company of young people for the study of the Scriptures and Christian fellowship – a Junior Christian Endeavour Society more than a century before such a thing was dreamt of! The young people were not confined to his own congregation, but were drawn also from the Established Church. From his book-lined study upstairs, the Professor would come down and mingle with his young comrades in study, illustrating this point to them, enforcing that, and gathering them all around the golden gates with him in prayer. It was typical of the spirit that animated him, and of his strong and well-grounded belief that the child held the hostages of the future.

The other picture is one presented by his fourth son, Samuel, who was only eight years of age when his father died. He carried with him the happy memory of sitting on the Professor's knee, and having his hair stroked with the feeble hands, and being called, 'My little prophet.' He has also another pleasant reminiscence of himself sitting on one knee and an older sister on the other, while the venerable parent, quitting for the moment the seclusion of his books, sang to them his favourite Latin song – the *Æquam Memento* (Remember with

[247]

tranquil mind) of Horace.[1] His great-grandson, the author of *Rab*, declared that it was murder to do an ode of Quintus Horatius Flaccus into English verse; but it may be permissible to render a part of this one into somewhat literal prose.

'Remember to keep your mind easy in hard times, and restrain it from exultation in good fortune. For, Dellius, you are sure to die, whether you live all your span in sorrow, or bless yourself with choice Falernian, lying in some grassy retreat the live-long festive day. So where the tall pine and the silver poplar interweave a hospitable shade with their boughs, and the swiftly flowing stream runs murmuring along its winding channel, bid them carry thee wines and perfumes, and the lovely blossoms of the short-lived rose, as long as your purse and your age and the mystic threads of the Sisters three permit,' etc.

It is a charming picture of the wearied and ageing Professor, sitting in the midst of his family, with his young children around him, and two of them on his knee, singing a song of one of the wittiest and gayest of Roman court-poets. From early morn he had been poring over his tomes in all languages, preparing works for the press, or developing his lectures to his students; and now he descends to enter into the children's gaiety, and delights them with his singing of an old Latin song. It reveals the human side of the learned theologian, captivating in its simplicity and tenderness.

His temperament was one that from the first was naturally serious; and his prolonged studies deepened its bias. It gave a gravity to his manners which those who were little acquainted with him mistook for severity. But, if gravity tempered his spirit, gloom found no place in its moods. Among friends he was cheerful as he was agreeable. His conversation preferred the flavour of a story with a touch of religion in it; but it was enlivened with pleasantry, and shafts of wit and raillery lit it up to the amusement and delight of his auditors.

[1] Horace, Book II, Ode III.

While he taught his children the joys of life, and would have them entertain no dull or jaundiced conception of it, he was equally alive to its higher demands and the call for the dedication of their gifts. Feeling the increasing infirmities of the years advancing upon him, and conscious that he could not surround the younger members of his family especially with his watchful counsel, he wrote a tender, affectionate message for them, which they might peruse when he departed. There were six of the younger branch of the household when he died, the eldest of whom was fourteen, and the youngest four. While commending certain books to be read, he makes most modest allusion to his own; 'perhaps,' he says, 'also my *Journal* may be useful to you.'

'MY DEAR CHILDREN,

'Believing that God hath made with me, and with my seed after me, His everlasting covenant, to be a God to me and to my seed, I did in your baptism, and often since, and now do, before God and His angels, make a solemn surrender of you all into the hands of my God, and my father's God, and of the God of your mother, and her father's God; and in the presence of that God, and as ye shall answer at His second coming, I charge you –

'1. To learn diligently the principles of our Christian and Protestant religion, from your Catechism, and Confession of Faith, but especially from your Bible. God's Word hath a light and life, a power and sweetness in it, which no other book hath, and by it your souls must be quickened and live, or you must be damned for ever; and the more closely you press the words of the Bible to your own hearts, and pray and think over them before God, you will find them the more powerful and pleasant. My soul hath found inexpressibly more sweetness and satisfaction in a single line of the Bible – nay, in two such words as these, *Thy God* and *My God*, than all the pleasures found in the things of the world, since the creation, could equal.

'2. Give yourselves to prayer. Jesus hath said, "Suffer little children to come unto Me, and forbid them not; for of such is the kingdom of heaven." "I love them that love Me; and those that seek Me early shall find Me." "Remember now thy Creator in the days of thy youth." "The Lord is good to them that seek Him." He is the hearer of prayer, and therefore to Him should all "flesh come." The Lord, "the Father of the fatherless," takes an especial pleasure in hearing the prayers of the fatherless young ones.

'When I was left destitute of a father, and soon after of a mother, the Lord dealt so with me; and though I was too bent on childish diversions, the Lord on some occasions made prayer more pleasant to me than any of them. By prayer improve the Lord as your Father, consulting Him and asking His direction in all your ways, and seeking His blessing on your learning, and on whatever you do agreeable to His will.

'3. Study earnestly to love, honour, and obey your mother, and to be a comfort to her. Much trouble hath she had in bringing you so far in the world, and much affection hath she showed you. She hath now a double charge and authority over you. The Lord now observes particularly what is done to her. Oh! for the Lord's sake, do not dishonour her, or break her heart, by your disobedience and graceless walk; otherwise the Lord's dreadful curse will light upon you, and ye will readily soon perish: for think what God hath said: Prov. 17. 25, "A foolish son is a grief to his father, and bitterness to her that bare him'; chapter 20. 20, "Whoso curseth his father or his mother, his lamp shall be put out in obscure darkness." See also Deut. 21. 18, 19; Prov. 10. 1; 13. 1; 15. 5, 20; 19. 13, 26; 28. 7, 24; 30. 17.

'4. Avoid as plagues every light, frothy, and wicked companion. Be not a disgrace to me and a cause of damnation to yourselves, by keeping company with idle talkers, swearers, drunkards, tipplers, frothy or lewd persons. Scarce anything more infallibly brings persons to misery in this world, or to hell in the next, than loose and trifling companions – Prov. 13.

20, "He that walketh with wise men shall be wise; but a companion of fools shall be destroyed"; chapter 28. 7, "Whoso keepeth the law is a wise son; but he that is a companion of riotous men shameth his father." See also Proverbs chapters 1, 2, 5, 6, 7, and 9, and 1 Cor. 5. 9, 11. Never make any your companions with whom you would not wish to appear at the judgment seat of Christ and with whom you would not wish to live for ever.

'5. Mind earnestly the infinitely important concerns of your eternal salvation. I hereby constitute the Addresses annexed to my *Shorter* and *Larger Catechisms* a part of my dying directions to you. Oh, ponder and practise them! Woe to you if, by your carelessness and wickedness, you thrust the grace of God out from among my posterity! Ah! my dear young children, shall I at the last day have to echo my *Amen* to Christ's sentence of your eternal damnation? In order to stir up your concern about eternal things, let me beseech you to read Boston's *Fourfold State*, Pearse's *Best Match*, Rutherford's *Letters*, Guyse's *Sermons to Young People*, Alleine's *Alarm*, and Baxter's *Call*; but beware of some legal directions in the last two. Read also the lives of Elizabeth Cairns, of Alexander Archibald, and especially the lives of Messrs. Thomas Halyburton, James Fraser, and James Hogg. Perhaps, also, my *Journal* may be useful to you; but above all, read the *Book of Inspiration*.

'6. Never affect conformity to the vain and vile fashions of this world. If you do, you disobey God, and hazard the ruin of your own souls – Rom. 12. 2, "Be not conformed to this world, but be ye transformed by the renewing of your mind"; James 4. 4, "Know ye not that the friendship of the world is enmity with God? whosoever therefore will be a friend of the world is the enemy of God." See also 1 Cor. 7. 31; 1 John 2. 15-17; 4. 5, 6; 5. 4, 19; John 7. 7; 15. 18, 19; Ps. 15. 4; 139. 21; 119. 53, 115, 136, 158.

'7. Never marry, nor take one step towards marriage, without much serious and solemn consultation of God, and patient waiting for His direction. By means of rash marriages was the old world defiled; and it was partly on this account that it was drowned, Gen. 6. In consequence of following these examples, Esau's posterity were cast out from the Church of God to all generations, Gen. 26. 34, 35; Judah's family was disgraced and killed, and it is to be feared that his two sons perished, Gen. 38; not only Jehoshaphat's family but even the kingdom of Judah was almost ruined, 2 Chron. 21., 22. How dreadful for your own souls, and for those of your children, if you take into your bosom an unconverted lump of wrath! For the Lord's sake let no beauty, no affability, no wealth decoy any of you into this dangerous snare, which may exclude the grace of God from your family till the end of time, 1 Cor. 7. 39; Deut. 7. 3, 4; Ezra 9. 2, 3, 12, 14.

'8. If the Lord give you families and children, bring them up for God. I have essayed to point out your duty in this respect, in my two sermons at Whitburn and Inverkeithing, which were printed; I pray you seriously to peruse these, and to comply with the advices given in the same.

'9. Set the Lord always before you as your Saviour, Witness, Master, Pattern, and future Judge. David said, Ps. 16. 8, "I have set the Lord always before me : because He is at my right hand, I shall not be moved." It is the command of God, 1 Cor. 10. 31, "Whether, therefore, ye eat or drink, or whatsoever ye do, do all to the glory of God."

'10. Adhere constantly, cordially, and honestly to the covenanted principles of the Church of Scotland, and to that testimony which hath been lifted up for them. I fear a generation is rising up which will endeavour silently to let slip these matters, as if they were ashamed to hold them fast, or even to speak of them. May the Lord forbid that any of you should ever enter into this confederacy against Jesus Christ and His cause!

'This from a dying father and minister, and a witness for Christ.

JOHN BROWN.'

Here it may be fitting to place the concluding part of the 'Short Memoir' of his life, which he penned in the eventide, when the shadows were beginning to lengthen. He is frank and fearless with himself, erring on the side of severity, with the thoughts inclined toward pessimism, which, declares Herbert Spencer, is one of the aspects of life that appears in old age. But the values he now puts on things have their interest; and the insight we obtain into his personal habits, as in reading, liberality, and conduct in public affairs, is refreshing.

'And now, after nearly forty years preaching of Christ and His great and sweet salvation, I think that if God were to renew my youth and put it entirely in my choice, whether I would be King of Britain, or be a preacher of the Gospel, with the Holy Ghost sent down from heaven, who had to beg his bread all the labouring days of the week, in order to have an opportunity of preaching on Sabbath to an assembly of sinful men, I would by His grace never hesitate a moment to take my choice. By the Gospel do men live, and in it is the life of my soul.

'When I consider what the Lord hath done for me, and what I have been doing against the Lord and His goodness, I know not whether to be most amazed at His kindness, or my rebellious treachery and ingratitude. God has been doing all He can to save, smile on, and favour me, and I have been acting to my uttermost in opposing and dishonouring Him. After all that He has done for me, I am good for nothing, neither to teach nor learn, neither to live nor die, but am both in heart and life evil, only evil, superabundantly evil, unto this very day. I am amazed to think how the Lord hath concealed my weakness and wickedness and even rendered them useful to me.

'Considering the dreadful pride of my heart, what a mercy that God, who gave me learning in so unexpensive a manner, annexed for a time such a sting of reproach to it; that my talents did not lie so properly in a quick and extensive view of

[253]

things at first (for in this I saw that I was inferior to many of my brethren) but rather in a close, persevering, and unwearied application to what I engaged in; that, notwithstanding all my eager hunting after most part of that lawful learning which is known among the sons of men, I was led generally to preach as if I had never read a book but the Bible. And the older I grew, I more and more aimed at this. An observation which I had made in the days of my youth that what touched my conscience or heart was not any airy flights or well-turned phrases, but either express scriptural expressions, or what came near to them, led me to deal much in Scripture language, or what was near it. My imagination being somewhat rank and inclined to poetic imagery when I commenced a preacher, sometimes led me into flighty thoughts or expressions. But the Lord made me ashamed of this, as a real robbing of Him in order to sacrifice to my own devilish or accursed pride. It was my mercy, too, that the Lord, who had given me some other talents, withheld from me a popular delivery, so that, though my discourses were not disrelished by the serious, as far as I heard, yet were not so agreeable to many hearers as those of my brethren. It was a pleasure to me to observe many of my brethren possessed of that talent which the Lord, to restrain my pride, had denied to me.

'When I consider how many whose parents were spared with them far longer than I had mine, and whose station in the world and means of education were far greater than mine, are in deep poverty, or, which is infinitely worse, have been left to turn out abandoned rakes, I am amazed to think by what kind and strange means the Lord hath carried through the poor young orphan till now, and taken him from following the ewes with young, and exalted him to the highest station in the Church of Christ, and by His mere grace made somewhat useful, not only in preaching and writing, but also in training up many for the ministry, whom I hope the Lord hath, or will make, far more useful in winning souls to Christ than ever I have been. Notwithstanding He left me a young orphan, without any relations on earth that were able to help me to any purpose, He carried me through to a larger stock of learning than many others who have the greatest plenty; and all this without my being obliged to be ever in debt to or dependent on any persons whatsoever. In this how plainly hath the Lord appeared as the Father of the fatherless, and the orphan's stay! This kindness of the Lord to me, as well as Ps. 68. 5, and 146. 9, and Jer. 49. 11, encourageth me to leave my present young family on Him without the least anxious care or fear. I cannot leave them many pence poorer than I was left myself; and though I would wish that God would render them more holy and useful in the world, I dare not wish them more easy, or more honourable, or wealthy, than God hath graciously made me.

'My vain curiosity hath led me into not a little useless reading to the mis-spending of much precious time. But even by this the Lord hath taught me what a mercy it was that when I had not a director in the choice of books, nor money to purchase the best, He hath led me into an acquaintance with the most useful ones, and did not permit me to take up with such as were erroneous or profane. From experience I have found that it is vain to attempt to be an universal scholar; that a few books, well chosen and carefully used, are better than a multitude of books; that multitudes of books are scarcely worth the reading, or, if read, one had better extract the useful hints into a notebook, and never more look into the books; that abridging of more useful books, especially if they be large, is very useful; that few plays or romances are safely read, as they tickle the imagination and are apt to infect with their defilement; and even those that are most pure, as of Young, Thomson, Addison, Richardson, bewitch the soul, and are apt to indispose for holy meditation, and other religious exercises, and so should be read at most very sparingly. In reading histories, the Lord often not only made me to take up the facts as the doing of the Lord, and as verifications of some part of His Word, but also made the stories to suggest some useful and sometimes very sweet thoughts respecting the redemption scheme.

'Notwithstanding my minding earthly things, the Lord so managed my wicked heart that it has rather been my care to husband well what He provided for me than to attempt a greedy catching of what did not come of its own accord, and notwithstanding my eager desire of books I chose rather to want them and much more other things than run into debt. Notwithstanding I had but 40 pounds of stipend for a considerable number of years, and then 45, and at last 50 in one of the dearest places of the country, the Lord gave me such contentment with it as made my lot preferable to some who had the double or near to it. It was also my mercy that my wives were averse to unnecessary wastefulness and cheerfully ready to add the interest of their money for the helping out of the stipend. When I was the first introducer of the administration of the Lord's Supper twice in the year, I reckoned it a providential favour that I then had no more than 20 shillings allowed me for extraordinary expenses on such occasions, which being the case no one could pretend that I pushed that more frequent administration of the ordinance in order to enrich myself. By such means the Lord hath so managed my heart that today I think none can say that they ever heard me complain of a small stipend, and I may add that we have never been in debt or in straits as some who had much more income. I have been helped to live as one that would gladly spend and be spent for my people, and aimed at seeking not theirs but them; yet not I, but the grace of God did all.

'My congregation's belief of this, I believe, not only disposed them to regard me, but even readily to concur with me in countenancing the erection of other congregations within our original bounds, while some other congregations, perhaps double our strength, opposed as for life any such thing within their bounds. By this means I have now, in my old age, the pleasure of seeing the Gospel fixed at Dunbar, North Berwick, and Tranent, all which places were in my original bounds, and

I hope and heartily wish with more success than by me. This pleasure I would not lose for I know not how large an advancement of my stipend. And yet, to the Lord's honour as well as that of my people, I have never lost a farthing by these disjunctions. I have always looked upon it as a great and hurtful blemish in ministers, especially Seceders, to appear greedy of gain, as if they wanted to serve not the Lord Jesus, but their own belly, or purse.

'I have also thought it a remarkable management of my mind by the Lord that, though I often grudged paying of a penny or two for a useless letter, I could have cheerfully bestowed as many or more pounds for promoting a pious purpose. For this end I for many years laid aside a certain part of my income when I got it; but when our family grew numerous, my wife could scarce attend to keeping two different purses. I think that having a different purse for the Lord is very proper in many cases. And from experience I can testify that liberality to the Lord is one of the most effectual means of making one rich. I have sometimes disposed more this way than it could be thought I was capable of, and yet I never found myself poorer against the year's end. Nay, when I think on matters, I wonder that my wealth, instead of being diminished, is not a little increased. There "is that scattereth and yet increaseth; and there is that withholdeth more than is meet, but it tendeth to poverty."

'I lament that I have been so deficient in effectual fervent prayer for my flock and for the Church of God; and that my discourses in conversation in my family or with others have not been more spiritual. My sense of my weakness and unskilfulness in pushing religious discourses made me keep company so little. And when at any time I was in company without something serious, it was painful for me to reflect on it. It was on this account, as well as because I thought feasting improper on such occasions, that I much disrelished all feasting at ordinations of ministers, at baptisms, or on Mondays after the Lord's Supper as little else than an ordinance of the devil,

I

calculated to erase every serious impression which had been made by the ordinance. I had little better opinion of making the dry disputes or curiosities of religion, the subject of conversation, especially on the Lord's Day.

'I lament that though I pretty often attended the Society meetings for prayer and spiritual conference, yet I did not do it more, especially after my settlement in the congregation. I am persuaded that ministers' encouraging of such meetings to the utmost of their power, and their catechizing and exhorting of children, after their settlement, are some of the best means they can use for promoting the welfare of souls. On things of this nature, I would wish all ministers' zeal and care were chiefly spent.

'In publick things I have been rather inclined to act up to my own views than to push others into a conformity to me. I had little relish for making ecclesiastical rules without great harmony. I had found no small difficulty to fix my sentiments on some things. This made me averse to urge my opinions on others unless where I had plain Scripture to support them. I laid it down as a rule, never to be very zealous in favour of anything in which my own self-interest or honour was in any respect concerned. I found it was dangerous in the lawful defence of self not to go too far. My sense of the forwardness of my temper, and that several of my brethren saw more quickly or further into a cause than I did, restrained me from obstinacy of judgment. My knowledge of the miserable effects of clerical contentions in the Christian Church, and my strong inclination to peace, I believe, sometimes led me to undue yielding or silence.'

Here the old yellow document ends, ten lines down from the top of the first half of the last page. It may have been his intention to add more; but there it stops. He usually crowds every inch of space, but the hand may have grown weary, or the heart may have dreaded the self-laudation that might follow. And so, thus abruptly, the 'Short Memoir' closes. It is all contained in eleven double-columned pages of seven inches by six, and a few lines. It reveals in its quaint simplicity his many struggles and shortcomings, and his strong opinions and convictions. Were it all that he had left behind him, posterity would never have known of the masterful spirit he possessed, or the vast professorial and literary work he executed, or the wide influence he wielded. But modesty ever drew down its thick folds when he began to dilate upon himself.

CHAPTER 25

Farewell Words and Table Talk

The intense, crowded life was now beginning to tell on the robust and sturdy frame. Up to the close of the year 1786, Brown's forceful and energetic spirit carried him through all his varied work with few signs of the advancement of the years. But for some time dyspepsia had begun to declare itself, and it became more acute as the months passed. In the beginning of 1787, it showed some of its worst symptoms. He was now in his sixty-fifth year, and the physical vigour could not combat illness with the ease with which it was wont to surmount it. His friends saw with regret that his health was not equal to the burden of work he manfully carried, and urged him to desist from part, at least, of his public service. But he answered with alacrity, 'I am determined to hold to the Church's work as long as I can. How can a dying man spend his last breath better than in preaching Christ?' To wear out was possible; to rust out was unthinkable.

It was early in this year, when he found himself not equal to his former tasks, that he penned his last letter to the Countess of Huntingdon, with whom by correspondence he had often held high counsel.

To the Countess of Huntingdon

'If I never write to you more, be these my last words. There is none like Christ, none like Christ, none like Christ; nothing like redemption through His blood, even the forgiveness of sins, according to the riches of His grace. There is no learning nor knowledge like the knowledge of Christ; no life like Christ living in the heart by faith; no work like the service, the spiritual service of Christ; no reward like the free-grace wages of Christ; no riches nor wealth like the unsearchable riches of Christ; no rest, no comfort, like the rest, the consolations of Christ; no pleasure like the pleasure of fellowship with Christ. Little as I know of Christ – and it is my dreadful sin and shame that I know so little of Him – I would not exchange the learning of one hour's fellowship with Christ for all the liberal learning in ten thousand Universities, during ten thousand ages, even though angels were to be my teachers. Nor would I exchange the pleasure my soul hath found in a word or two about Christ, as *thy* God, *my* God, for all the cried-up pleasures of creation since the world began. For what, then, would I exchange the being for ever with Christ, to behold His glory, to see God in Him as He is, and enter into the joy of my Lord?'

On February 25th, 1787, he occupied his pulpit for the last time, conducting services three times that day. In the morning he preached from Luke 2. 26, 'It was revealed unto him by the Holy Ghost, that he should not see death, before he had seen the Lord Christ.' He seemed to be conscious that he was addressing his flock, drawn from miles around, for the last time, and he bade them an affectionate farewell. In the afternoon he again addressed them, after the strain of the morning. In the evening his audience was largely composed of those residing in Haddington, principally members and adherents of the Established Church. As he climbed the pulpit for the third time he was scarcely able to support himself, but with more than usual earnestness he delivered his message, his last sermon, from Acts 13. 26, 'To you is the word of this salvation sent.' In a manner that touched all hearts, he again referred to his presence in the pulpit as never likely to be repeated, and bade an affectionate adieu to those who had so diligently waited on his ministry. It was a Sunday long remembered in Haddington.

But, withdrawn from the pulpit, he yearned over his flock. They were much in his thoughts during these latter weeks, and he poured out his heart in the following communication to them, throbbing with a yearning for their highest good. It was found among his papers after he had passed away.

'MY DEAR HEARERS.

'Having through the patience and mercy of God, long laboured among you, not as I ought, far, far from it, but as I could, I must now leave you, to appear before the judgment seat of Christ to give an account of my stewardship. You cannot say that I ever appeared to covet any man's silver or gold, or apparel, or ever uttered one murmur about what you gave me; or that I sought yours, not you. You cannot charge me with idling away my devoted time in vain chat, either with you or others, or with spending it in worldly business, reading of plays, romances, or the like. If I had, what an awful appearance should I soon have before my all-seeing Judge! You cannot pretend that I spared either body or mind in the service of your souls, or that I put you off with airy conceits of man's wisdom, or anything else than the truths of God. Though I was not ashamed, as I thought Providence called me, to give you hints of the truths presently injured, and for the support of which is the declared end of the Secession, yet I laboured chiefly to show and inculcate upon your consciences the most important truths concerning your sinfulness and misery, and the way of salvation from both through Christ, and laboured to hunt you out of your lying refuges, and give your consciences no rest but in Christ and Him crucified. The delight of my soul was to commend Him and His free and great salvation to your souls, and to direct and encourage you to receive and walk in Him. I call heaven and earth to record against you this day, that I laboured to set life and death, blessing and cursing, before you, and to persuade you to choose life that ye might live. By the grace of God, I have endeavoured, however poorly, to live holily, justly, and unblameably among you. And now I leave all these discourses, exhortations, instructions, and examples, as a testimony for the Lord against you, if you lay not your eternal salvation to heart, as the *one thing needful*, the better *part* which shall *never be taken from you*.

'But I have no confidence in any of these things before God as my Judge. I see such weakness, such deficiency, such unfaithfulness, such imprudence, such unfervency, and unconcern, such selfishness, in all that I have done as a minister or a Christian, as richly deserves the deepest damnation of hell. I have no hope of eternal happiness but in Jesus' blood, which *cleanseth from all sin*, in redemption through His blood, even the forgiveness of my sins, *according to the riches of His grace*. It is the everlasting covenant of God's free grace, well ordered in all things and sure, that is *all my salvation and all my desire*.

'Now I die firmly persuaded [of the truth] of those things which I preached unto you. I never preached unto you any other way of salvation than I essayed to use for myself. I now, when dying, set to my seal that God is true. After all that I have said of the sinfulness of your hearts, I have not represented to you the ten-thousandth part of their vileness and guilt. Knowing, in some measure, the terrors of the Lord, I endeavoured to persuade you that it was a fearful thing to fall into the hands of His wrath. But who knoweth the power of His wrath? Knowing, in some measure, the deceitfulness of sin, and the devices of Satan, I laboured to warn you of them. But what especially delighted my heart was, to set before you the excellencies, the love, the labours of our Redeemer, and God in Him, giving Himself, and applying Himself to sinful men; and to represent to you the work of God on the heart in the day of His power, and the exercise of the heart in its diversified frames. What I saw, and tasted, and handled, both of the bitter and the sweet in religion, declared I unto you. Little as I am acquainted with the Lord, I will leave it as my dying testimony, that there *is none like Christ, there is nothing like fellowship with Christ*. I dare aver before God, angels, and men that I would not exchange the pleasures of religion

[263]

which I have enjoyed, especially in the days of my youth, for all the pleasures, profits, and honours of this world, since the creation till the present moment, ten thousand times told. For what, then, would I ever exchange my entrance into the joy of a being for ever with my Lord? Truly God hath been good to a soul that but poorly sought Him. Oh! what would He be to yours, if you would earnestly seek Him! With what heart-ravishing power and grace He hath testified against my wicked and unbelieving heart, that He is God, even my God! And whom have I in heaven but Him? nor is there any on earth whom I desire besides Him. My heart and flesh fail, but God is the strength of my heart and my portion for ever. Left early by both father and mother, God hath taken me up, and been the orphan's stay. He hath given me the heritage of them that fear Him. The lines have fallen to me in pleasant places. I have a goodly heritage. The Lord is the portion of mine inheritance and of my cup; He maintaineth my lot: Yea, mine own God is he, my God that doth me save.

'Had I ten thousand worlds in my offer, and these secured to me for ever, they should be utterly contemned. "Doubtless I count all things but loss for the excellency of the knowledge of Christ Jesus my Lord; and I do count them but dung to win him, and be found in Him, not having mine own righteousness, which is of the law, but the righteousness of God which is through faith."

'Now, when I go to give my account to God, think what it must be! Alas! must it be that, in too great conformity to your careless neighbours, some did not attend the means of grace at examinations, in meetings for prayer and spiritual conference, as ye ought? Must it be that, after labouring so many years among you, I left less lively religion in the congregation than I found in it at first? Must it be that ye were called, but you made light of the marriage with Christ, and of His great salvation? Must it be that ye contented yourselves with a form of godliness, without knowing the power of it? Must it be that some few, trampling on their most solemn engagements, forsook me, having loved this present world? Must it be that others were not careful to train up their seed for the Lord? Must it be, that ye often heard the most searching sermons, or the most delightful, and went away quite unaffected? Or must it be that you were awakened, that your souls looked to Jesus and were enlightened; that ye believed with your heart unto salvation; that ye harrowed in the seed of the truth, which I sowed among you, by serious meditation and fervent prayer; that ye laboured to win souls to Christ? Alas! I fear many of you will go down to hell with a lie in your hand, with all the gospel sermons and exhortations you ever heard in your conscience, to assist it to upbraid, gnaw, and torment you! My dearly beloved hearers, shall I see you next in everlasting fire prepared for the devil and his angels? Shall I see those faces all in flames at the last day, and those eyes, which often looked at me, looking lively bright horror at the judgment-seat of Christ? Must I hear the Redeemer bid you depart from Him as cursed, into the everlasting fire, prepared for the devil and his angels? And must I, who have so often prayed for your salvation, and preached for your salvation, add my hearty AMEN to the sentence of your eternal damnation? God forbid!

'Let me then beseech you, now, without a moment's delay, to consider your ways. Listen to the Lord's invitations! Believe His self-giving declarations and promises, which, times without number, have, with some measure of earnestness, been sounded in your ears. For the Lord's sake, dare not, at your infinite peril, to see me again in your sins, and refusers of my glorious Redeemer and Master! Oh! give Him your hearts, give Him your hearts! I never complained of you giving me too little. Nay, I thought myself happier than most of my brethren as to all outward matters. But I always thought and complained that you did not use my Master Christ as I wished in your hearts, lives, and houses. And now I ask nothing for myself, or any of my family, but make this my only dying request to you, that you would now receive my Master Christ into your hearts and houses. Could my soul speak back to you from the eternal state, could all my rotting bones and sinews, and every atom of my body, speak back to you from the grave, they should all cry, "Oh that you were wise, that you understood this, that you would consider your latter end!" Oh that you would give my Master, Christ, these ignorant, guilty, polluted, and enslaved hearts of yours, that He, as made of God unto you wisdom, righteousness, sanctification, and redemption, might enter in and fill them for evermore with His grace and truth! Oh, say not to a dying, a dead minister, but to a living Redeemer, and His Father, and blessed Spirit, NAY.

'Dearly beloved, whom I wish to be my joy and crown in the day of the Lord, suffer me to speak from the dead to you. Let me obtest you, by all your inexpressible sinfulness and misery, by all the perfections, words and works of God, by all the excellencies, offices, relations, labours, sufferings, glory, and fulness of Christ, by all the joys of heaven and horrors of hell, now to make serious work of the eternal salvation of your souls. Try what improvement you have made of all my ministrations. Call to mind what of my texts, sermons, or other instructions you can; and pray them over before the Lord, applying them closely to your own conscience and heart. Wash yourselves thoroughly in the blood of Jesus Christ from all the sins of holy things since you and I met together.

'I recommend to you, young persons, my two addresses annexed to my *Catechisms*; and to you, parents and masters, my address in the *Awakening Call*, and my sermons on *Raising up Children to Christ*, as a part of my dying words to you. They will rise up in judgment against you, if you contemn them.

'With respect to your obtaining another minister, let me beseech you, by much fervent prayer, get him first from the Lord. And let it be your care to call one whose sermons you find to touch your consciences. May the Lord preserve you from such as aim chiefly to tickle your fancy, and seek themselves rather than Jesus Christ the Lord! Let there be no strife among you in calling him. And when you get him, labour at his entrance to receive his message from Christ with great greediness. Let your vacancy make you hungry and thirsty for the Gospel. And let all hands and hearts be intent on raising up a seed for Christ in poor withered and wicked East Lothian.

'Oh! how it would delight my soul to be informed, in the manner of the eternal state, that Christ had come along with my successor, conquering and to conquer! How gladly should I see you and him by hundreds at the right hand of Christ at the great day, though I should scarcely have my ten! Oh, if Christ were so exalted, so remembered among you, as to make me scarcely thought of! I desire to decrease, that He may increase.

' "Now unto Him that loved us, and washed us from our sins in His own blood, and hath given us everlasting consolation and good hope through grace, be honour and glory, dominion and blessing, for ever and ever.

' "This is a faithful saying, and worthy of all acceptation, that Christ Jesus came into the world to save sinners, of whom I am chief."

'Your once affectionate pastor,   JOHN BROWN.'

In the five months that intervened before his end, the restraint that Brown placed on any personal expression of spiritual feeling seemed to be removed. Like John Woolman in his last illness, he 'uttered many lovely and comfortable expressions.' Says an acknowledged authority in letters as in imperial affairs, 'We want to know how a master man talked, and, if possible, what he thought; what was his standpoint with regard to the graver issues of life, what he was in the hours of ease, what he enjoyed, how he unbent.' We have had glimpses of what the master man of Haddington was in his hours of ease, and how he unbent. He enjoyed nothing so much as hours in his library among his books. It is now, thanks to his son, Ebenezer, that we hear him converse, and especially on the deeper matters of life.

Ever since the Abernethy calumny, Brown was very sparing in references to himself. Now and again he did unbend, as once, well remembered by his students, when urging them not to be satisfied with a mere speculative acquaintance with the truths in the 'System of Doctrine,' or a storing of them in their memories, but to have them engraven on their hearts by the Spirit of God, he said: 'I recollect that, when sitting on the braes of Abernethy, hearing Mr. Wilson of Perth [one of the Secession Four], I got more insight into the marrow of the Gospel, "thy God" and "my God," than I ever got before or since. Alas! that it was so long ago!' That he lived among faith's high altitudes was the ready conviction of all with whom he came in contact. It was characteristic of him to say, as he walked with a friend, and a loud clap of thunder rolled overhead, 'That is the low whisper of my God.' His difficulties, as it has been said, were not so much of an intellectual as of a spiritual nature. His attainments in personal holiness were far short of his ideal. When he stood before the Love that redeemed him, the intensity of its white light seemed to darken the shadow cast by his many shortcomings. In preaching, while never failing to exhibit the charm and the joy and the glory of the Christian calling, he often depicted with a strong, severe hand the blackness and the horribleness of whatever sin touched. He was wittingly or unwittingly interpreting himself. And now that life's battle was practically fought, he was more communicative regarding his own inner life, and unbosomed himself in a way that left a deep impression. His son, Ebenezer, the minister of Inverkeithing, was frequently by his side during these months; and he noted down much of the table talk that fell from his lips. It is illuminative and striking, though often it flashes a description of the speaker himself that makes one start and shudder. He speaks with a freedom on topics that many today might deem too sacred to be uttered. This, which may seem strange to us, was quite characteristic of the times when the veil was uplifted on the inner life.

On March 2nd, the week after he had laid down the pulpit

service, a friend remarked to him that with care he might yet recover; in a moment came the answer, 'If Christ be magnified, whether in my life or death, this is the great matter.'[1]

On the day following, when the reading of history was discussed, the old historian enunciated his principle in studying the records of the past.

'Often we read history as Atheists or Deists, rather than as Christians. To read of events without observing the hand of God in them, is to read as Atheists; to read and not observe how all events conduce to carry on the work of redemption, is to read as Deists.'

He mused on the theme; and in the evening he referred again to the subject.

'A piece of history hath sometimes amused me when my natural spirits were low; but now I find no pleasure except in meditating on the promises. I wish to begin with that in Genesis, "The seed of the woman shall bruise the head of the serpent," and to delight myself with it, and all the rest that follow, to the end of the Revelation of John.'

The learning accumulated with so much zest in his life-time seemed to obtain another adjustment when the burden of the grasshopper was felt, and the eye peered into the other world. Brown, reviewing the past, affirmed:

'If there were such a thing as exchange of learning I should willingly quit with all my acquaintance with languages, and other branches of knowledge, to know experimentally what that meaneth, "I am crucified with Christ; nevertheless I live; yet not I, but Christ liveth in me; and the life which I now live in the flesh, I live by the faith of the Son of God, who loved me, and gave Himself for me."'

[1] A fuller record of his talk is given in the Appendix.

[269]

As he talked with his sons, John and Ebenezer, who like himself served in the ministry, the one at Whitburn, the other at Inverkeithing, he was consumed with an eagerness for their devotion to their calling. More than once in these closing months he reverted to this, and to the delight and joy he himself had had in the ministerial career – except these bonds.

'No doubt I have met with trials as well as others; yet so kind hath God been to me, that I think, if God were to give me as many years as I have already lived in the world, I would not desire one single circumstance in my lot changed – except I wish I had less sin.' 'Labour, labour for Christ while ye have strength,' was his passionate entreaty. 'I now repent that I have been so lazy and so slothful in His service. Oh! commend Jesus. I have been looking at Him for these many years, and never yet could find a fault in Him, but what was of my own making; although He hath seen ten thousand faults in me. Many a comely person I have seen, but none so comely as Christ; many a kind friend I have had, but none like Christ in loving-kindness and tender mercies.'

Speaking about sermons, he alleged:

'So far as ever I observed God's dealings with my soul, the flights of preachers sometimes entertained me; but it was Scripture expressions which did penetrate my heart, and that in a way peculiar to themselves.'

His sons left him for a week or so. While they were away, he wrote to John at Whitburn the following interesting letter:

To Rev. John Brown, Whitburn

'When I get an opportunity, I have some thoughts of making a trial of the medicine which you mention, though my hopes of being better by it are not very high. My life and health seem now to pass like a declining shadow; nor dare I repine at the

[270]

matter. God hath, in some measure, satisfied me with old age; I would therefore be longing to see His salvation. I observe several things relative to my family, which urge my carnal heart to wish continuance; but my death can make no vacancy in my family, and far less in the Church, which Jesus cannot easily fill up. What I desire is, to have the presence of God in my trouble, and to be enabled to act for His glory. I can hardly bear the thought of being consigned to be a useless weight on this earth. But I must not quarrel at His disposal; He cannot but do right; nor would I wish to attempt making straight what He has made crooked. Redemption through His blood, even the forgiveness of sins, according to the riches of His grace, is what I ever desire to enjoy; and I wish to leave the circumstances of my departing to His high sovereign will. If grace reign through Jesus' righteousness to eternal life to me and mine, I ask no more. I believe I shall never be perfectly well till I be with the Lamb in the midst of the throne. In the meantime, I earnestly desire to die as a wax-taper, sending forth a sweet smell of Him whose garments smell of myrrh, and aloes, and cassia '

On their return on March 20th, his sons found him physically weaker, the memory not so tenacious, but the vision as keen, and the judgment on things sharp as ever. 'Men may talk of the sovereignty of redeeming love as they will; but had it not been sovereign, infinitely sovereign, I had been as surely lost as if I were in hell already. How these words, "He loved me, and gave Himself for me," once penetrated my heart and made me cry, "Bless the Lord, O my soul, and let all that is within me be stirred up to bless His holy name."'

The various incidents of his daily life were a continuous source of searching and exhilarating remarks – it might be the morning when he awoke, the washing of his face, the breakfast with which he was served, or the meals of the day, the carriage exercise in which he participated, the converse of friends – they were all to him avenues to the incomparable riches of grace. 'Wonderful, wonderful subject, grace,' as he once exclaimed, at an afternoon repast. 'Wonderful, wonderful means, by which it vents the righteousness of Christ! and wonderful, wonderful issue, eternal life.'

He was grateful for all the attention bestowed upon him by his wife and children and expressed his appreciation of it in warm terms, but it was only an avenue to a higher domain. 'Yet I must go back to this, "Whom have I in heaven but Thee? and there is none upon earth I desire beside Thee."' One of his younger children, Peggy, who three years later followed him to his rest, slipped into his room to inquire as to his welfare. Drawing her near him, he laid his hands upon her head, 'Now my little dear, mind to pray to God; your father must soon leave you, but cry unto Jesus, "Thou art my Father and the guide of my youth"; and then, though you will not have a room like this to come and see your father in, you will be taken to a far better Father's room.' The anguish of parting with his children was soothed by the recollection of his own early days, and the guiding hand that had been upon him. As he said to another of his younger children, 'I do not think that I was much older than you, when God caused me to claim Him; and God hath been good to me.' The dark sorrows that had marked his journey, he acknowledged, had not been without their rich compensation. 'I think the early death of my father and mother, the death of a wife and of children, in a remarkable manner wrought for my good. I could not but notice, that when God took away these, He always supplied their room with Himself.'

The vicissitudes of his career indeed tested the Word on which he planted his hopes, and on which he wrote so extensively. Passages of it seemed to embody his very experiences, like the ninety-first psalm with its dark outlines fringed with gold of promise. 'I know a man to whom almost every line of that psalm has been sweet. I think if ever God touched my heart, He went through that psalm with me.' But life to him was enriched and gladdened above all with the treasures of his Master, Christ. 'Oh! What must Christ be in Himself, when He sweetens heaven, sweetens Scriptures, sweetens ordinances, sweetens earth, and even sweetens trials. What must that Christ be in Himself!'

We have here access to the inner springs that were so long concealed from outer gaze. It was a period of patient waiting that for the first time in that crowded existence enabled others to see whence emanated the energy that never paused, and the confidence that never wavered. These months when the pen ceased and the voice in public was silent were not without their recompense: 'They also serve who only stand and wait.'

CHAPTER 26

The Close

Brown's increasing weakness told its tale on some of his faculties, but the inner soul glowed with a brighter flame. Daily, if the weather showed no drooping or weeping skies, he took carriage exercise. It revived him; and the tokens of bursting spring spoke their gladdening message of higher things to an observer long accustomed to see nature sparkling with spiritual emblems. His church was close by, in which he had ministered for thirty-six years; but to attend the services now was becoming too exhausting for his enfeebled frame. Once he passed within its portals on a week-day and looked round, and his heart filled with emotion as the fragrant memories of hours spent there rushed back upon him. 'Weak as I am, I would try to preach yet, if I had none to preach in my stead. Oh! what sweet fellowship with Christ I have had here! That pulpit hath been to me the best place in all this house.'

In the meadow adjoining the church behind the manse, he was often wont to stroll. As he paced it now slowly with his sons, he would call attention to places where visions divine broke upon his soul, and made the spots to him as hallowed ground.

'On certain occasions my soul hath been so transported here that, as the Apostle speaks, "whether I was in the body, or out of the body, I could scarcely tell." Perhaps it is superstitious in me, but I confess I have a peculiar love for these very spots."

The book-lined study that used to enthrall him from early morn to the latest hours seemed to lose its charm, and he seldom crossed its threshold. 'You never go in there now,' said his son to him as they passed the door. 'No; the closet I wish now is the place of God's immediate presence. There the face of God will serve me instead of all my books.' Regarding the numerous works he himself produced out of that study, some of which were to pass into many editions, a friend advised him to grant an assignation of his rights for the good of his family.

'No, no; I would not wish that ever there should be the least appearance of the world in me. I can trust my family to Providence; and if, when I am in heaven, it appear that there was one converted by means of anything I ever wrote, I will mark down a hundred pounds; if there should be two, I will say there are two hundred pounds; and, if twenty, there is something of more value than two thousand pounds. That is the reward which I wish.'

The astonishing memory he possessed and so assiduously cultivated began to lock its doors, and sometimes he faltered through lack of its help. But the other life, he was convinced, would quickly repair the loss. 'Were I once in heaven, a look of Christ will cure my broken memory, and all my other weaknesses.'

While memory might fail, the spirit was all alive. The simplest occasions flashed out starting thoughts. The fire was being stirred and its bright glow lit up the room.

'Oh! to have my heart stirred and set in an eternal flame of love to that dear Son of God, of whom I think I can say, "He loved me and gave Himself for me"; and I am sure, in point of worthlessness, He might as well have loved Beelzebub himself.'

He amazed his son one day by saying – it may have been occasioned by some unfortunate bankrupt in Haddington being pilloried in public, as was the case with monetary defaulters in those days:

'I confess I should not like to stand at our town cross with a paper on my breast, declaring that I was a bankrupt to men; but I think I would love to stand in the most public place in heaven having all the redeemed pointing to me as the greatest sinner that ever was saved; yea, I think their very staring at me, as the chief debtor to free grace, would rejoice my heart.'

In the beginning of April, his eldest son returned to his charge at Whitburn, and he wrote him the following letter:

To Rev. John Brown, Whitburn

'I am at present in a weak and languishing condition; but as it is the doing of the Lord I desire to be resigned, and would gladly be content, whether death or recovery be the issue. Indeed, the desire of my heart is that, if it be His will, I should depart and be with Christ, which is far better than being in this sinful world. But it would be improper for me to set up my ignorant and corrupt will as a rule to the Most High. I wish to be at entire and cordial resignation to His will, who hath so graciously performed all things for me. Let Him recover or let Him kill me, as is most for His glory; I know that it shall be in infinite love to my soul. I desire to take all kindly from His hand; and I hope that He will sweeten all with believing views of His everlasting love to me. To leave a multitude of kind relations, hearers, and neighbours on earth is an easy matter, in order to depart and to be with Jesus for ever. When I write, perhaps, my last letter to you, I would commend Him who is white and ruddy, the chiefest among ten thousand and altogether lovely. Rather, oh that the Holy Ghost would enable you and your children to come and see Him! I am sure that is a pleasant and enriching sight. May never one of you get rest in your minds, till you obtain such a blessed discovery! I give it, perhaps as my last words to you and your children, that there is none like Christ, there is none like Christ, there is none like Christ.'

Thy Synod of his Church was convened to meet in Edinburgh on May 1st that year. For twenty years he had sat at the clerk's table, and witnessed and shared in many exciting debates, when sometimes the calm of deliberation was broken by the storm of passionate discussion. The advent of the Synod was always eagerly anticipated; but it suggested to him now another general assembly – that of the first-born for which he yearned. 'No idle words, no angry speeches, no sinful ignorances, no haughty pride there. But, after all, it is a great mercy that Jesus, the great manager of the Church, can overrule even our contentions here for His own glory.'

The approaching Divinity Session, however, was giving him some concern. His place at the clerk's table could easily be filled by another member; but his post as Professor could not be so speedily arranged for. He was doubtful if his health would permit of his discharge of the manifold duties of the chair in the autumn; and he requested his son, John, who was Moderator of his Church that year, to represent his circumstances to the Synod. The letter he sent him contains his request and shows the trend of his thoughts, and the slackening of time's bonds upon him.

To the Rev. John Brown, Whitburn

'My weakness still continues; nor, indeed, is my mind anxious about this, but a Christ-glorifying death, and a being for ever with the Lord. My concern, too, is that all my relations should have my place on earth delightfully supplied by the knowledge, care, and fellowship of Jesus Christ, even Him whom, notwithstanding all my present and now long-continued carelessness and wickedness, I still hold to be Jesus Christ, my Lord. Oh! could my soul enter into the full meaning of these words as I wish! But I hope that I shall be allowed this attainment by and by. Already my poor soul, in a manner hovering between time and eternity, cries, NONE LIKE CHRIST! AND NONE BUT CHRIST FOR ME! And may I and all my relations and friends be His henceforth and for ever! It is no small comfort to have my relations on earth so kind and agreeable to me; but my superlative desire, I think, is to be with Jesus

[277]

and His ransomed millions above. That such a sinner, and originally such a mean sinner, should be so kindly treated by so many brethren and friends, doth and may amaze me. But oh how sweetly doth Jesus and His Spirit exceed them all! Now I in some sweet measure feel and see that there is no friendship like that of Father, Son, and Holy Ghost.

'This week my bodily appetite is no better; but little matter if God would enable me to drink up a river of His redeeming blood, and to feed full on Jesus' flesh – on all the fulness of God.

'At the meeting of the Synod let my weakness be represented to them; and if they judge that it has disqualified me for teaching the students, I heartily agree to be laid aside from this work, and that one more fit should be chosen. It is Jesus Christ whom I wish to be exalted; and the best means for saving sinners, I wish to take place.

'I hope the brethren will take care to supply my congregation with sermon, as want of this would sink my spirits. I have been but a dry tree myself among them; and oh! it would rejoice my heart to hear of Jesus' power being felt, and His glory seen, by the ministry of my brethren helping me! I do not wish to be a burden to them; and if Providence bring me back to any measure of strength, I shall inform the supplier. The longer I live, I see myself the less worthy of being regarded by anybody.

'Wishing all the blessings of time and eternity on your family, and that the Lord may render you and your brother, and all my pupils more faithful, diligent, and successful in the ministry, than I have been,

'I remain yours, etc.'

His son, John, as retiring Moderator, preached the opening sermon of the Synod, when it met in Bristo Church, Edinburgh, on May 1st, choosing as his text Prov. 11. 30, 'He that winneth souls is wise.' He intimated to the court that his father's enfeebled health prevented him attending the Synod meetings, and the Rev. David Greig, Lochgelly, Fife, was appointed to take his place at the clerk's table. He also indicated his father's desire that some one should be appointed to take charge of the students at the coming session, as he was afraid his health would not be equal to the strain. The Rev. George Lawson,[1] Selkirk, one of Brown's former students, was appointed to undertake this duty. The Synod not only sympathetically acceded to their old Professor's requests, but also provided supply for his pulpit, authorizing the Presbytery of Dunfermline to preach to his congregation in the month of May, the Presbytery of Kelso during June, the Presbytery of Edinburgh during July, and the Presbytery of Glasgow during August, thus arranging for the occupancy of his pulpit up to the next meeting of Synod.[2] It was a touching expression of the Church's esteem for his devoted labours; but their thoughtful kindness in making provision was not required so long as they anticipated.

During May his health did not seem to improve, but sufficient strength availed to enjoy carriage exercise. 'How strange that I, a cottager's son, should have a chaise to ride in; but oh! how much more strange that I should have a "chariot of salvation to ride in!" ' One day they said, 'You cannot go out today because of the rain.' 'Oh,' said he, 'if God would but send His new covenant chariot, Death, to carry me hence before the end of the day, I would not mind the weather, whatever it might be.'

Toward the end of the month his sons, who had been with him after the Synod Session, returned to their charges for a few days. They had been, before assistance was provided by the Synod, supplying his pulpit occasionally; and he was wishful that they might return and continue their help, which was so welcome, though the Presbyteries appointed were doing their duty. He wrote to Ebenezer as follows, the last letter, most likely, he ever penned:

[1] Rev. G. Lawson, D.D., was appointed his successor in the Professoriate, and the Divinity Hall was removed to Selkirk.
[2] Minutes of the Associate Synod, vol. iv, pp. 2038 ff.

'I am, and have been since you went away, much as when you saw me. Still weak, but desiring to wait for the salvation of God, which, I know, will make me strong in due time; His afflicting hand lies very mercifully on me. How pleasantly His glorifying hand, in a short time, will lie on me, I with humility wish to know, as soon as it is for His glory, and my own and others' good. Oh! study early fellowship with Christ! It is sweet in days of trouble to look back to this.

'I hope you will not grudge to preach for me another Sabbath; and may that sweet Jesus Christ and His Spirit give you and me many days of fellowship with them, which I am sure and glad they can give us. My allowed inclination is to serve the Lord on earth, or to praise Him in heaven, as He thinks most for His honour, for a time; though, saving His will, I would cheerfully prefer the latter. Oh! to be with Christ in heaven appears to me a double, triple heaven for such a sinner! This, with my kind compliments to all my brethren about you.

'Yours affectionately, etc.'

The sons returned in the beginning of June. The 4th of June was the birthday of the King, George III. The bells rang out a merry peal. He inquired what it meant. 'Oh! when will that glorious solemnity arrive, when all the artillery of heaven shall be let off! that day of Jesus, when angels and the saints shall join in a general shout to His honour.' Some time after, as the bells continued to ring, He said, 'Blessed be God that we have a better King's birthday to celebrate, "Unto us a child is born, in the city of David, a Saviour who is Christ the Lord." On account of that event, the Gospel bells have been sounding for ages past, and they will ring louder and louder still.'

Someone asked him whether he did not think he should feel a stranger when he got into the world of spirits. 'No,' said he, 'I am sure that everybody there will be ready to treat me well for Christ's sake.' It had been his frequent practice to travel in the leafy month of June to Stow for communion services. A friend remarked, 'You are not journeying thither this year.' 'No,' he answered, 'I wish to be travelling to God, as my exceeding joy.' Within three days his wish was realized; the royal chariot he had longed for was awaiting him. On the morning of June 19th, his increasing feebleness rendered the voice weak. On an appeal being addressed to him the answer showed the ambit of his thoughts, 'The Lord hath His own way of carrying on His work.'

The last words he uttered were the summation of his life: 'MY CHRIST.'

After four hours the silence that is unbroken reigned. On Tuesday, June 19th, 1787, he passed to his rest, in the sixty-sixth year of his age, the thirty-sixth of his ministry, and the twentieth of his professorship. On the following Saturday, amid crowds of mourners from the town and district, all that was mortal was laid to rest in the churchyard of Haddington. A simple tombstone in obelisk form was erected to mark the spot where he lies, on which is inscribed the following record:

TO

THE MEMORY

OF

MR. JOHN BROWN

36 YEARS MINISTER OF THE GOSPEL AT HADDINGTON, AND 20 YEARS PROFESSOR OF DIVINITY UNDER THE ASSOCIATE SYNOD. AFTER MAINTAINING AN EMINENT CHARACTER FOR PIETY, CHARITY, LEARNING AND DILIGENCE, HE DIED, REJOICING IN HOPE OF THE GLORY OF GOD, AND ADMIRING THE RICHES OF DIVINE GRACE TO HIM AS A SINNER, THE 19TH DAY OF JUNE, 1787, AGED 65 YEARS

Beneath are recorded the deaths of Janet Thomson, his first wife, who died May 10th, 1771, aged 38 years, and Violet

Croumbie, his second wife, who died March 21st, 1822, aged 77 years, and the words, 'They rest among the blessed dead who die in the Lord.'

On the Sunday following his death, the Rev. John Henderson, Dunbar, preached the funeral sermon in the church at Haddington; and in many pulpits throughout the country, especially where men ministered who had been under his own tuition, tributes were paid to the memory of one who, though so inadequately equipped at the outset, became a master in learning and in particular in the Scriptures. His own Church at its first Synod meeting after his death recorded its high appreciation of his character and worth:

'The Synod,' it chronicled, 'unanimously agreed to take this opportunity of testifying their respect to the memory of the Rev. John Brown, their late Professor, whose eminent piety, fervent zeal, extensive charity, and unwearied diligence in promoting the interests of religion, will be long remembered by this court, especially by those members of it who had the happiness of studying divinity under his inspection.'

The record is the more striking that such appreciations were exceedingly rare incidents in the Church procedure of those days.

The utterances of these later weeks reveal the spring of his varied activities, and the irresistible call he felt to utilize the moments and the gifts he possessed for the highest purposes. The age in which he lived had cross-currents running strongly. Many of these in Brown's opinion were not conducive to real progress; and he was not alone in this contention. Many were deeply concerned as to the manifest sapping of the nation's strength by the vices and frivolity of the period, and the laxity in the Church that prevailed. Brown valiantly contributed his share in arresting the threatening decay, and vitalizing the religious forces of the country. His views were neither narrow nor superficial, though always intensely held. From the days when he began to master languages by searching into their basal formations, he delighted to probe down to root causes. What he wrote accordingly was the expression of a full mind charged with deep conviction. His life and labours planted against the background of his century—a century that is remarkable both by its bias for the past and by its eagerness to advance—reveal a man of consecrated spirit, intellectual vigour, and boundless energy, who spared not himself in the service of his fellows. If genius be the art of taking pains, he had it in abundance. Knowledge, sacred knowledge in especial, beckoned him on with its tempting light; and he followed with great zest, noting every step with minute care. The heights to which he rose in its pursuit, have in the onward march of the generations been left behind; but he bravely prepared the way for others to follow. He opened up the Scriptures to vast multitudes, and gave an impetus to learning that is felt through his descendants to this hour.

> So when a good man dies,
> For years beyond his ken,
> The light he leaves behind him lies
> Upon the paths of men.

APPENDIX

A RECORD OF THE LAST SAYINGS
OF JOHN BROWN

After Sunday, February 25th, 1787, he was unable to preach. His son, the Rev. Ebenezer Brown, noted some of his utterances, in those latter months. It may be felt, as his grandson says, that he spoke in a 'hyperbolical' way, especially when he referred to sin, and to himself. It was, however, no affectation on his part, but a vivid, overwhelming sense of the divine glory and the divine goodness, such as led another and a greater to regard himself as the chief of sinners.

March 4th. – An acquaintance said to him it was pleasant to see Hervey[1] insisting so much on grace reigning through righteousness. 'Yes,' he replied, 'that is the doctrine which is good to live with, and good to die with.'

On the Sunday, he was able to attend church. On returning he remarked, 'What a happy life might a Christian have, if he were always persuaded of the love of God which is in Christ Jesus our Lord!'

In the evening he was asked if he felt better, and calmly came the reply: 'I am no worse; but I do not wish to have a will in that matter; only I would not desire to live, and yet not be able for Christ's work; though, perhaps, were God so ordering it, He would enable me to bear that too.'

March 6th. – He called the two eldest of his sons, John and Ebenezer, into his room. They were returning to their homes, Whitburn and Inverkeithing, and he urged them to undertake

---

James Hervey, 1714-58, author of *Meditations and Contemplations* (1746), *Theron and Aspasio* (1755), etc. His works were at one time in great repute.

their work 'with both hands earnestly.' 'No doubt, I have met with trials as well as others; yet so kind hath God been to me, that I think, if God were to give me as many years as I have already lived in the world, I would not desire one single circumstance changed, except that I wish I had less sin.'

The sons returned in a fortnight. On March 20th, Ebenezer noted that greater weakness had set in. The memory was impaired, but not the judgment; and he conversed as if earthly things were left behind.

'I have often wondered at the favour which men have shown to me, but much more at the favour of God to such a grievous sinner.'

'Oh! to be with God, to "see him as He is, to know Him even as I am known"; it is worthy, not merely of going for, but of dying for, to see a smiling God.'

'About the year—, God said to my soul, "I have loved thee with an everlasting love"; and how faithful hath He been to that since!'

'There would not have been more grace shown in the redemption of the chief of devils than in saving me; the same price would have ransomed them, the same strivings would have overcome them.'

'Men may talk of the sovereignty of redeeming love as they will; but had it not been sovereign, infinitely sovereign, I had as surely been lost as if I were condemned already.'

'Were it not that God foresaw our sins and provocations from eternity, He never could have continued His love to me, the grievous sinner, the arrant rebel; yet I think He is now preparing me for being ever with Himself. Oh! what is that! I have done all that lies in my power to condemn myself, and though I will not say that God hath done all that He could to save me, yet I am sure He hath done a great deal.'

'If angels and men knew the raging enmity of my heart, what would they think of redeeming love, which hath pitched on me!'

'What a miracle to see me, the arrant rebel, sitting on the

throne with Jesus! And I hope I shall be seen there. What cannot Jesus do!'

'How these words. "He loved me and gave Himself for me," once penetrated into my heart, and made me cry, "Bless the Lord, O my soul, and let all that is within me be stirred up to bless His holy name!"'

A friend asking him if he had any appetite for his supper, he replied, 'Yes! O for as good an appetite for the fulness of God as I have for earthly victuals.'

One remarked to him that, under all his weakness, his mind seemed very composed. 'Indeed I am composed; God hath put a bridle in my mouth; and though I have been a most perverse wretch, yet He hath strangely restrained me; and how amazing! He hath done this chiefly by loving-kindnesses and tender mercies; and is not that a strange bridle for such an imp of hell as I have been?'

'I cannot say that I have found God's words and eaten them; but truly His words have found me, and have been given me, and have been to me the joy and rejoicing of my heart.'

'That is a sweet little sentence, 'We shall be for ever with the Lord." How sweet, FOR EVER with the Lord! And that which makes the wonder is this, that it is WE that are to enjoy this happiness; WE pitiful wretches are to be for ever with God our Saviour – God in our nature!'

'How amazing the mystery of redemption, in which those who richly deserved death are exalted to the throne of God, and that by the blood of our Lord Jesus Christ!'

'Oh! to be brought to this point –

"Then will I to God's altar go,
    To God MY chiefest joy:
Yea, God MY God, Thy name to praise
    My harp I will employ." '

'I desire to depart and to be with Christ, which is far better; and though I have lived sixty years very comfortably in this world, yet I would gladly turn my back on you all, to be with

Christ. I am sure Christ may say of me, "These sixty years this wretch hath grieved Me." '

March 21st. – In the evening he fell asleep communing with his Master; in the morning he was still with Him, and his first words were: 'Oh! it is pleasant to enjoy fellowship with Christ. Any small acquaintance I have had of Him convinceth me of this. And, how much more pleasure might I have had had it not been for my own folly and wickedness; I think that I could now willingly die to see HIM, who is "white and ruddy, the chiefest among ten thousand." '

When at breakfast, he turned to his two sons in the ministry and addressed them with peculiar earnestness. 'Oh! labour, labour for Christ while ye have strength. I now repent that I have been so lazy and so slothful in His service. Oh! commend Jesus. I have been looking at Him for these many years, and never yet could find a fault in Him but what was of my own making; though he hath seen ten thousand, thousand faults in me. Many a comely person I have seen, but none so comely as Christ; many a kind friend I have had, but none like Christ in loving-kindnesses and tender mercies.'

A little later the old spirit with which he was wont to plead with his students seemed to awaken within him, and he appealed to them again with unwonted emphasis. 'I know not whether I shall ever see you together again or not; but oh! labour, labour to win souls to Christ; there is none like Christ, there is none like Christ, there is none like Christ! I am sure a poor worthless wretch He hath had of me; but a precious Christ I have had of Him. Never grudge either purse or person for Christ; I can say this, I never was a loser by any time spent, or by any money given for Him.'

'Oh! the pains which God hath been at to save me, and the pains which I have been at to destroy myself! But He hath partly gained, and I hope that He will completely gain the victory.'

On returning from a carriage exercise, he remarked as he crossed the threshold of his house, 'Reading tires me, walking tires me; but were I once with Jesus, fellowship with Him will never tire me. "So shall we be ever with the Lord."'

In the afternoon he lay down to rest; on awaking he was asked how he was. 'I am no worse; I am just a monument of mercy, and that is a great deal for such a sinner, especially when I add, that I am hoping for "redemption through Christ's blood, even the forgiveness of my sins, according to the riches of His grace."'

'I was young when left by my parents, yet their instructions, accompanied with God's dealings, made such impressions on my heart as I hope will continue with me to all eternity. I have served many masters, but none so kind as Christ; I have dealt with many honest men, but no creditor like Christ; and had I ten thousand bodies, they should all be employed in labouring for His honour.'

Two or three friends were sitting around him, and their conversation led him to speak of himself as a debtor to grace. 'Now, sirs, I have sinned longer, and in more aggravated forms than any of you; but what sins cannot the blood of Christ wash out! What cannot mercy forgive! "The Lord passed by, and proclaimed His name, The Lord, the Lord God, merciful and gracious, long-suffering and abundant in goodness and truth." How astonishing that the Spirit of God should enter into our vile hearts, contrary to our strivings! Even so it seemeth good in His sight! Let praise flow, for ever flow!'

March 22nd. – He had no sooner sat down to breakfast than, like a person enrapt, he broke into the following lines, repeating them thrice, changing the original words, *they* and *them*, into *we* and *us*.

> We with the fatness of Thy house
> Shall be well satisfied;
> From rivers of Thy pleasure Thou
> Wilt drink to us provide.

Then he added, 'How strange that "rivers of pleasure" should be provided for the murderers of God's Son, and the contemners of His Word!'

One of his sons remarked that he seemed to be quite in-different about things mundane. 'Indeed, I am so; only I wish you, my sons, my friends, my congregation, the Church, and all the world, so far as is consistent with the decree of God, were with Christ. From all other things my mind is weaned; yet if the influence of God's Spirit were to be withdrawn for a moment, oh how horribly my heart would blaspheme!'

To a youth of his flock, the son of a loyal member, he tenderly said, 'Well, mind these words, "Thou art my God, I will prepare Thee an habitation; my father's God, I will exalt Thee." We should reckon him a madman who would throw away a father's estate, but he is much more foolish who throws away a father's God.'

The day, he was told, was cold, and a drive would be better postponed. 'Oh to win to the everlasting day of fellowship with Christ! Then we shall reflect with pleasure on all our cold and sorrowful days here.'

Washing his face in water made him exclaim, 'Oh to be washed in the water of life.' It was remarked that he looked better than he did. 'It may be,' he replied; then, with a smile, 'However, when I am conformed to the image of Christ, I shall look far better still.'

Finding he required assistance to step into the carriage waiting to take him for an outing, he turned to his helpers and bade them see the propriety of the advice: 'Let not the wise man glory in his wisdom, neither let the mighty man glory in his might, let not the rich man glory in his riches; but let him that glorieth glory in this, that he understandeth and knoweth Me, that I am the Lord which exercise loving-kindness, judgment, and righteousness in the earth.'

When he returned, he was asked how he was, 'Well, well, for such a sinner.'

To another who inquired if he felt himself any stronger he replied, 'I cannot say that I am, but I am just as well as my heart could wish, if I were but free of sin.'

When a third acquaintance asked a similar question, he

K

answered, 'I am well; for it is with body and soul as it pleaseth God; and what pleaseth Him, as a new-covenant God, I desire to say pleaseth me too.' When he returned, a saying of Dr. Evans[1] was read showing his resignation to the rod. 'Well, that is just what I would have to be at too. What kindness has God heaped upon me since the year—! What kind strugglings! What kind smilings! What kind overlookings of my outrageous wickedness! He hath shown Himself to be God, and not man, in His dealings with me.

'In my mad attempts He hath often stopped me; my mad wishes He hath refused to grant; and my mad words He hath often seemed to overlook.'

He was asked if he remembered preaching on the text, Psalm 73. 22, 'So foolish was I, and ignorant; I was as a beast before Thee.' He replied, 'Yes, I remember it very well; and I remember, too, that when I described the beast, I drew the picture from my own heart. But oh! amazing consideration, "Nevertheless, I am continually with Thee; Thou hast holden me by my right hand!"'

In the evening, when a friend proposed to assist him to undress, he said, 'Very well; I would not wish to be a man of strife on the borders of eternity, and especially when I am sure that the redeeming God is mine own, as that there is an eternity.'

March 23*rd*.—Reference was made to another sermon, Isaiah 46. 4, 'Even to your old age, I am He'—one of the sermons, he tells us in his *Memoir*, he delighted in preaching. He remembered well discoursing on it, and added, with a lit-up countenance, 'I must say, that I never yet found God to break His word in this; no, notwithstanding all the provocations which I have given Him.'

He was walking in the meadow adjoining the manse; the wind was boisterous, and he encountered it with difficulty. He turned to his companion and said, 'I find I am but weak, but—

---

[1] John Evans, D.D. (1680-1730), minister first among the Independents, later of the Presbyterian Church, at Wrexham and London, author of *Practical Discourses regarding the Christian Temper*.

> "Soon may the storms of trouble beat
> The house of bondage down,
> And let the prisoner fly." '

From his afternoon's rest he awoke with the words, 'What a wonder that I have not slept into eternal life! Rather, what a wonder if I should thus sweetly sleep into eternal life!'

When he sat down to tea, he could not refrain from discoursing on spiritual things. 'God is love; there is no enmity in Him at all.' 'There are three things which are very sweet – the sovereignty, the freeness, and the fulness of divine grace.'

An acquaintance asked him if he really wished to recover. 'I rather wonder that I have so much health and strength as I have. Many of my fellow-sinners, and many less sinners than I, are now roaring in the place of torment, without any hopes of deliverance, while my body is easy, and my heart in some measure filled with His praise. The strength which I now wish is strength "to walk up and down in the name of the Lord."'

March 24th. – At breakfast, he looked round on his household and said, 'Oh, sirs! when shall I take the last Christian meal with you? I am not weary of your company, nor have I any cause; but I would fain be at that, "I will go to God's altar, even unto God, my exceeding joy."'

He was told that his eldest son, John, had gone home to Whitburn. How happy, he remarked, he should be, if the time of his departure into the eternal world was come. 'About the year—, these words were sweet to my soul, "There remaineth a rest for the people of Good."' 'Are you not willing to live and preach Christ?' he was asked. 'I would love to preach Christ, if I live; but, as to my life, I have no will in that matter. I wish to have my inclinations subordinate to the will of God.'

A friend told him that the Gospel was spreading in the Church of England. 'Oh! well, well may it spread. The Gospel is the source of my comfort, and every sinner is as welcome to this source as I. And, how pleasant, that neither great sins nor great troubles do alter these consolations! These words were once impressed upon my heart, "Where sin abounded, grace did much more abound." How it delighted me to see God taking advantage of my great sinfulness, to show His great grace!' Oh! the sovereignty of God! I think that He hath used more means to bring down the enmity and rebellion of my heart, than He hath used for a hundred beside.'

On receiving a glass of wine, he said, 'How astonishing that God's Son should get gall and vinegar to drink when His thirst was great, and yet that I should have such wine, when my thirst is by no means excessive!' On another occasion, when being similarly refreshed, he remarked, 'I long to drink of the new wine in my Father's kingdom, which will neither hurt head nor heart. Oh! that I had all the world around me, that I might tell them of Christ!'

A friend reminded him that, through his instrumentality as a teacher of divinity, over a hundred ministers were engaged in preaching Christ. 'Had I ten thousand tongues, and ten thousand hearts, and were I employing them all in commendation of Christ, I could not do for His honour as He hath deserved, considering His kindness to such a sinner.'

When at tea, he expressed his gratitude to those about him: 'I am much obliged to you all, and [turning to his wife] particularly to you for your kindness to me; yet I must go back to this, "Whom have I in heaven but Thee? and there is none upon earth that I desire beside Thee." '

' "He hateth putting away" – I am sure I have found that; for, oh! the provocations which I have given to God to cast me off; and yet to this day He crowneth me with loving-kindness! How astonishing the necessity of the love of the Son of God! Once I thought that I got a ravishing sight of the necessity of His loving me, the sinner. He said, "Other sheep I have; them also I *must* bring." '

'Oh! His kindness, His kindness! I have shared of His frowns, as well as of His smiles; little frowns in comparison of what I deserved. Yet, even when I abused these frowns, as well as His smiles, He hath overcome me with tender mercies.'

To some who asked him if he was any worse, he answered,

'I am weak, but I am well, considering that I am such a sinner. I may say, "Goodness and mercy have followed me all the days of my life"; and I hope to "dwell in the house of the Lord for ever."'

Someone speaking to him about his supper, he exclaimed, 'Oh! to be there, where they "hunger no more, neither thirst any more; but are filled with the fatness of God's house!"'

To one of his younger children he affectionately said, 'Now cry to God, "Thou art my Father." I do not think that I was much older than you when God caused me to claim Him; and oh! God hath been good to me! It is long since He said, "Leave thy fatherless children; I will preserve them alive, and let thy widows trust in Me." As I know not but I am dying of this distress, I have essayed to cast you on the Lord; see that you cast yourself on Him.'

March 25th. – 'Long ago I thought to have known by experience what is meant by "dying in the Lord"; that is a lesson, however, which I have not yet learned, but I will not quit hopes of learning it still.'

'These words were once sweet to my soul, "I am less than the least of His mercies." I thought that I was not worthy of the smallest favour, yet I aimed to apprehend the greatest gift. Oh! amazing scheme, redemption! Amazing contrivance of it by God the Father! Amazing work of the Son purchasing it! Amazing application of it by the Holy Ghost! And amazing possession of it by men!'

'It is now many years since God put me into the state that I could not totally apostatize from Him; though no thanks to me, for I have done my utmost against Him, and yet He hath held me. I know not if there ever was a sinner such a perverse wretch as I.'

March 26th. – Being asked how he had slept, he replied in his usual fashion. 'Good rest for such a sinner.' The friend said, 'You know that He giveth His beloved sleep.' 'It is true, but sure, God hath no cause to love me.'

'Long ago Jehovah silenced me with this, "Is there anything

too hard for the Lord?" and to this day I have never found out the thing, though perhaps I have resisted His Spirit more than ever a sinner did.'

'I wish to be at that point, "He hath put to me the everlasting covenant ordered in all things and sure; for this is all my salvation, and all my desire."'

'I am entirely at the Lord's will,' he remarked to a friend, who answered him, 'Such resignation is not the attainment of every Christian.' 'This is rather,' he humbly said, 'what I would be at, than what I have attained.'

Speaking about the students of divinity who had been under his charge, he remarked, 'I wish them all more serious and diligent than ever I have been. I hope, however, that God will not cast me off as a slothful and wicked servant. I am sure that He "hateth putting away."'

A friend said to him, 'It is an unspeakable mercy that God does not deal with us according to our works,' to which he replied, 'Ah! if God were to deal with men that way – I will not except the Apostle Paul – the hottest place in hell would be the lot of us ministers.'

'My mind is now so wavering, that I have little remembrance of what is past, little apprehension of what is present, and little foresight of what is future. But, oh! what a mercy, that when once the everlasting arms of Jesus are underneath, He will not lose His hold. "Israel shall be saved in the Lord with an everlasting salvation!"'

'Here is a wonder – a sinner saved by the blood of God's own Son! There are wonders in heaven, and wonders on the earth; but the least part of redemption work is more wonderful than them all.'

March 27th. – Some of his family expressed wishes for his recovery. 'I wish that God may do what is most for His glory, and for the good of my soul. Were it left to me whether I would choose life or death, I would not turn a straw for either, but would refer it wholly to God Himself. All my days I have been rebelling against and vexing His Holy Spirit, yet I may say this has been the sum of His conduct toward me, "He wrought for His name's sake, that it should not be polluted."'

'Oh! how God hath exemplified that law in His conduct toward me, "If thine enemy hunger, feed him; if he thirst, give him drink"; and in so doing I hope He hath heaped hot, melting coals of fire upon my head!'

One of his brother ministers called to see him. He was grateful for the visit, but it made him wish that of a Greater. 'Now, I am obliged to you for your kindness; but entreat Christ to pay me a visit. I do you no wrong when I say, that I would not give half an hour's visit of Christ for days, months, or years of yours.'

'Anything that I know about religion is this, that I have found weakness and wickedness about myself; and grace, mercy, and loveliness about Jesus.'

A friend remarked to him that we must run deeper and deeper in debt to divine grace. 'Yes,' he replied, 'and God is a good creditor; He never seeks back the principal sum, and indeed puts up with a poor annual-rent.'

As a few friends dined with him, he broke out with these words. 'Well, sirs, may we all at last meet at the table above, and enjoy a feast there; no pain, no complaining, no trouble there, but there is everlasting peace and joy.'

It was Tuesday of the week, but he thought it was Saturday. He was asked, Did he long for the Sabbath? 'I do,' he said, 'weary for the Sabbath; and I would fain be wearying for the everlasting Sabbath. Then I shall have no need of the assistance of preachers; nor will I even need the blessed Bible itself. God's face will serve me for preachers and Bible too.'

March 28*th.* – 'Oh that is a strange text, "God so loved the world, that He gave His only-begotten Son, that whosoever believeth in Him should not perish, but have everlasting life." This declaration would set all our hearts on fire, if they were not infernally frozen; and, indeed, closely applied by the Holy Ghost, it would set them on fire, even though infernally frozen. He once applied it with such power to my soul, that I think the application would have inflamed the heart of a devil, had it been so spoken to him.'

In conversation with his sons in the ministry, he again besought them for a whole-hearted consecration to their work. 'Oh! labour, labour to win souls to Christ. I will say this for your encouragement, that when the Lord led me out to be most earnest in this way, He poured most comfort into my own heart, so that He gave my reward in my bosom; and when I have tried to help vacancies, He hath repaid me well with glimpses of His glory. Were the Lord to make me young again, I think I would study to devise other means for gaining souls than those which I have used, and prosecute them with more activity than ever I did.'

An acquaintance inquiring about his welfare, 'I am but weak, but it is delightful to find oneself weak in the everlasting arms. Oh! how much do I owe my Lord!'

'What a mercy that once within the covenant, there is no getting out of it again! Now I find my faculties much impaired.' 'No,' said his friends, 'it is only your memory that is at fault.' 'Well,' he said, 'how marvellous that God hath continued my judgment, considering how much I have abused it; and continued my hope of eternal life, though I have misimproved it! "But where sin hath reigned unto death, grace hath reigned through righteousness unto eternal life by Christ Jesus our Lord."

'My memory is much failed, but, were death once over, I will remember God's heaping of mercies on me, and my multiplied provocations of Him; and when I view the first on one side, and the last on the other, on a new covenant footing—I will sing thanksgiving to God for ever.'

One alleged that, if he was not happy hereafter, many had reason to be afraid. 'I have no other ground to be happy than what is by redemption through the blood of Christ, and that is suited to you as well as to me.'

An interesting conversation took place as to his eagerness to depart and the anxiety of those around him that he might recover. It was urged that he might yet serve the Church, and feed his flock and be a father to his household. It seemed as if these things concerned him not, and that he had no desire to continue with them, and cared not what befell his family or the Church. Did it not seem selfishness on his part to wish to be rid of this life and go hence? 'I own,' he acknowledged, 'I do sway to one side; for I "desire to depart and be with Christ, which is far better," and you selfishly wish me to live with you. Indeed it may be selfishness with us both. I confess it may be selfishness in me to wish to be with Christ; but oh! that God had never seen any other selfishness in me than that!'

'Oh! to have all our troubles sanctified to us! and then, when in the other world, we will with pleasure look back and see, that "through fire and water He brought us to the wealthy place."'

One of his children said to him, 'Father, we would fain have you live.' 'Well,' he answered, 'I believe so; but I would fain be with Christ.' 'But,' said the little voice, 'would you not wish to take us with you?' 'It is not I,' he gently said, 'but Christ who must do that. However, as to my departure, I will not set the time of it to God; He is wise, and I am a fool.'

In 1764, he had been seriously ill, and said then that he wished to be gone. He was reminded what service he had rendered to multitudes since then. 'How strange that God should make use of one so sinful as I to do good to others; but I believe that He was wiser than I; and I shall see this more clearly when in the eternal state.'

Ralph Erskine's poem, 'The Work and Contention of Heaven,'[1] which had had great vogue at that time and retained

[1] In Ralph Erskine's poem the contention was what rank of all the ransomed race owed 'highest praise to sovereign grace.' The children so early on 'the happy shore,' the saint of years, the sinner above many, the sufferer, and various others are depicted as contending for the honour. At last it is agreed that all should 'praise upon the highest key,' and

> Their discord makes them all unite
> In raptures most divinely sweet;
> So great the song, so grave the base,
> Melodious music fills the place.

its popularity for half a century longer, was read to him. 'Well, though I should never wish to see contention in the Church on earth, yet I should be willing to join in Ralph's contention above. Were I once in heaven I think that I would contend with the best of them; and I know that our contention there will not raise heats, but excite love to one another.'

On receiving a glass of wine, he with a smile said to his friends, 'Now, sirs, I wish you all new wine in the kingdom of our Father at last, and new wine from the kingdom of our Father while you are on the way to it.'

At supper, with his usual cheerfulness, he repeated the lines:

> They with the fatness of Thy house
> Shall be well satisfied, etc.

and then added, 'If earth transformed, partly by the instrumentality of men, is so delicious, oh! what must the fatness of God's house be, the flesh and blood of the Son of God!'

March 29th. – Among the first words he uttered this morning were 'What a rebellious child I have been to God! and what a kind Father He has been to me! I need not go farther than myself to see that "God is love," for even in my trouble He treats me as a mother doth her sucking child.'

A friend took occasion to say, 'I suppose you make not your labours for the good of the Church the ground of your comfort?' At once he replied with earnestness, 'No, no, no! it is the finished righteousness of Christ which is the only foundation of my hope. I have no more dependence on my labours than on my sins. I rather reckon it a wonder of mercy that God took any of my labours off my hand. "Righteousness belongeth unto Him, but unto me shame and confusion of face."'

Walking through the house, with the sun streaming in upon his face, he, in an elated mood, repeated the lines of the 89th Psalm:

> ' "In brightness of Thy face, O Lord,
> They ever on shall go.
> They in Thy name shall all the day
> Rejoice exceedingly;
> And in Thy righteousness shall they
> Exalted be on high."

Oh that will be sweet, when the redeemed of the Lord shall walk thus in heaven'; and then, with tears in his eyes, added, 'And I am sure that I may think shame to appear among them; but the more shame and disgrace I deserve, the more glory God will get. Oh, what strange things God hath done to save me! By afflictions in my own body, by the deaths of my parents, by bringing me to ordinances, by reproofs of conscience, He hath striven with me for my salvation.

Behind the manse was the meadow from which a little distance off was visible the church[1] of the other branch of the Secession, of which Robert Chalmers,[2] who hailed from Dennyloanhead, Stirlingshire, was minister. Brown, looking at the church of his young brother, could not forbear expressing his vital interest in the good of souls while discounting his own efforts. 'I would be happy if my Anti-burgher brother had ten [souls] for my one, as crowns of joy at the last day, though I must say that I would wish to have as many as possible; but oh! it will be a strange honour for such a wretch as I to have half a dozen.'

March 30th. – To one who inquired about his welfare, he answered, 'I sit here an instance of human frailty, and, I would fain add, an amazing instance of God's kindness in redemption.'

In his hearing some persons were discussing an ill bargain, when he broke in, 'How happy to have an interest in Christ! That is a bargain which will never break; and by that we, though naturally heirs of hell, are entitled to eternal life.'

Often he said, 'I find that I am not strong; but oh! it is a wonder that I am not damned! I bless God that I know at least this much about religion – I am convinced that I am as a beast before God.'

[1] The church was discontinued for public worship in 1880, and the building is now used as a public reading-room and library.
[2] Robert Chalmers's two daughters were married, the one to Dr. M'Crie, the biographer of 'John Knox' (second wife), and the other to his son, Professor M'Crie, of the English Presbyterian Theological College, London. In this church Samuel Smiles was baptized and brought up (*The Autobiography of Samuel Smiles*, p. 8).

March 31*st*. – 'I remember that, about the year—' I was breathing out slaughter against the Lord Jesus; but that was always the turn of the tale, "Yet I obtained mercy." If I were offered the crown of Britain, instead of the fellowship with Christ which I then enjoyed, I would not hesitate a moment about choosing the latter.'

'The debt of grace is a strange kind of debt. Were I even now two or three hundred pounds in debt to any man, it would considerably distress me; but the views of my debt to free grace remarkably refresh my heart.'

April 1*st*. – 'Were I once in heaven, a look of Christ will cure my broken memory, and all my other weaknesses. There I shall not need wine nor spirits to recruit me; no, nor shall I mind them, but as Christ was through them kind to me.'

April 3*rd*. — Sitting down in the meadow behind the manse, the sun shining in his face, he cried out in a kind of transport, 'Oh! how pleasant to be for ever beholding the Sun of Righteousness in heaven! and how pleasant, even in time, to see Him by faith!'

One of his brethren in the ministry called upon him, and in course of conversation declared, 'We cannot well do without you.' 'Oh yes,' said the old Professor, 'you can easily want me, and I would wish to be with Jesus. Meantime, I am wholly at the Lord's disposal. If the Lord would make me useful in the Church, I have no objections against living; but if not, I would rather die.' His friend asserted that the Lord had been very kind to him. 'Yes,' he said, 'God hath been heaping favours upon me, the sinner, these forty years past; and I will say, to His honour, that He hath made my days of affliction always the happiest. Indeed, I think that I have seldom had very sweet days, except when I have met with affliction one way or another.' He then asked him if he felt no uneasiness at leaving his family and congregation. 'I cannot say that I feel any such uneasiness; not but that I regard them, but I know that God in Christ can infinitely more than supply my room. I might be spared, and be of little use to them; but God

[300]

will be infinitely useful. My parents were taken from me when I was young, and God has been far better to me since than they could have been.' 'What think you,' said the friend, 'of the present state of the Church?' 'The Church is at present in a very poor condition; but the Lord can revive her. I have often found that when wicked lusts and wicked devils have caused great disorder in my heart, the Lord hath brought order out of confusion. This partly encourages me to believe that, though wicked men and wicked devils cause disorder in the Church, yet the Lord will make all things to work together for good to His own elect. I do not expect to see it; yet it is the joy of my heart that the time is coming when the kingdoms of this world shall become the kingdoms of our Lord and of His Christ. Dead Churches shall yet be quickened, apostate Churches shall yet be recovered, and Churches shall be planted where there were none before.'

April 4th. – He apparently felt his weakness increasing. 'My legs are of little use, my head is of little use, and my hands are of little use; but my God in Christ is the same to me now as ever.'

Speaking about the Synod, the supreme court of his Church which was convened to meet in the beginning of May, and of which he was clerk, he expressed his doubt of being able to attend it, and then he added, 'Oh, if the Spirit of God would bring me to the General Synod of the Church of the first-born, that would be far better! No idle words, no angry speeches, no sinful ignorance, no haughty pride there. After all, it is a mercy that Jesus, the great manager of the Church, can overrule even our contentions here for His own glory.'

April 5th. – He walked in the meadow attached to the manse, and pointed to several spots where his soul had exulted with views of divine grace. 'Yea, on certain occasions my soul hath been so transported here that, as the apostle speaks, "whether I was in the body, or out of the body, I could scarcely tell." Perhaps it is superstitious in me, but I confess I have a peculiar love for these very spots.'

When he came into the house, he was somewhat exhausted, and expressed himself, not as one oppressed with the weariness of fatigue, but as buoyed up with another longing. 'That will be a pleasant journey, "The ransomed of the Lord shall return, and come to Zion with songs and everlasting joy upon their heads; they shall obtain joy and gladness, and sorrow and sighing shall flee away." '

In speaking about mercy, he said, 'I could wish to live and die a deep, deep debtor to mercy, and that none of my works should ever be mentioned, but as manifestations of mercy in enabling such a sinner to do anything for the honour of the God of mercy, and for promoting the work of mercy in the welfare of others.'

To an acquaintance who came to ask for his welfare he said, 'Well, you see I am a prisoner here in my own house; but oh! that is a happy – I do not choose to call it imprisonment – a happy sort of confinement, in a Redeemer's arms, and in the covenant of grace.'

April 6th. – He was afraid lest, in his physical weakness, he might in conversation overstep the bounds of prudence, and frequently requested his watchful and devoted partner to guard him against any such forgetfulness, for which indeed there was no necessity. 'I hope you will take care, when I am speaking to any acquaintance, that I do not say anything trifling to them. It is not my honour that I mind in this; but I should be vexed, now that I am a dying man, if I should say anything to the dishonour of Christ, to the grief of the godly, or to be a stumbling-block to the wicked. Indeed, it would be ill on my part to act thus.'

A brother minister being in conversation with him, Dunfermline was mentioned, whereupon he said that in his rovings he was often about that place, and he recollected the time when he went over the hills of Cleish, from Gairney Bridge, to hear that great man of God, Mr. Ralph Erskine, whose ministry, he thought, was brought home by the Spirit of God to his heart. On returning thanks for the meal that followed, he said, 'We thank Thee, O Lord, that since we rove in our weakness, we rove about those places where we think we met with the God of Bethel, and saw Him face to face.'

April 8th. – Being asked how he was now, he replied, 'I am weak; but the motto of each of my days is, "He hath not dealt with us as we have sinned, neither rewarded us according to our iniquities." '

Sitting down in the meadow, and finding his eyes unable to bear the bright shining of the sun, looking up he smilingly said 'Oh! how pleasant to be in that place where they are so overcome with the glory of the Sun of Righteousness that they have to cover their faces with their wings!'

He was talking about young men entering the ministry, and the greatness of their calling, when he declared, 'Well, though pride prevails much in my heart, yet I think I would trample it thus far under my feet, as that I would be glad to see all my students, and not my students only, but all the faithful ministers of Jesus, bringing hundreds or thousands of souls with them to heaven, though I should but have five or six.'

He went into his church, which adjoined the manse, and looking round him said, 'Now, weak as I am, I would try to preach yet, if I had none to preach in my stead. Oh! what sweet fellowship with Christ I have had here! That pulpit hath been to me the best place in all the house.'

A young surgeon paid him a visit, and he took occasion to offer him some counsel. Persons in his profession had excellent opportunities of conversing with dying persons about their eternal interests; their patients would probably pay more attention to religious hints from them than from others; while they endeavoured to restore physical health, they should never forget to apply to Christ for spiritual healing themselves. As he was evidently becoming hoarse with speaking, one of the family reminded him that he was exerting himself, and desired him to forbear a little. 'Well,' he said, 'I shall say no more now; but, oh! to be at that –

"My mouth the praises of the Lord
To publish cease shall never;
Let all flesh bless His holy name
For ever and for ever." '

His sons left him for a few weeks to attend to their own congregational duties and to arrange for the approaching meeting of the Synod. After the Synod meetings, the sons returned to Haddington, and Ebenezer records some further sayings of his father, which afforded a very near view of his inner life.

May 6th. – Lying on his back in bed, and being very weak, he said in a low tone of voice, 'Here is a lecture on that text, "Vanity of vanities, all that cometh is vanity and vexation of spirit"; for what a poor useless creature am I now! But oh! what a mercy that Christ can raise glory to Himself out of mere vanity!' In uttering these last words, he seemed quite overcome.

When a friend alleged to him that he appeared to be sunk in his spirits, he replied, 'I am so; but it is not in the least through any terror, but just through weakness.'

Being asked if he was not afraid to enter into a world of spirits, he answered, 'No; a persuasion that Christ is mine makes me think that, when I appear in that world, as a new incomer, all the spirits there will use me well on Christ's account.'

To a kind remark that his increasing weakness did not daunt him, and that he seemed quite calm and confident of victory, 'Yes,' he said, 'I really am so; for in my body I am not much pained; and, as to my mind, it is composed, or rather cheerful. I mean not that I have what the world calls mirth; but I possess a sort of cheerfulness which ariseth from views of certain texts of Scripture.'

May 7th. – 'As I have had fulness all my days, I believe that I could not now easily bear with pinching want; yet, I think, to publish the Gospel of Jesus I could willingly meet with want or anything else.'

He was able to enjoy a carriage drive, and was refreshed by the glad signs of spring on every hand. The spirit of the

Christian Journal awoke within him. 'I think I should love to see that promise accomplished, "The wilderness and the solitary place shall be glad for them; and the desert shall rejoice and blossom as the rose; it shall blossom abundantly, and rejoice even with joy and singing. The glory of Lebanon shall be given unto it; the excellency of Carmel and Sharon; they shall see the glory of the Lord, and the excellency of our God." I should love to see all this ere I die, though I would wish that it may not be long till the event take place. I should love, when I depart to heaven, to be able to tell this news to redeemed millions that the Holy Ghost has been remarkably poured out in East Lothian, and that there was not a family in which the worship of God was not observed. I daresay it delights the redeemed above to hear of Christ's glory being displayed, and of souls being saved on earth.'

To his wife this was a prolonged period of anxiety; and the thought of separation had its dark clouds for her. She would rather that he would turn his eyes toward possible recovery. 'Now, no doubt, you do not wish to hear about my departure; but "Thy Maker is thy husband; the Lord of hosts is His name." He can infinitely more than supply the want of me.'

May 8th. – Addressing one of his sons he said, 'Now I am easy whether ever you or any of the family be what the world calls rich; but I should wish you all to be the fearers of God. Next to seeing Christ as He is, I think that I would desire to see you, and hundreds at your back, all debtors to free grace. Oh! I would be happy to say, "Lord, here am I and the children whom Thou hast given me."'

'Ever since God dealt convincingly with my heart, I never had any comfort in the thought that my sins were little, but in the belief that the virtue of Christ's blood is infinite – blood that "cleanseth from all sin"; and in the consideration of God's mercy being higher than the heavens.

'I once thought that text, "I will have mercy on whom I will have mercy," had just been made for me; and that it was so full of grace, just that it might suit my condition. Were it possible for His Majesty and me to become young again, and were it left to my choice whether I would have his lot or my own, I would, without hesitation, choose my own. If I have not got such grand entertainment for the body as he, I have got feasts on texts of Scripture, the like of which perhaps he never obtained; "Goodness and mercy have followed me."'

Talking about death, he said, 'It might be written on my coffin, "Here lies one of the cares of Providence, who early wanted both father and mother, and yet never missed them!"'

May 9th. — Speaking of submission to the rod, he said, 'I would not wish that foolish question ever put to me, "Would you go to hell, if that were the Lord's will?" for it is God's promise, securing my salvation, that has much influence in making me resigned. God said to me, "I am the Lord thy God"; and if He were not to be mine for ever, he would forfeit His word — which is impossible.'

Two young ladies called upon him. When he asked how they were, and receiving the answer, 'Very well,' he said, ' "It is of the Lord's mercies that we are not consumed"; and oh! never say to your own consciences you are very well, until you have good evidence of your interest in Christ. Be earnest to have acquaintance with Jesus; no connection so glorious as union with Christ; no pleasure like that which is enjoyed in fellowship with Him.'

The remarkable surrender of the man is instanced in reply to one who thought that he was improving in health. 'All my wish is, that if God spare me, I may have gifts to serve Him while I live; and if I die, I wish to praise Him while I have any being.'

May 10th. — Hearing some talk about endorsing a bill, he said, 'Oh how pleasant! the bills of God's promises are my heritage. I have often forgotten them; but I am sure Jehovah minds them; and I know, too, that the Spirit of God will never deceive me.'

Referring to his weakness, he asserted, 'God deals so tenderly with me in my affliction that indeed I think the strokes, as it were, go nearer His heart than they do mine.'

May 11*th.* – 'The command is, "Owe no man anything." What a mercy that there is no such precept as this, "Owe the Saviour nothing!" or even this "Study to owe Him as little as possible!"'

May 14*th.* – He acknowledged that his extraordinarily retentive memory was becoming impaired, but, shutting his eyes he devoutly uttered the prayer, 'Lord, I am a stranger on this earth; hide not Thy commandments from me.' The day was wet, and there was no likelihood of the daily drive. 'Well,' said he, 'if God would send His new covenant chariot, death, and transport me to heaven ere night, I should be happy, let the day be what it will.'

'Oh! what a mercy that my admission into eternal life does not in the least depend on my ability for anything; but I, as a poor sinner, will win in leaning on Christ as the Lord my righteousness – on Christ, "made of God unto me righteousness, sanctification, and redemption!" I have nothing to sink my spirits but my sins and these need not sink me either, since the great God is my Saviour.'

His calm serenity evinced itself in a reply to an inquiry as to his welfare. 'I am sitting here trying to wait for the salvation of God. I should love that my departure were nearer than perhaps you wish; but I will not murmur.'

Passing from one room to another he exclaimed in a sort of transport, 'Oh! it will be pleasant to enter into Christ's light room above! Surely when I am there, and when I reflect on the opportunities which I enjoyed in this world, I shall wonder at myself as a fool, for the misimprovement of them. But what shall I say? When Christ is the way to heaven, "a wayfaring man, though a fool, cannot err therein."'

To a young man he was tendering advice to honour his father and mother, and was reminded that they were both dead. 'Oh!' he said, 'what a mercy that you can never tell me that my friend Jesus is dead, when so many of my earthly acquaintances are gone! If you say of Him that He was dead, I can answer, But now He is "alive, and lives for evermore; and hath the keys of hell and of death."'

Speaking about the manner in which the Gospel-call is addressed to men, he declared, 'It has been my comfort these twenty years, that not only sensible sinners, but the most stupid are made welcome to believe in Christ.'

When he lay down on his bed, he was asked how he was now. 'I lie here in the everlasting arms of a gracious God.' 'Are you not afraid,' said the friend, 'to appear at the tribunal of God?' 'Were I looking to give the account in my own person, considering my sins, I might indeed be terrified; but then I view Christ the Judge as my Advocate and my Accountant, and I know that I do not owe more debt than He has paid.'

June 5th. – An acquaintance who was leaving him remarked that he would probably be seeing some of his brethren in the ministry soon. 'Tell them that it is my desire that they may win souls for Christ, for now I am not able, though ever so willing; meantime, you must say Christ hath been a kind Master to me. Many a visit He hath given to me already; and I expect to be with Him in heaven by and by. Tell them, too, that I desire their prayers, that, with submission to the divine will, I may "depart to be with Christ, which is far better."'

His breakfast, he declared, was a memorial to him of his spiritual provision. On returning from his daily outing, which he was still able to take, his heart seemed to glow with praise at the love and goodness of God. 'Oh! the sovereignty of grace! How strange that I, a poor cottager's son, should have a chaise to ride in; and, what is far more wonderful, I think God hath often given me rides in the chariot of the new covenant. In the former He hath raised me from the dunghill, and set me with great men; but in the latter He hath exalted the man, sinful as a devil, and made him to sit with the Prince of the kings of the earth. Oh! astonishing! astonishing! astonishing!' Being offered a little wine, he objected to taking it. 'I am afraid that it will hurt me; and I would not wish to hurt that head which, as well as my heart, is Christ's. Let Him do with it as He pleaseth, but I would not wish to have any hand in hurting it myself.'

'No doubt I would love to be at my public work again; and, had it been any other than God that had restrained me, I would not have taken it well; but, as it is the Lord, I desire to submit.'

'Were God to present me with the dukedom of Argyle on the one hand, and the being a minister of the Gospel with the stipend which I have had on the other, so pleasant hath the ministry been to me, notwithstanding all my weakness and fears of little success, I would instantly prefer the latter.'

To some acquaintances who came to visit him he said, 'Here, sirs, take warning that ye must die. Now I think it is come to dying work with me; but if Jesus hold me up, though I die, all is well. "Blessed are the dead who die in the Lord."'

A minister asked him what was the best method one could take when a consideration of his own sinfulness terrified him in preaching. He said to him, 'Attempt to believe, just as a sinner, as the chief of sinners. Those promises have been sweetest to me which extend to men, if they are out of hell. "It is a faithful saying, and worthy of all acceptation, that Christ Jesus came into the world to save sinners, of whom I am chief." Once these words were sweet to my soul. I thought, ill as I was, I could not be worse than the chief of sinners. Conscience said that I was the most wicked wretch that ever breathed, and that I had showed myself to be such, especially by rebelling against convictions, and by trampling on Christ's alluring words; yet, since Christ came to save sinners, even the chief, why, thought I, should I except myself?'

His feebleness he realized as he moved through the house, when it seemed as if at any step he might slip and fall. 'I am now very weak; but were I in heaven I shall "renew my strength." There I shall mount up with wings as an eagle; I shall run and not be weary; I shall walk and not faint. No staggerings there.'

Gathering them that evening round the family altar, he said,

'It would be pleasant if our experiences in ordinances were such here, as that they would fit us for the exercise of heaven; our prayers here, a stretching forth of our desires for the employment of God, and of the Lamb; and our praises here, a tuning of our hearts for the songs above.'

June 6th. – His willingness and almost eagerness to depart suggested to one the question, 'Are you not sorry to part with your family?' 'I must own I have a concern about my wife and children; but when my heart enters properly into these words, "Be with the Lord," the leaving of them diminishes into a very small point; and although affection for them is as strong as ever, I hope that when I am away, Christ will far more than supply my room to them; and then, you see, we shall be better on all hands.'

His relatives rendering him assistance from time to time, drew from him the remark, 'I really wonder at the kindness of men to me; but especially I am amazed, when I reflect that it is all the kindness of my God through them.'

When his young children were gathered round him on any occasion he would appeal very tenderly to them. 'There is none so glorious as Christ; "He is altogether lovely." If you could put all the gold and silver into one heap, the glory of Christ would far exceed all. I say this, having, I think, seen Jesus; but, as yet, I have seen Him only "through a glass darkly"; after this I hope to see Him "face to face."'

To one of his sons in the ministry he urged, 'Try to run as deep in Christ's debt as possible; and take His own way of paying, by acknowledging His kindness. And when you mind your own debt, remember your father's debt too; say "Thou art my God, I will praise Thee; my father's God, I will exalt Thee!"' Later he said to him, 'Labour, labour to win souls to Christ; souls are well worth the winning, and Christ is far more worthy of them too. It gives me pleasure now to think that I did not indulge myself in idleness in my Master's service; not but that I was idle, only I do not remember indulging myself in it.'

June 15th. – It was invariably his custom, at this time of year, to render assistance at the great communion at Stow. Stow had a warm corner in his heart ever since the day it called him to its ministry. 'You are not travelling thither now,' said a friend. 'No, I wish to be travelling to God as "my exceeding joy." In the meantime I must say, that at Stow I have had such sweet hours, that neither Christ nor I shall ever forget them.'

He was asked what he thought of free grace after his long record in the Ministry. 'I have altered my mind about many things, but I am of the same mind that ever I was as to grace and salvation through Christ.' 'Where are all your anxieties about the Church?' said one to him. 'I have left my anxiety about it, and about everything else, on the Lord; and indeed, were it not for a God in my nature, I would reckon the present case of the Church very hopeless; but in the view of Christ, I am persuaded that she will yet remarkably revive on earth.'

June 17th. – Extreme weakness was now manifest; but as the outward man decayed, the inward man was renewed. Scarcely able to speak, he turned to a brother minister with a smile, 'Oh! Mr. —, "the Lord is my strength and my song; He also is become my salvation."'

June 18th. – As he seemed oppressed by the increasing feebleness, a friend said to him, 'I hope the Lord is not forsaking you now.' 'No, God is an unchanging rock.' Being asked by another how he was, 'Oh! it is strange that the Lord Jesus encourageth us to pray even at the last!'

Some of his relations stood by his bedside, and, fixing his eyes upon them, he spoke to them with touching pathos. 'Oh! sirs, dying work is serious, serious indeed! and that you will soon find, strong as you now are.'

June 19th. – He appeared to be frequently engaged in speaking; but, owing to the weakness of his voice, it was only a few of the words that could be understood. Upon a friend saying to him, 'You seem to be sore distressed,' the answer appeared to be, 'The Lord hath His own way of carrying on His own work.

The last words he was heard to utter were: 'MY CHRIST.'

BIBLIOGRAPHY OF JOHN BROWN'S
WORKS

1758. *A Help for the Ignorant*; or An Essay toward an easy, plain, practical and extensive explication of the Assembly's Shorter Catechism. Editions, 1761, 1781, 1800, 1811.

1759. *A Brief Dissertation concerning the Righteousness of Christ*. Pamphlet.

1764. *Two Short Catechisms Mutually Connected*. 4th edition, 1769; 9th, 1779; 14th, 1786; 23rd, 1795. The first part, *A Short Catechism for Young Children*, published separately. New editions, 1824, 1826, etc.

1765. *The Christian Journal*; or, Common Incidents, Spiritual Instructors. 6th edition, 1792; new editions, 1808, 1824, etc.

1766. *An Historical Account of the Rise and Progress of the Secession*. 7th edition, 1793.

1767. *Letters on the Constitution, Government, and Discipline of the Christian Church*.

1768. *Sacred Typology*; or, a Brief View of the Figures and Explications of the Metaphors contained in Scripture. New editions, 1782, 1791, 1802; edition corrected from the author's manuscript, 1803; new edition, 1813.

1769. *A Dictionary of the Holy Bible*. Two vols. 2nd edition, 1778; 5th, 1807; 6th, 1816; edition revised by his son, William Brown, M.D., 1865; with contributions by Professor John Eadie, D.D., 1868.

1769. *Religious Steadfastness Recommended*. Sermon.

1771. *A General History of the Christian Church, from the Birth of our Saviour to the Present Time*. Two vols.

1775. *The Psalms of David in Metre*, with Notes exhibiting the Connection, explaining the Sense, and for directing and animating the Devotion. Other editions, 1793, 1812, 1825, 1836, 1837, 1858.

1778. *The Self-interpreting Bible.* Two vols. 26 editions issued, the last in America in 1897, 1909.

1779. *The Oracles of Christ and the Abominations of Antichrist Compared*; or a Brief View of the Errors, Impieties, and Inhumanities of Popery.

1780. *The Absurdity and Perfidy of all Authoritative Toleration of Gross Heresy, Blasphemy, Idolatry, and Popery in Britain.* Two Letters to a Friend.

1780. *The Re-Exhibition of the Testimony, Vindicated* in opposition to the unfair Account given of it by the Rev. Adam Gib. Pamphlet.

1780. *The Duty of Raising up Spiritual Children to Christ.* Sermon.

1781. *An Evangelical and Practical View of the Types and Figures of the Old Testament Dispensation.*

1781. *The Christian, the Student, and Pastor, exemplified in the Lives of Nine Eminent Ministers of Scotland, England, and America.*

1782. *A Compendious View of Natural and Revealed Religion.* 2nd edition, 1796.

1782. *The Young Christian*; or, the Pleasantness of Early Piety.

1783. *Practical Piety exemplified in the Lives of Thirteen Eminent Christians, and illustrated in Cases of Conscience.*

1783. *The Necessity and Advantage of Earnest Prayer for the Lord's Special Direction in the Choice of Pastors.* Pamphlet.

1784. *The Harmony of Scripture Prophecies, and History of their Fulfilment.* New edition, 1800.

1784. *A Compendious History of the British Churches in England, Scotland, Ireland, and America*, with an

Introductory Sketch of the History of the Waldenses.
Two vols. New editions, 1820, 1823.

1784. *Devout Breathings, and Four Solemn Addresses.*

1785. *Thoughts on the Travelling of the Mail on the Lord's Day.* Pamphlet.

1785. *Life and Spiritual Experiences of Elizabeth Wast.*

Six Letters on Gospel Preaching.
Ten Letters on the Exemplary Behaviour of Ministers.

Tracts
    I Christ being made of God to us Sanctification.
    II The Grace of God, and Jesus Christ, the All of Redemption.
    III A Contrast of the Purchase and Application of Redemption.
    IV Reflections of a Soul shut up to the Faith.
    V Reflections of a Christian upon his Spiritual Elevations and Dejections.
    VI Reflections of a Candidate for the Ministerial Office.
    VII Reflections of One entered into the Pastoral Office.
    VIII Reflections of a Minister encouraging himself in Christ.
    IX On Conditional Election and Free-will.
    X The Parliament Dissolved.
    XI The Grand Poll.
    XII On a Sinner's Marriage with Christ.
    XIII On the Glorious Work of Mercy
    XIV Holy Resolutions in View of Marriage.
    XV State of Britain's Debt to God.
    XVI Britain's Sole Preservative in an Outpouring of the Spirit.
    XVII Christ the Best Minister of State.
    XVIII A Brief Chronology of Redemption.
    XIX Blanchard's Travel Excelled.

Strictures on Ordination Vows.

Translation of Drelincourt's *Charitable Visits.*

Pleasant and Practical Hints from Samuel Rutherford.

A Brief Dissertation concerning the Righteousness of Christ.

Apology for the more Frequent Administration of the Lord's Supper. 1804.

Devout and Practical Meditations. *Christian Repository,* November, 1816.

The Composition of Pulpit Discourses. *Christian Repository,* November, 1817.

To a Young Person under Serious Impressions. *Christian Monitor,* March, 1825.

Index